HOUSEHOLD AND FAMILY RELIGION IN PERSIAN-PERIOD JUDAH

ANCIENT NEAR EAST MONOGRAPHS

General Editors
Alan Lenzi
Juan Manuel Tebes

Editorial Board
Reinhard Achenbach
C. L. Crouch
Roxana Flammini
Esther J. Hamori
Christopher B. Hays
René Krüger
Graciela Gestoso Singer
Bruce Wells

Number 18

HOUSEHOLD AND FAMILY RELIGION IN PERSIAN-PERIOD JUDAH

An Archaeological Approach

by

José E. Balcells Gallarreta

 PRESS

Atlanta

Copyright © 2017 by José E. Balcells Gallarreta

All rights reserved. No part of this work may be reproduced or transmitted in any form or by any means, electronic or mechanical, including photocopying and recording, or by means of any information storage or retrieval system, except as may be expressly permitted by the 1976 Copyright Act or in writing from the publisher. Requests for permission should be addressed in writing to the Rights and Permissions Office, SBL Press, 825 Houston Mill Road, Atlanta, GA 30329 USA.

Library of Congress Cataloging-in-Publication Control Number: 2017940546

Printed on acid-free paper.

I am most blessed by the great family that surrounds me, and for the love and support that they provide every day. To my father and mother-in-law, Jim and Kay, for your encouragement, editing support, and continued prayers. To my sister and brother-in-law, Ana and Miguel, for helping with whatever was needed. To my parents, Juan and Léonie, for your support with so many things. To my children, Christopher, Ana, and Katrina, for your encouragement and wonderful memories along the way; thank you for your willingness to relocate in support of my studies. To my dear wife, Carole, for your unending love, patience, and support during these past years; you never gave up no matter what, and believed in me and our ultimate purpose. To you all I dedicate this study.

CONTENTS

ILLUSTRATIONS ix
ACKNOWLEDGEMENTS xi
ABBREVIATIONS xiii
INTRODUCTION 1
   The Need for Research 1
   State of Research 2
   Project Scope 3
1. METHODS AND DEFINITIONS 7
   1.1 Social-Scientific Theories and Methods and Their Contributions to Biblical Studies 7
      1.1.1 Texts and Methods 9
      1.1.2 Archaeology of Ritual and Religion 11
2. PERSIAN PERIOD RITUAL IN EZRA 21
   2.1 Significance 21
   2.2 Background of Ezra-Nehemiah 22
      2.2.1 Provenance 22
      2.2.2 Geographical Boundaries for Yehud 23
      2.2.3 Judah and the Southern Levant under Persian Rule 27
      2.2.4 Persian Influence on Religion 31
      2.2.5 Language 35
      2.2.6 Demographic Changes: Social and Ethnic Groups 37
      2.2.7 Identity Formation 39
   2.3 Analysis of Ezra 40
   2.4 Review of Other Persian Period Biblical Texts 47

3. PERSIAN PERIOD RITUAL ARTIFACTS FROM TELL EN-NAṢBEH HOUSEHOLDS 49

3.1 Significance of Tell en-Naṣbeh 49

3.2 Persian Period Tell en-Naṣbeh 52

3.3 Archaeology Related to Ritual and Religion 56

    3.3.1 Ritual Artifacts 64

4. PERSIAN PERIOD ARCHITECTURE AND NATURAL LANDSCAPE FROM TELL EN-NAṢBEH 81

4.1 Ritual Loci: Architecture and Natural Landscape 81

5. PERSIAN PERIOD RITUAL MATERIAL CULTURE FROM OTHER YEHUD SITES 121

5.1 Shephelah Sites 121

5.2 Archaeology Related to Ritual and Religion 122

    5.2.1 Ritual Loci: Architecture and Natural Landscape 122

6. SUMMARY AND CONCLUSIONS 133

APPENDIX A: TELL EN-NAṢBEH MATERIAL CULTURE DISTRIBUTION FOR STRATUM 2 145

APPENDIX B: TELL EN-NAṢBEH STRATUM 2 BUILDING RECONSTRUCTIONS 159

APPENDIX C: PHOTOGRAPHS OF TELL EN-NAṢBEH RITUAL ARTIFACTS STRATUM 2 169

APPENDIX D: TELL EN-NAṢBEH STRATUM 2 BUILDING SPECIFICATION 177

BIBLIOGRAPHY 179

ANCIENT SOURCES INDEX 189

MODERN AUTHORS INDEX 191

ILLUSTRATIONS

Figures

Figure 1. Approximate geographical area of Yehud. 25
Figure 2. World powers during the sixth century BCE. 28
Figure 3. The extent of the Persian Empire. 30
Figure 4. Tell en-Naṣbeh Stratum 2 architecture. 53
Figure 5. Excavator's distribution of possible ritual artifacts. 65
Figure 6. Tell en-Naṣbeh Building 74.01. 87
Figure 7. Tell en-Naṣbeh Building 110.01. 89
Figure 8. Tell en-Naṣbeh bedrock elevations in northern areas. 91
Figure 9. Tell en-Naṣbeh Outer Gate. 97
Figure 10. Tell en-Naṣbeh Outer Gate complex. 99
Figure 11. Ancient map of Tell en-Naṣbeh and its surroundings. 118
Figure 12. Map of Tel Lachish with Buildings 106 and 10. 125
Figure 13. Details of Buildings 106 at Tel Lachish. 127
Figure 14. TEN Building 74.01. 160
Figure 15. TEN Building 93.03. 161
Figure 16. TEN Building 110.01. 162
Figure 17. TEN Building 125.01. 163
Figure 18. TEN Building 127.01. 164
Figure 19. TEN Buildings 127.03 (left), 144.01 (center). 165
Figure 20. TEN Building 145.02. 166
Figure 21. TEN Building 160.10. 167
Figure 22. TEN Building 194.01. 168
Figure 23. Altar fragment; Bldg. 144.01, Rm. 324, x27 170
Figure 24. Incense altar fragment; Bldg. 110.01, Rm. 378, x41. 171
Figure 25. Pillar base figurine fragment; Bldg. 93.03, Rm. 366, x29. 172
Figure 26. JPF; Bldg. 93.03, Rm. 369. 173
Figure 27. Animal figurine fragment; Bldg. 160.10, Rm. 463, x20. 174
Figure 28. Rattle fragment from Bldg. 110.01, Rm. 400, x19 175
Figure 29. Zoomorphic vessel; Bldg. 144.01, Rm. 331, x8 176

Tables

TABLE 1 Population estimates for Judah and Jerusalem 38
TABLE 2 Ritual Typologies in Ezra 45
TABLE 3 Tell en-Naṣbeh Stratum 2 architectural remains......................... 56
TABLE 4 Typologies possibly related to ritual loci................................... 59
TABLE 5 Typologies possibly related to ritual artifacts............................. 60
TABLE 6 Altars and stands at Tell en-Naṣbeh 68
TABLE 7 Figurines and statuettes at Tell en-Naṣbeh 72
TABLE 8 Zoomorphic vessels at Tell en-Naṣbeh...................................... 78
TABLE 9 Building 110.01 Stratum 2 material culture................................ 93
TABLE 10 Outer gate complex Stratum 2 ritual material culture............. 102
TABLE 11 Building totals for Stratum 2 146
TABLE 12 Building 74.01 Stratum 2 material culture.............................. 147
TABLE 13 Building 93.01 Stratum 2 material culture.............................. 148
TABLE 14 Building 93.03 Stratum 2 material culture.............................. 149
TABLE 15 Building 110.01 Stratum 2 material culture............................ 150
TABLE 16 Building 125.01 Stratum 2 material culture............................ 151
TABLE 17 Building 127.01 Stratum 2 material culture............................ 152
TABLE 18 Building 127.03 Stratum 2 material culture............................ 153
TABLE 19 Building 144.01 Stratum 2 material culture............................ 154
TABLE 20 Building 145.02 Stratum 2 material culture............................ 155
TABLE 21 Building 160.10 Stratum 2 material culture............................ 156
TABLE 22 Building 194.01 Stratum 2 material culture............................ 157
TABLE 23 TEN Stratum 2 building characteristics.................................. 178

ACKNOWLEDGEMENTS

This research represents the culmination of several years of investigation. I have had the opportunity to interface with some wonderful people that have influenced and/or contributed to my discoveries and thinking.

The Tell en-Naṣbeh collection from Badè Museum played a significant role in this investigation. A key aspect of being able to utilize the architecture from this site in my research is connected with the renewed study of the stratigraphy and its associated dating completed by Dr. Jeffrey Zorn. I am thankful to him for his past and present research on Tell en-Naṣbeh, and for the support and advice that he provided during my project.

I wish to express my gratitude to Dr. Aaron J. Brody for his generous gift of time, wise guidance regarding archaeology and the Badè Museum collection, and support in so many other ways. Thank you to Dr. John Endres, S.J. and Dr. Benjamin Porter for your encouragement, for reading this manuscript, and for providing suggestions to improve it. To Dr. Gina Hens-Piazza and Dr. Jean-François Racine for your advice, encouragement, and assistance. I am grateful to the Badè Museum and the Pacific School of Religion for the continued support of the exploration of biblical studies and archaeology. The Tell en-Naṣbeh collection is a truly special gift for others to explore and enjoy.

I grateful for the support that I received from the Hispanic Theological Initiative. I wish to say thank you to Joanne Rodriguez, Angela Schoepf, and other HTI staff for their educational programs, mentorship, financial support through the Luce Fellowship, and willingness to support me in whatever way was needed. Thank you also to Dr. Guillermo Ramírez for serving as my mentor in this program. I also want to extend a special thank you to Ulrike Guthrie for her assistance in editing this study and for always providing great comments.

I was fortunate to receive a grant from the University of Southern California West Semitic Research Project during my investigative phase for training on Reflectance Transformation Imaging (RTI). I wish to thank Dr. Bruce Zuckerman, Dr. Marilyn Lundberg, Johnna Tyrrell, and Kenneth Zuckerman for the hospitality, lending of the RTI equipment to use at the Badè Museum, and training me to be a better photographer.

I wish to extend my appreciation to Dr. Alan Lenzi and to Nicole Tilford of the SBL Press for accepting this study for publication in the ancient Near East Monograph Series. I also wish to thank the two anonymous reviewers who offered many insightful comments to help improve this manuscript.

ABBREVIATIONS

ABD	*Anchor Bible Dictionary*
BAR	*Biblical Archaeology Review*
BASOR	*Bulletin of the American Schools of Oriental Research*
BASORSup	Bulletin of the American Schools of Oriental Research Supplements
BCE	Before the Common Era
BibSem	The Biblical Seminar
bldg	Building
ca.	Circa
ConBOT	Coniectanea Biblica: Old Testament Series
CE	Common Era
cx	Complex
diam	Diameter
FAT	Forschungen zum Alten Testament
fig.	Figure
fn.	Footnote
h	Height
IEJ	*Israel Exploration Journal*
JHebS	*Journal of Hebrew Scriptures*
JPF	Judean Pillar-Figurine
JSOTSup	Journal for the Study of the Old Testament Supplement Series
l	Length
LSTS	The Library of Second Temple Studies
m	Meter
mm	Millimeter
NEA	*Near Eastern Archaeology*
NEAEHL	*The New Encyclopedia of Archaeological Excavations in the Holy Land*
NEAF	*Near Eastern Archaeology Foundation Bulletin*
NICOT	New International Commentary on the Old Testament
NIDB	*New Interpreter's Dictionary of the Bible*
o	Outer
OBO	Orbis Biblicus et Orientalis

OIS	Oriental Institute Seminars
PEF	Palestine Exploration Fund
PIBA	Proceedings of the Irish Biblical Association
rm(s)	Room(s)
SHANE	Studies in the History of the Ancient Near East
SMNIA	Tel Aviv University Sonia and Marco Nadler Institute of Archaeology Monograph Series
TEN	Tell en-Naṣbeh
Transeu	*Transeuphratène*

INTRODUCTION

The Need for Research

The Persian period biblical and nonbiblical textual traditions serve as valuable sources to study and understand the religion, or religions, of ancient Judah, especially early Judaism.[1] Among their many valuable contributions, these texts as literary compositions reflect how ancient authors and editors recorded the religious practices and rituals in the Levant during the Persian period. As scholar of ancient religions Rainer Albertz notes, "[the Persian period was] one of the most productive eras in the history of Israelite religion."[2] Yet, while these texts narrate some of these details, there are still gaps in our understanding of how these ancient societies conceptualized the sacred and incorporated religious practices into daily life. Biblical texts typically provide the story from the viewpoint of what became the desired religious practices of the institutionalized or official religion at the Jerusalem temple through the writing of the elite.[3] Given that the vast majority of ancient populations were illiterate, such written

---

[1] Most scholars recognize the dating of the Persian period to be from 539 to 332 BCE. See Mary Joan Winn Leith, "Israel among the Nations: The Persian Period," in *The Oxford History of the Biblical World*, ed. Michael D. Coogan (New York: Oxford University Press, 1998), 367. Also, Ephraim Stern, "Chronological Tables: The Historical Archaeological Periods," *NEAEHL* 5:2126. I use the term early Judaism to highlight the Jewish religious practices and observances specific to the Second Temple period, dating from 587 BCE to 70 CE, rooted in the communities in the region of Judah or with diaspora ties to the region.

[2] Rainer Albertz, *From the Exile to the Maccabees*, vol. 2 of *A History of Israelite Religion in the Old Testament Period* (Louisville, KY: Westminster John Knox, 1994), 437.

[3] See Aaron J. Brody, "'Those Who Add House to House': Household Archaeology and the Use of Domestic Space in an Iron II Residential Compound at Tell en-Naṣbeh," in *Exploring the Longue Durée: Essays in Honor of Lawrence E. Stager*, ed. J. David Schloen (Winona Lake, IN: Eisenbrauns, 2009), 45.

sources skew our knowledge towards the elite class of these societies.[4] Individuals and social groups that were not part of this elite class are ignored or marginalized because of their illiteracy, socioeconomic class, location, and possible language barriers. These included women, widows, the poor, et cetera. So while textual information is useful for understanding household and family religious practices and rituals in the Levant during the Persian period, we cannot view these sources as normative as they leave common households and families out of the scholarly picture and overlook the material culture related to ritual and religion. Thus, household archaeology holds much promise in the study of family rituals and religion.

State of Research

While earlier research tended to reconstruct a monolithic view of Israelite and Judean religion, more recent scholarly inquiry portrays the diversity of religious ideas and ritual practices.[5] This broader perspective provides an opportunity to explore religious practices and rituals at the household and/or family level(s).[6]

More specifically, past scholarship that has researched ancient religious practices and rituals has been limited in two areas. First, these studies have minimally incorporated the data from material culture and relied mostly on

---

[4] For a discussion of literacy and schools in ancient times see Philip J. King and Lawrence E. Stager, *Life in Biblical Israel* (Lousville, KY: Westminster John Knox, 2001), 300–317.

[5] See for example Francesca Stavrakopoulou and John Barton, *Religious Diversity in Ancient Israel and Judah* (London: T&T Clark, 2010).

[6] See for example Rainer Albertz, "Personal Piety," in *Religious Diversity in Ancient Israel and Judah*, ed. Francesca Stavrakopoulou and John Barton (London: T&T Clark, 2010). Also, Rainer Albertz and Rudiger Schmitt, *Family and Household Religion in Ancient Israel and Levant* (Winona Lake, IN: Eisenbrauns, 2012). Other authors and works include: John P. Bodel and Saul M. Olyan, eds., *Household and Family Religion in Antiquity*, Ancient World: Comparative Histories (Malden, MA: Blackwell, 2008). Karel Van der Toorn et al., "Religious Practices of the Individual and Family," in *Religions of the Ancient World: a Guide*, ed. Sarah Iles Johnston, Harvard University Press Reference Library (Cambridge, MA: Belknap Press of Harvard University Press, 2004), 423–37. Beth Alpert Nakhai, "Varieties of Religious Expression in the Domestic Setting," in *Household Archaeology in Ancient Israel and Beyond*, ed. Assaf Yasur-Landau et al., Culture and History of the Ancient Near East, 50 (Leiden: Brill, 2011). Carol L. Meyers, "Household Religion," in *Religious Diversity in Ancient Israel and Judah* (London: T&T Clark, 2010). Karel Van der Toorn, *Family Religion in Babylonia, Syria, and Israel: Continuity and Changes in the Forms of Religious Life*, SHANE (Leiden: Brill, 1996).

textual information; and second, the research on household and family ritual and religion has focused primarily on the Bronze and Iron Ages, leaving out the crucial later Persian period.[7] This study therefore particularly addresses these two lacunae as it investigates household and family rituals and religious practices in the Persian period.

How does one then investigate rituals and religious practices with sensitivity to exploring these at the family level? Research in this area since 2000 has broadened its scope to include more interdisciplinary theories and approaches and thus also subfields and criticisms from the social-sciences, such as anthropology, history, sociology, political science, economics, archaeology, cultural studies, and linguistics. In this study, I will draw from some of these methods to the extent that they complement this investigation.

Project Scope

This study briefly analyzes various Persian period biblical texts to demonstrate that textual evidence provides only a limited view into household and family ritual and religion during the Persian period in Judah. It then presents the contributions of non-textual alternatives. Specifically, this study investigates the ritual artifacts from Persian period Tell en-Naṣbeh in their excavated contexts, as a case study by which to understand the religious ideas and practices of households in Persian period Judah. Tell en-Naṣbeh is associated with the biblical settlement of Mispah of Benjamin, an important regional center in its Persian period phase mentioned in Nehemiah.[8] Ritual objects in the collection from Tell en-Naṣbeh include human and animal figurines, incense altars, stands, chalices, zoomorphic vessels, rattles, and amulets. This study also focuses attention on ritual aspects of stamp seals and scarabs, as well as profane objects that may have had ritual use or significance, such as lamps, iron knives, and

---

[7] The Bronze Age dating ranges between circa 3600 to 1200 BCE and the Iron Age between circa 1200 to 586 BCE. This chronology follows Stern, "Chronological Tables," *NEAEHL* 5:2126.

[8] Aaron J. Brody, "Mizpah, Mizpeh," *NIDB* 4:116–17. I am utilizing the spelling of Mispah and other archaeological site names as suggested in Society of Biblical Literature, *The SBL Handbook of Style*, 2nd ed. (Atlanta: SBL Press, 2014), 30. For sites not found in this handbook, I refer to the spelling per Michael Roaf, *Cultural Atlas of Mesopotamia and the Ancient Near East* (New York: Facts on File, 1990). For other style matters, see *Chicago Manual of Style*, 16th ed. (Chicago: University of Chicago Press, 2010).

beads found in ritualized contexts.⁹ The study investigates profane objects in their household contexts in order to determine the basic functionality of the rooms in which ritual objects were found. Tell en-Naṣbeh, a three-hectare site located twelve kilometers north of Jerusalem, was excavated by William F. Badè of Pacific School of Religion for five seasons between 1926 and 1935, and it provides us with one of the broadest examples of a Persian period settlement in the northern territory of Yehud.¹⁰ This study draws heavily on a contextual analysis of ritual objects from this settlement.

Unlike scholarship that focused on official or state religion, I utilize archaeological evidence from religion and domestic contexts to investigate the existence of household religion and rituals in Persian period Tell en-Naṣbeh, along with other contemporary sites in Yehud. This inquiry sheds light on ways in which families engaged in religious practices and rituals at the household level using figurines, altars, and other ritual artifacts. I specifically investigate how individuals and groups that were not part of the elite class participated in such rituals.

Archaeological records and data collection from excavations in the early 1920s to1930s present limitations and challenges to a modern-day researcher. This is the case with Tell en-Naṣbeh, even though its excavation methods received numerous accolades from scholars, as the site followed what were considered cutting-edge techniques for excavation and record keeping in its time.¹¹ This study points out these limitations and challenges as they become

---

⁹ See Carol L. Meyers, *Households and Holiness: The Religious Culture of Israelite Women*, Facets (Minneapolis, MN: Fortress, 2005). Also, Carol Meyers, "Terracottas without Texts: Judean Pillar Figurines in Anthropological Perspective," in *To Break Every Yoke: Essays in Honor of Marvin L. Chaney*, ed. Robert B. Coote, Norman K. Gottwald, and Marvin L. Chaney, The Social World of Biblical Antiquity (Sheffield: Sheffield Phoenix, 2007).

¹⁰ See William Frederic Badè, *A Manual of Excavation in the Near East: Methods of Digging and Recording of the Tell en-Nasbeh Expedition in Palestine* (Berkeley, CA: University of California Press, 1934). Also, Chester Charlton McCown et al., *Archaeological and Historical Results*, vol. 1 of *Tell en-Nasbeh Excavated under the Direction of the Late William Frederic Badè* (Berkeley, CA: Palestine Institute of Pacific School of Religion and American Schools of Oriental Research, 1947).

¹¹ Tell en-Naṣbeh research has been updated with the detailed 1993 study by Jeffrey Zorn on the stratigraphy and architecture of the site. He updates the assumptions for the dating of the architecture and facilitates working with the features or architectural elements. See Jeffrey R. Zorn, "Tell en-Nasbeh: A Re-evaluation of the Architecture and

relevant to the analysis of evidence. With regards to the artifacts at the Badè Museum and the accuracy of the original classification on millimeter cards, I have checked whenever possible their attribution and have evaluated them critically in relationship to photographs, drawings, or the artifacts themselves.

Archaeological data presented from Tell en-Naṣbeh, and other sites in the Shephelah region of Yehud demonstrates that household religion was practiced in Persian period Judah.[12] This diversifies our understandings of early Judaism in this period, which is typically reconstructed primarily on biblical and other ancient textual data that focuses on official Judean religion practiced in and around the Jerusalem temple.

Chapter 1 suggests that social-scientific methods, specifically the archaeology of ritual and religion, provide a solid academic method for this study. It supports this by reviewing past uses of social-scientific approaches, and in particular those of anthropology and archaeology, and discusses how these have contributed to the field of biblical studies. The chapter explores definitions of key terms such as ritual, religion, family, and household, and opts to side with definitions that remain broad and flexible. I present Bell's six ritual typologies as an investigative framework in textual and archaeological studies.

Chapter 2 introduces the reader to the contextual background of Persian period Judah to provide a historical and cultural base for the study of biblical text and the archaeology of this period. It discusses issues of geographical boundaries in Yehud, Persian methods of administration at the provinces, Persian influences on local religion, language, social and ethnic groups, and the identity of the people in Ezra. These elements contribute to a more complete understanding of the biblical texts and the archaeology of ritual and religion. The chapter selects Ezra as a test case to evaluate how this text can contribute to research in family and household ritual and religion, and it suggests that this text shows minimal data to analyze this type of investigation. Other studies validate this further with similar conclusions.

Chapter 3 introduces Tell en-Naṣbeh as a strategic settlement of the Persian period in the province of Judah. It discusses the Persian period material culture of the southern Levant with a focus on the archeology of ritual and religion, as a vehicle to explore the religious practices and rituals at the family and household level. The chapter covers the scholarly literature related to this topic and concludes that there is need to further explore the material culture related to

---

Stratigraphy of the Early Bronze Age, Iron Age and Later Periods" (Ph.D. Dissertation, University of California, Berkeley, 1993).

[12] I discuss my reason for selecting the Shephelah in the introductory paragraphs of chapter 5.

family and household rituals. I suggest some categories and typologies for ritual artifacts after finding gaps with existing ones. I utilize this framework to analyze artifacts of Tell en-Naṣbeh possibly related to ritual and/or religious practices. I consider artifacts that have been associated with ritual in the past, but I also search for clues in areas that have been overlooked or ignored. The analysis demonstrates that the collection of Tell en-Naṣbeh does include artifacts that have been associated with ritual and religious practices.

Chapter 4 presents in detail the architecture and natural landscapes of Tell en-Naṣbeh as potential sources of ritual and/or religious practices. I investigate areas with possible connections to domestic settings, such as houses and household areas. The analysis shows that ritual and religious practices did occur at the family and the household level in Persian period Tell en-Naṣbeh.

Chapter 5 briefly discusses ritual and religious archaeological evidence from several sites in the Shephelah during the Persian period as a supplementary study to Tell en-Naṣbeh's investigations. It utilizes a similar method of analysis as in chapters 3 and 4. I conclude that other sites in the Shephelah do not offer as wide an array of ritual and religious material culture from the Persian period at the family and household level as Tell en-Naṣbeh does, and this makes Tell en-Naṣbeh an important contributor to study these types of questions.

1. METHODS AND DEFINITIONS

This chapter asks: What methods provide a solid academic approach to study household and family rituals and religious practices from Persian period Tell en-Naṣbeh and how should these methods be utilized? I investigate approaches that have proven successful in other similar projects, and I use this information to create an appropriate framework for analyzing the archaeology of ritual and religion at the family and household level.

1.1 Social-Scientific Theories and Methods and Their Contributions to Biblical Studies

Since the late nineteenth century, biblical scholars have successfully used social-scientific theory and methods, specifically those of cultural anthropology, to expand biblical research.[1] Some of the early pioneers include: Mary Douglas, Emile Durkheim, Clifford Geertz, Claude Lévi-Strauss, W. Robertson Smith, and Victor Turner. The importance of cultural anthropology as an interpretative vehicle in biblical studies has resurfaced more recently with supporters exhorting other scholars to explore this discipline. For example, Thomas Overholt notes the benefits of incorporating this type of exegetical lens:

> Two kinds of benefit may result from using anthropological methods and materials. On the one hand, fieldwork reports will prove to be rich sources of comparative materials for helping us to understand specific phenomena.... On the other hand, theoretical constructs developed by anthropologists provide

---

[1] T. M. Lemos, "Cultural Anthopology," in *The Oxford Encyclopedia of Biblical Interpretation*, ed. Steven L. McKenzie (Oxford: Oxford University Press, 2013), 157. For an example of using anthropology in the study of religion, see Emanuel Pfoh, "Introduction: Anthropology and the Bible Revisited," in *Anthropology and the Bible: Critical Perspectives*, ed. Emanuel Pfoh, Biblical Intersections 3 (Piscataway, NJ: Gorgias, 2010).

insights into the nature of society and social processes and can be valuable in our attempts to interpret ancient texts.[2]

Even with these and other benefits of using archaeology in biblical studies, the field of religious studies has not fully tapped into the potential archaeology has to enhance research.[3] The use of archaeology in the study of religion for the early stages of humanity is almost a required endeavor.[4]

Anthropology provides a means to investigate the contextual world of the Bible overcoming the gap between modern reader and ancient time, religion and culture.[5] Biblical texts contain multidimensional expressions of cultures and therefore, these should be researched through different exegetical methods.[6] Anthropological methods which focus on trying to understand the way in which ancient people and religions operated provide a critical framework to deal with these various factors. The inclusion of an interdisciplinary approach becomes more critical when investigating issues of household and family religion rather than, say, other aspects of daily life because of religion's complexities—rituals, prayer, offerings, beliefs, cultic artifacts and their meaning. As Albertz notes in his recent study, "comprehensive examination of the history of the family and household religion of ancient Israel and its neighbors requires the consideration and integration of a variety of approaches, such as biblical studies, religious history, archaeology, epigraphy, iconography, cultural anthropology, and sociology."[7]

Recognizing the benefits of such a multi-faceted approach, the present study focuses on the archaeology of ritual and religion as methods and incorporates other approaches as they benefit the inquiry. The sociology and anthropology of religion and textual studies on the religious ideas and practices of early Judaism also inform this study in order to gain a more complete and contextual view of

---

[2] Thomas W. Overholt, *Cultural Anthropology and the Old Testament*, Guides to Biblical Scholarship Old Testament Series (Minneapolis, MN: Fortress, 1996), 1.

[3] Rosemary A. Joyce, "What Should an Archaeology of Religion Look Like to a Blind Archaeologist?," *Archaeological Papers of the American Anthropological Association* 21 (2012): 184.

[4] Mar Llinares García, *Los Lenguajes del Silencio: Arqueologías de la Religión*, Akal Universitaria (Madrid: Akal Ediciones, 2012), 11.

[5] Overholt, *Cultural Anthropology and the Old Testament*, viii.

[6] Robert Wortham, *Social-Scientific Approaches in Biblical Literature*, Texts and Studies in Religion (Lewiston, NY: Mellen, 1999), 23.

[7] Albertz and Schmitt, *Family and Household Religion in Ancient Israel and Levant*, 17.

the Persian period rituals and practices at the household and/or family level, which heretofore has not been a focus of inquiry. The study relates these observations to households at Tell en-Naṣbeh, as well as to the material culture of key Judean/Shephelah excavation sites that contain significant Persian period ritual material culture. Comparative approaches with other Judean sites enhance the understanding of the function for these ritual elements. As part of this research, I investigate newer trends in the field that focus on the archaeology of religion and ritual, and ritual studies. These studies balance out the picture of religion from the biblical and extrabiblical texts that focus on temple-based official theology and ritual.

1.1.1 Texts and Methods

Although the social sciences offer numerous theoretical options to assist our understanding, there are a number of potential pitfalls to avoid while implementing them.[8] Due to its editorial tradition a biblical text may contain perspectives that may be better interpreted with other non-textual sources.[9] Well-balanced research examines data from multiple sources and is critical and honest about each one's inherent biases and limitations realizing that these methods do not offer a one-size-fits-all solution. Thus, a researcher does well to implement the theory that best fits the investigative objectives.

In addition, archaeologists who deal with ritual and religions should develop a balanced schema since investigations solely based on material culture may not provide the most complete picture.[10] Biblical scholars can contribute to the fields of anthropology and archaeology of ritual and religion by making the study of religion more complete. For example, they can share their expertise in biblical exegesis, ancient languages, and epigraphy. In many cases ancient religious texts can inform and introduce a better understanding of rituals in a faith community. In addition, biblical scholars can introduce human spiritual

---

[8] Robert R. Wilson, *Sociological Approaches to the Old Testament* ed. Gene M. Tucker, Guides to Biblical Scholarship (Philadelphia, PA: Fortress, 1984), 28–29.

[9] Certain scholars criticize the use of social-scientific approaches. Emanuel Pfoh, for example, excoriates the reliance on texts in interdisciplinary social-scientific studies. He argues that here the main function of anthropology and sociology would be to see how these "can modify and enhance our representations of Israel's historical past without relying or depending slavishly on the Bible's depictions." He explains that most social-scientific biblical scholars have not separated themselves and their interpretations from their personal background. See Pfoh, "Introduction: Anthropology and the Bible Revisited," 6–7.

[10] Timothy Insoll, *Archaeology, Ritual, Religion* (London: Routledge, 2004), 33.

components that are an important aspect of ritual and religious life that material culture at times does not reflect.

I would argue that both extremes, the one of not using the text and the other of relying solely on the text, may lead to lost opportunities in research. Instead, in each investigation one needs to carefully evaluate its sources of data and one's possible scholarly biases, and see how best to approach the project given the circumstances.[11]

Thanks in part to the fact that there is a fairly well established past use of anthropology in biblical studies, scholars have learned to adapt methods to better serve their analysis. For example, the use of modeling and mapping has the potential to help with the interpretation of biblical texts.[12]

The adoption of anthropological exegetical theories and methods does not solve all the interpretative problems or please all critical audiences. For example, in biblical scholarship the historicity of the Tanak remains contested. Like many other disputed positions, there is a range of opinions spanning, on the one hand, scholars who see the Tanak as a textual witness encapsulating historical events and, on the other, those who perceive this text as a myth and lacking historicity. As it relates to anthropology, this issue surfaces in connection with the biblical texts' ability to reflect social reality.[13] In this case, it is prudent to keep in mind that anthropology may assist with the interpretation of the Hebrew Bible without necessarily arguing that such texts are historically accurate. Rather, anthropology illuminates the context for these biblical texts.[14] There is a need for modern scholars to be sensitive to past interpretations of ancient people and culture.[15]

This perspective aligns well with this study and the need to find contextual approaches to investigate the other. This pertains to women, foreigners, or other marginalized people and their involvement in rituals and religious practices at the household level.

---

[11] T.M. Lemos offers various helpful critiques and suggestions to anthropologists and biblical scholars. See Lemos, "Cultural Anthropology," 162–63.

[12] Overholt, *Cultural Anthropology and the Old Testament*, 10.

[13] For an example of this critique see ibid., 18–19.

[14] Ibid. Llinares García comments on history's tendency to privilege the text, leaving out the material culture and its contributions. See Llinares García, *Los Lenguajes del Silencio*, 27.

[15] Louise J. Lawrence, "A Taste for 'The Other': Interpreting Biblical Texts Anthropologically," in *Anthropology and Biblical Studies: Avenues of Approach*, ed. Louise Joy Lawrence and Mario I. Aguilar (Leiden: Deo, 2004), 10–11.

Therefore, anthropological theories and methods provide a valuable critical tool for exploring ritual and religious practices in the biblical texts, as well as in the material culture. These views incorporate the understanding of religion as a system of symbols and religion's ability to carry culture and symbols.[16] The complexities of rituals and religions call for a multi-dimensional perspective that allows and considers these complexities.[17]

1.1.2 Archaeology of Ritual and Religion

The study of the archaeology of ritual and religion integrates several academic disciplines. While the collective effort in interdisciplinary research has deepened the discussions, at the same time it has also identified areas of disagreement since disciplines tend to approach definitions, theories, methods, and the analysis of data from a slightly different perspective.[18] Methodologically, we must be careful on how archaeologists' views and definitions of ritual and religion strongly influence how and where we see these occurring.[19] Therefore, we need to define our terms in a self-conscious manner, while keeping an open mind to new areas and potential pitfalls.

1.1.2.1 Definition of Ritual and Religion

What is considered a religion? What constitutes a ritual? Even though these are fundamental and perhaps seemingly simplistic questions, they have been at the forefront of scholarly discussions in the social-scientific fields of archaeology, anthropology, religious studies, and others. The way researchers define and interpret, and hence, limit terms such as ritual and religion, affects how one approaches the inquiry.

---

[16] Clifford Geertz, *The Interpretation of Cultures: Selected Essays* (New York: Basic Books, 1973), 90–93. Wortham, *Social-Scientific Approaches in Biblical Literature*, 6, 13.

[17] For example, Insoll, *Archaeology, Ritual, Religion*, 77.

[18] Rosemary Joyce effectively traces its development and summarizes important historical influences, trends, and contributors. See, Rosemary A. Joyce, "Archaeology of Ritual and Symbolism," in *International Encyclopedia of the Social and Behavioral Sciences*, ed. James D. Wright (Oxford: Elsevier, 2015).

[19] See, ibid.

The challenge of how to define religion attracts much conversation, and what seems clear is that there is no consensus in sight.[20] We need to define religion in a way that does not place it as an isolated box representing activities that do not affect the rest of a person's daily life. Our view of religion needs to incorporate a more holistic approach that looks beyond ritual objects.[21] Joyce sheds light on this area:

> the study of religious images, objects, spaces, and material practices' develops from a new understanding that religion is about the sensual effects of walking, eating, meditating, making pilgrimage, and performing even the most mundane of ritual acts … what people do with material things and places, and how these structure and color experience and one's sense of oneself and others.[22]

We tend to develop preconceived ideas of what religion is and where we find it.[23] I agree with maintaining an open mind and propose a simple definition for religion along the line of: a belief in or worship of a higher being.

Advocating for the insights derived from the cognitive-science and neuroscience, Colin Renfrew argues that the study of ritual and religion, perhaps, could benefit from a cognitive approach.[24] He states, "The most coherent insights into the belief systems of the past must come, if we exclude from the discussion the information available from written texts, from the analysis of symbolic systems."[25] He further argues that by definition, every religion "involves a system of beliefs which offers answers to profound existential questions," such as "Where do we come from? Where are we? Where are we going?"[26] These are foundational questions that define the religion and the beliefs that each holds as part of its core. It is precisely these beliefs that

---

[20] See, Colin Renfrew, "The Archaeology of Religion," in *The Ancient Mind: Elements of Cognitive Archaeology*, ed. Colin Renfrew and Ezra B.W. Zubrow (Cambridge: Cambridge University Press, 1994), 47.

[21] Insoll, *Archaeology, Ritual, Religion*, 150. Insoll suggests the use of the simplest of definitions, and ultimately questions the need of a definition at all, when he states, "Is religion as a concept really only the result of a desire to classify what is in effect an unclassifiable and indivisible facet of life for much of the world's population today and in the past? See, ibid., 6.

[22] Editorial Statement, *Material Religion apud* Joyce, "What Should an Archaeology of Religion Look Like to a Blind Archaeologist?," 184.

[23] Ibid., 187.

[24] Renfrew, "The Archaeology of Religion," 53.

[25] Ibid.

[26] Ibid., 48.

challenge archaeologists as they try to recover these from the archaeological record. Llinares García comments on this view: "todas las sociedades y religiones tienen un sistema de representaciones mentales que intenta dar cuenta y otorgar un sentido a la totalidad del mundo."[27] In addition to these mental representations she suggests that each society has a system of moral prescriptions that regulate conduct, and these along with rituals often leave traces in the archaeological record.[28]

Academics who study religion by defining and thinking of it as something strongly connected to a belief system tend to focus the inquiry with a cognitive approach. These scholars try making connections to see how these beliefs would be manifested in the material remains via rituals or other components. Moreover, a researcher's background, perspective, and investigation agenda all influence the questions and methods that he or she asks and employs. We tend to find what we investigate since we focus on trying to explain those research questions.[29]

The desire to define ritual with some precision varies. Catherine Bell, a religious studies scholar who did significant theoretical work on ritual, argues that archaeologists would be better served by maintaining an open mind about what ritual is, and allowing the definition to be simple.[30] She further questions other scholars' complex definitions of ritual when she writes, "several speakers argued that we need to define ritual so we can better talk to one another, *as if our problems interpreting a ritual site lay in communicating with one another.*"[31] Bell promotes Colin Renfrew's simple definition: "rituals are those activities that address the gods or other supernatural forces."[32] Yet Evangelos Kyriakidis, an archaeologist working on ritual sites in Greece, finds that Bell's simple definition is insufficient and insists that, "the lack of a definition of ritual is responsible for a great deal of the problems any discussion of the topic

---

[27] Llinares García, *Los Lenguajes del Silencio*, 143.

[28] Ibid., 144.

[29] Catherine M. Bell, *Ritual: Perspectives and Dimensions* (New York: Oxford University Press, 2009), 21.

[30] Catherine M. Bell, "Response: Defining the Need for a Definition," in *The Archaeology of Ritual*, ed. Evangelos Kyriakidis, Cotsen Advanced Seminars 3 (Los Angeles, CA: Cotsen Institute of Archaeology, University of California, Los Angeles, 2007), 278.

[31] Ibid., 283.

[32] Ibid., 278.

faces."[33] He further argues, "to make ritual useful, to study it, learn from it, and to convey this learning, one needs to have a clear idea of what it is."[34] Kyriakidis defines ritual as, *"an etic category that refers to set activities with a special (not-normal) intention-in-action, and which are specific to a group of people."*[35] I suggest that Kyriakidis's attempt to make ritual's definition more specific has resulted in the opposite, as it introduces a number of elements that invoke vagueness. For example, what is a "not-normal" action? How does this address the issue that people in the ancient Near East may have incorporated rituals into their daily living making such actions quite "normal" to them?[36] I propose that a broad view of the term is most helpful when investigating aspects of ritual, symbols, and religion as a whole. Therefore, I prefer to adopt a definition of ritual that remains broad: "rituals are those activities that address the gods or other supernatural forces."[37] With this in mind, it appears prudent to allow some flexibility in regards to defining and working with ritual.

Issues of ritual definitions aside, it is important to recognize the relationship between religion and ritual. Religions display their practices in various forms and ritual may be one of them. While religions may manifest themselves through rituals, not all rituals are religious. It is precisely this relationship that presents challenges to archaeologists.[38]

---

[33] Evangelos Kyriakidis, "Archaeologies of Ritual," in *The Archaeology of Ritual*, ed. Evangelos Kyriakidis, Cotsen Advanced Seminars 3 (Los Angeles: Cotsen Institute of Archaeology, University of California, Los Angeles, 2007), 289.

[34] Ibid., 290.

[35] Ibid., 294.

[36] Timothy Insoll identifies some of these potential problems when he cites and supports Jonathan Smith's definition of ritual as, "a 'focusing lens' for the sacred, one which need not only be concerned with the odd but also with 'routine action.'" See Insoll, *Archaeology, Ritual, Religion*, 10. Also, Renfrew, "The Archaeology of Religion," 47.

[37] Bell, "Response: Defining the Need for a Definition," 278. Bell ultimately argues in her seminal book that "talk about ritual may reveal more about the speakers than about the bespoken … ritual is not an intrinsic, universal category or feature of human behavior—not yet, anyway. It is a cultural and historical construction that has been heavily used to help differentiate various styles and degrees of religiosity, rationality, and cultural determinism." See Bell, *Ritual: Perspectives and Dimensions*, ix, xi.

[38] Renfrew perceives this when he notes, "it is probably fair to say that most considerations of the archaeological correlates for religion or for religious ritual have not made sufficient distinctions between evidence of ritual practice in general and that of specifically religious ritual practice." See Colin Renfrew, "The Archaeology of Ritual, Cult, and of Religion," in *The Archaeology of Ritual*, ed. Evangelos Kyriakidis, Cotsen

It is fair to say that the distinction of secular and religious context in ancient times adds another layer of complexity. One may think of a particular place or artifact as belonging to a ritual context, but in reality these may have been part of a nonreligious frame of reference. The challenge comes in how ritual tends to manifest itself in the archaeological record. Ritual, both secular and religious, appears through the repetition of formal acts.[39] These reoccurrences may provide an indication of past ritual.

1.1.2.2 Components of Ritual

How then can archaeologists identify and retrieve evidence of ritual or religious practice?[40] Elements seen in ritual provide a framework to start discussing possibilities. At a high level and in agreement with Bell, Renfrew describes ritual observances as "time-structured in at least two senses:" first, in specific time of day, year, et cetera, and second, in "Internal time-structured with sequences of actions, repetitions, and assigned durations."[41] He lists sixteen archaeological indicators for ritual that fall in four overarching areas: (1) Focusing of attention; (2) Boundary zone between this world and the next; (3) Presence of the deity; (4) Participation and offering.[42] Some of these indicators may be present in secular rituals as well, and not all may be manifested in every ritual, but the list provides a guideline for archaeologists to consider. I find that some of his indicators provide a valuable lens to examine instances of ritual. Marcus in her research in Mesoamerica develops an alternative list of ritual components that may be useful for ritual studies in the Near East. These components include: "(1) One or more performers; (2) An audience; (3) A location (temple, altar, et cetera); (4) A purpose; (5) Meaning; (6) Temporal span (hour, day, week); (7) Actions; (8) Foods and paraphernalia ... used in the performance of rites."[43] I utilize both of these lists in my analysis of ritual in the following chapters as guides in identifying potential aspects of ritual even though some rituals may not involve all of these components.

Advanced Seminars 3 (Los Angeles: Cotsen Institute of Archaeology, University of California, Los Angeles, 2007), 114.

[39] Joyce Marcus, "Rethinking Ritual," in *The Archaeology of Ritual*, ed. Evangelos Kyriakidis, Cotsen Advanced Seminars 3 (Los Angeles: Cotsen Institute of Archaeology, University of California, Los Angeles, 2007), 46.

[40] I use the term ritual in the religious context, unless otherwise stated.

[41] Renfrew, "The Archaeology of Ritual, Cult, and of Religion," 116.

[42] Renfrew, "The Archaeology of Religion," 51–52.

[43] Marcus, "Rethinking Ritual," 48.

1.1.2.3 Typologies of Ritual

Scholarship over the years has debated the definition of a ritual, and how rituals may be studied. Classification is a commonly accepted approach within anthropology and archaeology.[44] The history of research on ritual typologies dates back to the 1960s. Durkheim, Turner, Grimes, and Bell suggest typologies and categories of ritual.[45] These recommendations range from two types (Durkheim and Turner) to sixteen (Grimes).[46] This study uses Bell's typological framework, as it fits well with the objectives of this project. It is also an approach that has been utilized successfully in a study that includes texts.[47] Furthermore, the list encompasses categories that have long been associated with religious traditions, including ancient Judaism.[48]

Bell's six ritual typologies are: (1) rites of passage, (2) calendrical rites, (3) rites of exchange and communion, (4) rites of affliction, (5) feasting, fasting, and festivals, and (6) political rites.[49] Bell describes rites of passage as "ceremonies that accompany and dramatize such major events as birth, coming-of-age initiations for boys and girls, marriage, and death. Sometimes called 'life-crisis' or 'life-cycle' rites, they culturally mark a person's transition from one stage of social life to another."[50] Even though it appears at first glance that these rituals are closely connected with a certain natural and biological order in life, Bell argues that these rites are more culturally determined, and there also seems to be a higher number of these rites associated with religious cultures than with secular ones.[51]

---

[44] For example, the field of archaeology developed typologies for such things as bowls and other artifacts, as a critical tool in analyzing these kinds of material culture.

[45] Bell, *Ritual: Perspectives and Dimensions*, 93–94.

[46] Bell settles on six categories as a simpler and more manageable number. She explains her reasoning for this decision and to some extent critiques larger typologies when she notes, "While often descriptively useful, these typologies are designed to support the particular theory being advanced and sometimes reinforce unconscious assumptions about ritual.... The more complete and nonreductive a system attempts to be, however, the more unwieldy it can be to use." She was quick to point out that her list of typologies is not meant to be a definitive one, but rather a pragmatic approach. See ibid.

[47] See for example, James R. Davila, "Ritual in the Jewish Pseudepigrapha," in *Anthropology and Biblical Studies: Avenues of Approach*, ed. Louise Joy Lawrence and Mario I. Aguilar (Leiden: Deo, 2004).

[48] Bell, *Ritual: Perspectives and Dimensions*, 94.

[49] Ibid., 94–129.

[50] Ibid., 94–95.

[51] Ibid.

Calendrical rites, as the name suggests, are closely associated with seasonal factors. These rites "give socially meaningful definitions to the passage of time, creating an ever-renewing cycle of days, months, and years.... They occur periodically and predictably, accompanying seasonal changes in light, weather, agricultural work, and other social activities." [52] The solar and the lunar calendars play an important part in these rites, each with its own way of marking time. Rites associated with the solar calendar occur on the same day every year, and those rites connected with the lunar calendar fluctuate year to year with the moon. The ancient Jewish calendar incorporates a number of events that integrate this latter type of rite, such as the Feast of Tabernacles.

Rites of exchange and communion "are those in which people make offerings to a god or gods with the practical and straightforward expectation of receiving something in return—whether it be as concrete as a good harvest and a long life or as abstract as grace and redemption."[53] Some of ancient Judaism's offerings fit well into this type of rite, such as gift offerings.

Rites of affliction "seek to mitigate the influence of spirits thought to be afflicting human beings with misfortune."[54] Bell argues that these rites also include broader understandings of affliction such as those seen in sin, pollution of menstruation, childbearing, and death. These are "morally neutral but still require purification ... [they] attempt to rectify a state of affairs that has been disturbed or disordered; they heal, exorcise, protect, and purify ... these rites also illustrate complex cultural interpretations of the human condition and its relation to a cosmos of benign and malevolent forces."[55] Sin offerings within ancient Judaism provide an example of this type of rite.

Feasting, fasting, and festivals comprise a type of rite that can overlap with rites of affliction, although the former tend to involve communal feasts or fasts with a different ritual logic. Bell comments that "the emphasis [is] on the public display of religiocultural sentiments.... In these rituals people are concerned to express publicly—to themselves, each other, and sometimes outsiders—their commitment and adherence to basic religious values."[56]

Political rites are "those ceremonial practices that specifically construct, display, and promote the power of political institutions (such as king, state, the village elders) or the political interests of distinct constituencies and

---

[52] Ibid., 102.
[53] Ibid., 108.
[54] Ibid., 115.
[55] Ibid., 115 and 119.
[56] Ibid., 120.

subgroups."⁵⁷ Bell argues that these rites define power in a two-dimensional way: through the use of symbols and actions based on values, and by showing the legitimacy of these values.⁵⁸

1.1.2.4 Family and Household Archaeology

What is household archaeology? What is a household and how is this different from a family? Research from the field of anthropology deals with these terms and concepts more broadly than scholarship that centers on Israelite religion(s). Thus, there are benefits in incorporating concepts from both fields. The origin of the term "household archaeology" goes back to 1982, when Richard Wilk and William Rathje "coin the phrase ... in their seminal issue of *American Behavioral Scientist*."⁵⁹ The field of household archaeology attracts multiple interdisciplinary followers and practitioners. Foster and Parker define it broadly in three ways: "1) a subdivision of settlement archaeology specializing in the study of spatial patterning at the household level; 2) a development from social archaeology presenting more humanized reconstructions of the past; or 3) simply as the study of household-based behaviors and relationships."⁶⁰ It is important to recognize in household archaeology that households were not static entities; rather, they were active and varied in how they organized, functioned and acted according to their geographical location and time.⁶¹

The definition of family is central to this field. Traditional views of this term define it as "a group of people related by descent or marriage."⁶² So

---

⁵⁷ Ibid., 128.

⁵⁸ Ibid., 129.

⁵⁹ Catherine P. Foster and Bradley J. Parker, "Introduction: Household Archaeology in the Near East and Beyond," in *New Perspectives on Household Archaeology*, ed. Bradley J. Parker and Catherine P. Foster (Winona Lake, IN: Eisenbrauns, 2012), 1.

⁶⁰ Ibid.

⁶¹ Ibid., 2.

⁶² Lynn Rainville, "Techniques for Understanding Assyrian Houses," in *New Perspectives on Household Archaeology*, ed. Bradley J. Parker and Catherine P. Foster (Winona Lake, IN: Eisenbrauns, 2012), 142. Albertz identifies challenges that researchers who investigate areas from the biblical text face when they try to reconcile the terms household and family with modern sociological definitions. When talking about family, he prefers to use the terms "nuclear" and "joint family households" instead. As he notes, "'Nuclear' can be generic 'parental' households or, in a sense perhaps better reflecting the patriarchal structure of Israelite society, 'paternal,' 'stem,' or 'fraternal' households. We additionally use the term 'extended family household' to denote a nuclear family plus

families form the smaller circle of social units, which extend to include other types of social classes who may not be blood related. These larger social units form households. They may be all in one house or in multiple houses.

Family and household archaeology provides valuable scholarship and an important contribution in identifying and interpreting issues of gender and ethnicity in the material culture, which in the past have not been part of investigations.[63] Even though gender and ethnicity in the archaeological record are challenging to recover, every effort should be made to shape a research methodological framework that allows questions to surface in an inclusive manner. Contextual and interpretative methods of archaeology provide this type of approach. Recognizing the importance of these studies, Albertz states, "these gender-oriented approaches and others like them have clarified the significance of women, particularly in their roles as wives and mothers, for Israelite family and household religion, in stark contrast to their restricted roles in the official cult of YHWH."[64] Moreover, literature on the Persian period lacks scholarly coverage on the role that women played in administrative and everyday life. Jason Silverman notes, "Women, of course, played important roles in society including intermarriage, child-rearing, and economic activities. A full examination of the position and role of women in Judaean-Iranian interaction deserves attention."[65] The roles that women played in ancient times make an important contribution in better understanding household and family rituals. Therefore, research in this area should include a framework to capture and analyze data with sensitivity to the roles of women and other marginalized individuals at various levels of the social stratum.

This chapter presents a discussion of the various methodological considerations, issues with definitions, and typologies of ritual that affect and inform this study. It focuses on social-scientific theories and methods and their

---

cohabitating single relatives beyond the one conjugal family unit (the couple and its children)." Albertz's suggestion of "extended family household" recognizes the potential for familial multigenerational arrangements, as well as singles or widows who continue to be part of the family. See Albertz and Schmitt, *Family and Household Religion in Ancient Israel and Levant*, 21–26.

[63] Phyllis Bird, Carol Meyers, and Sue Ackerman are three scholars challenging other scholars to rethink their projects in order to develop research agendas that include women's role in ancient societies and religious practices.

[64] Albertz and Schmitt, *Family and Household Religion in Ancient Israel and Levant*, 10–11. See, Meyers, *Households and Holiness*, 19.

[65] Jason M. Silverman, "Iranian-Judean Interaction in the Achaemenid Period," in *Text, Theology, and Trowel: New Investigations in the Biblical World*, ed. Lidia Matassa and Jason M. Silverman (Eugene, OR: Pickwick, 2011), 135.

use in studies that investigate ritual and religion. Having established anthropology and the archaeology of ritual and religion as appropriate investigative methods, the following chapters elucidate family and household ritual and religious practices in Persian period Yehud.

2. PERSIAN PERIOD RITUAL IN EZRA

The objectives of this chapter are: (1) to introduce a brief history of the Persian period in Yehud; (2) to provide a contextual framework by discussing issues such as language, social and ethnic factors, possible Zoroastrian influences, and identity formation; (3) to analyze Ezra as a representative text from the Persian period. I ask the questions: How much data and what kind of information can I derive from this analysis to assist in an investigation of family and household ritual and religion in the Persian period? How does the context influence and affect the text, and how does this relate to my investigation of family and household ritual and religion?[1]

2.1 Significance

Why explore Ezra in connection with family and household ritual and religion? First, texts from the Persian period continue to gain importance, as scholars determine that significant portions of the Tanak were either written or underwent final editorial review during this period.[2] And second, Persian period texts, and in particular Ezra-Nehemiah, have not been subjected to social-scientific and anthropological critical methods. As Jacques Berlinerblau notes, "biblical scholarship must venture into these [social-scientific] waters in order to engage the issues of 'Israelite popular religion.'"[3]

---

[1] I also briefly researched the text of Nehemiah as part of this investigation, although the scope of this study limits its analysis to the text of Ezra. This author supports the proposal that Ezra-Nehemiah in all likelihood was a unified source in the early stages of transmission. See for example Jacob M. Myers, *Ezra Nehemiah: Introduction, Translation, and Notes* ed. William Foxwell Albright and David Noel Freedman, The Anchor Bible, vol. 14 (Garden City, NY: Doubleday, 1965), xxxviii–xxxix.

[2] Sara Japhet, *From the Rivers of Babylon to the Highlands of Judah: Collected Studies on the Restoration Period* (Winona Lake, IN: Eisenbrauns, 2006), vii.

[3] Jacques Berlinerblau, "The 'Popular Religion' Paradigm in Old Testament Research: A Sociological Critique," in *Social-Scientific Old Testament Criticism: A*

There are a number of options to identify manifestations of ritual in texts. Using Bell's six categories of ritual, the following analyzes Ezra to determine the extent of evidence for ritual in the text.[4] Because social and cultural influences are part of understanding ritual, prior to analyzing ritual in Ezra, this chapter begins with a broader contextual discussion of this text: its position within the history of the Persian period, a brief survey of contemporary religions and languages, and an overview of the sociocultural context surrounding the southern Levant during this period.

2.2 Background of Ezra-Nehemiah

2.2.1 Provenance

The authorship and dating of the text in Ezra-Nehemiah represents one of the most challenging issues in biblical scholarship.[5] For well over one hundred years, various formulations have developed to try and explain who wrote the text. Among the most recent discussions and commentaries are theories that divide scholarship, making it all the more difficult to find consensus. For example, Jacob Myers suggests that Ezra would be the likely candidate, although he allows other views in his discussion and dates the text to ca. 400 BCE.[6] F. Charles Fensham proposes three theories for authorship and concludes that the Chronicler probably fit as the most likely option.[7] He does not provide conclusive details for the dating of the text. Hugh G. M. Williamson credits authorship to an editor or compiler other than the Chronicler, and sees the process of text composition extending over two phases; the first includes the joining of Ezra-Nehemiah, and the second the prefacing of Ezra 1–6 into the rest of Ezra-Nehemiah.[8] His dating for the text ranges between ca. 400 and 300

Sheffield Reader, ed. David J. Chalcraft, BibSem 47 (Sheffield: Sheffield Academic, 1997), 53.

[4] Bell, *Ritual: Perspectives and Dimensions*, 93–135.

[5] This difficulty includes the two, as most scholars consider both to come from a single source. Sara Japhet plays an instrumental role in dividing authorship of Ezra-Nehemiah and 1 and 2 Chronicles.

[6] Myers, *Ezra Nehemiah*, LXIII and LXX.

[7] F. Charles Fensham, *The Books of Ezra and Nehemiah*, NICOT (Grand Rapids, MI: Eerdmans, 1982), 2–3.

[8] Hugh G. M. Williamson, *Ezra and Nehemiah* ed. R. N. Whybray (Sheffield: Sheffield Academic, 1987), 43.

BCE.⁹ Joseph Blenkinsopp offers a good discussion of the alternatives, and concludes that 1–2 Chronicles share commonalities with Ezra-Nehemiah, and therefore there is the likelihood that the Chronicler authored both of these texts.¹⁰ His analysis does not offer a definitive dating. The commentary by Lester Grabbe focuses on the literary critical issues and his close reading of the text, without addressing the authorship and dating of the texts.¹¹ Likewise, Gordon Davies's rhetorical critical commentary lacks discussion on authorship and dating.¹² Keith Schoville credits authorship to an editor or compiler, but not necessarily the Chronicler.¹³ He aligns himself with Williamson in this regard and dates the text to ca. 300 BCE.¹⁴ Finally, Andrew Steinmann offers a detailed discussion in which he suggests four proposals for authorship, and argues for a position of neither Ezra nor Nehemiah as authors of the present form of the books.¹⁵ He dates the text to ca. 335 BCE.¹⁶ It is important to note that the text of Nehemiah recounts the events that take place in the fifth century BCE and that most scholars attribute the dating to around the fourth century BCE.¹⁷ This gap in chronology is not unusual for Second Temple period literature, and in fact becomes fairly common in this literature.

For the purposes of this study, I follow the broad consensus that dates the authorship or compilation of Ezra-Nehemiah to the late Persian period at ca. fourth century BCE. Events portrayed in the book are set in the early Persian period at ca. fifth century BCE. Attribution or editing is of less importance for my study.

2.2.2 Geographical Boundaries for Yehud

The area that constituted the geographical boundary for the province of Yehud remains elusive. There is a lack of direct primary evidence in support that Judah

---

⁹ Ibid., 46.

¹⁰ Joseph Blenkinsopp, *Ezra-Nehemiah: A Commentary* (Philadelphia, PA: Westminster, 1988), 47–54.

¹¹ Lester L. Grabbe, *Ezra-Nehemiah* (New York: Routledge, 1998).

¹² Gordon F. Davies, *Ezra and Nehemiah*, Berit Olam (Collegeville, MN: Liturgical Press, 1999), 28–29.

¹³ Keith Schoville, *Ezra-Nehemiah* (Joplin, MI: College Press, 2001), 28–29.

¹⁴ Ibid., 28.

¹⁵ Andrew E. Steinmann, *Ezra and Nehemiah* (Saint Louis, MI: Concordia, 2010), 2, 12.

¹⁶ Ibid., 21.

¹⁷ Winn Leith, "Israel among the Nations," 373.

was a province during the Persian period.[18] The existence of the province comes from Ezra 5:8 and Neh 1:3, 7:6, 11:3, and from Yehud seals and seal impressions.[19] Still, most scholars support the assumption that these sources provide an accurate portrayal of Yehud as a province.[20] The elusiveness surfaces in determining certain borders. Fantalkin and Tal summarize the state of research in this area well when they comment, "The boundaries of Yehud are one of the most debated issues in the study of the Persian Period in the region of Israel."[21] A survey of the literature dealing with the issue of geographical boundaries shows scholarly agreement on the central region and the northern and eastern borders.[22] There are various proposals for the western border; the debate is about whether or not to include the Shephelah as part of the province, as well as the region of Lod and Ono on the northwest corner of Yehud.[23] Like the western side, the southern border seems to be subject to discussion, although most scholars would position it between Beth-Zur and Hebron.[24] Figure 1 illustrates approximate borders according to the interpretation of this study.

---

[18] For example, Lester L. Grabbe, *A History of the Jews and Judaism in the Second Temple Period*, LSTS (London: T&T Clark, 2004), 134.

[19] Ibid.

[20] For example, Grabbe, Lipschits, Williamson.

[21] Alexander Fantalkin and Oren Tal, "Redating Lachish Level I: Identifying Achaemenid Imperial Policy at the Southern Frontier of the Fifth Satrapy," in *Judah and the Judeans in the Persian Period*, ed. Oded Lipschits and Manfred Oeming (Winona Lake, IN: Eisenbrauns, 2006), 179. Refer to pp. 179–180 for a brief discussion on the "Central Place Theory" application to the boundaries of Yehud.

[22] Grabbe provides a survey up to 2004. See bibliography for more recent sources.

[23] Grabbe, *A History of the Jews and Judaism in the Second Temple Period*, 135. Charles E. Carter, *The Emergence of Yehud in the Persian Period: A Social and Demographic Study*, JSOTSup 294 (Sheffield: Sheffield Academic, 1999). Amos Kloner, "The Identity of the Idumeans Based on the Archaeological Evidence from Maresha," in *Judah and the Judeans in the Achaemenid Period: Negotiating Identity in an International Context*, ed. Oded Lipschits, Gary N. Knoppers, and Manfred Oeming (Winona Lake, IN: Eisenbrauns, 2011). John W. Wright, "Remapping Yehud: The Borders of Yehud and the Genealogies of Chronicles," in *Judah and the Judeans in the Persian Period*, ed. Oded Lipschits and Manfred Oeming (Winona Lake, IN: Eisenbrauns, 2006).

[24] Grabbe, *A History of the Jews and Judaism in the Second Temple Period*, 155. Anson F. Rainey and R. Steven Notley, *The Sacred Bridge: Carta's Atlas of the Biblical World*, Second Emended and Enhanced ed. (Jerusalem: Carta, 2014), 295. Yohanan Aharoni, *The Land of the Bible: A Historical Geography*, 2nd rev. ed. (London: Burns & Oates, 1979), 416–17.

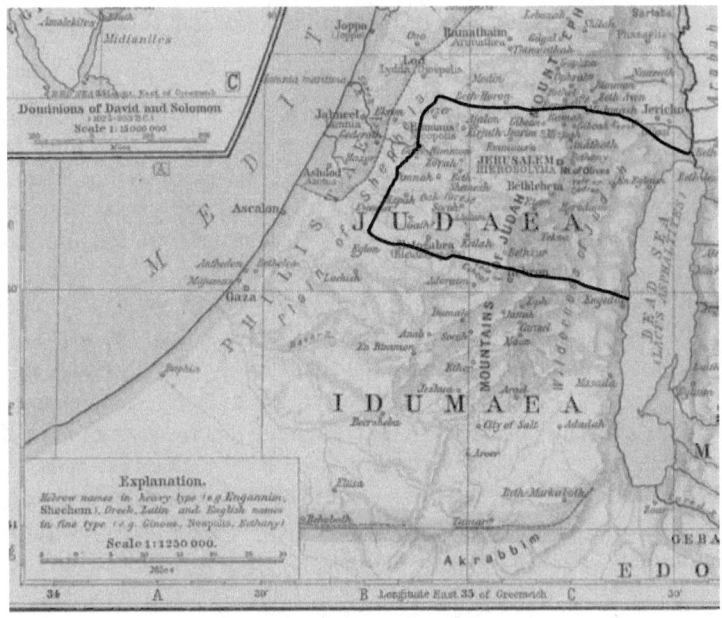

Figure 1. Approximate geographical area of Yehud.

Source: Shepherd, *Reference Map of Ancient Palestine*, 1923. Courtesy of the University of Texas Libraries, University of Texas at Austin. Historical maps PCL Map Collection.

As John Wright convincingly argues, however, positioning definitive borderlines is not the best way to reconstruct the actual boundaries of Yehud during the Persian period.[25] Wright suggests that in the past, borderlines were porous, less definitive:

> Recent maps that depict Yehud as a precisely bounded territory belong to a tradition of map-making that originates as recently as 1718. Borders are not ontologically real but are human constructs of the imagination. The concept of borders arises with the emergence of a particular form of polity—the modern nation-state. Depictions of borders for Yehud, therefore anachronistically

---

[25] Wright, "Remapping Yehud," 70–72. See also a general, but helpful discussion on cartography on I. W. J. Hopkins, "Nineteenth-Century Maps of Palestine: Dual-Purpose Historical Evidence," *Imago Mundi* 22 (1968): 30–36.

retroject a modernist, European polity onto the social realia of the sixth-fourth centuries B.C.E.[26]

According to Wright, it is this issue that makes it so difficult for scholars to agree on definitive borders; thus, he proposes the idea of a frontier based on ethnos and not nation-state as a more accurate reflection of the situation and representation of the dynamics and familial relations during this time.[27]

I question the benefit of a precise borderline in assisting with this investigation of the archaeology of ritual and religion of Yehud, and more specifically the area of the province known as the Shephelah. This position reflects my examination of the literature, as well as my studies done while visiting these locations in the Shephelah and the southern frontier of Yehud. Sites within these regions show a mixed material culture suggesting various ethnic groups and the possibility for religious practices that were directed toward different deities. For example, Maresha, a settlement in the southern border, that traditionally has been associated with the Edomites and categorized from the territorial perspective as Idumean, appears to show the presence of multiple religious practices suggesting varied ethnoi. Amos Kloner identifies both Edomites and Jews living and worshiping at the settlement.[28] Would including this settlement enrich not only the local understanding of ritual and religion at this locality but also the regional view during this time? In my opinion this inclusion would benefit this type of study and, therefore, I reject the idea of definitive borderlines for the study of household and family ritual. A number of archaeologists have been, and are currently excavating sites around the edges of the Shephelah, at settlements which were not excavated previously or that were excavated a century ago in the early 1900s.[29] Their findings will contribute to the understanding of this contested region. Perhaps even looking at this information in conjunction with other historical data will bring clarity to this issue in the future. Fantalkin and Tal study some of the historical and political components taking place during the Persian period, and suggest that definitive established borders do not occur until after 400 BCE when Egypt broke away from the Persians.[30]

---

[26] Wright, "Remapping Yehud," 70.

[27] Ibid., 70–71.

[28] Kloner, "Identity of the Idumeans," 563–64, 570, 572.

[29] For example, Oded Lipschits, Yuval Gadot, and Manfred Oeming in Tel ʿAzekah, Aren Meier in Tell eṣ-Ṣafi, Adi Erlich and Amos Kloner in Maresha.

[30] Fantalkin and Tal, "Redating Lachish Level I," 188.

In general, the Shephelah represents the foothills between the coastal plains to the West, and the Judean highland to the East. Traditionally, it covers the land which was part of the territory allotted to Judah. The northern edge reaches Gezer, and the southern portion approaches Tel Lachish. From a topographical perspective, it tends to include the low-rolling hills of between approximately 500 and 1,500 feet in elevation. These form part of a zone surrounded by roads and valleys which provide easy access to the coastal plains.[31] There seems to be agreement that Gezer, Tel Batash, Tel 'Azekah, Tell eṣ-Ṣafi (Gath), Tel Zayit (Khirbet Zeitah el-Kharab), Maresha, and Tel Lachish form part of the Shephelah. These last two sites at times are mentioned as part of the jurisdiction of Idumea and not Yehud, although this association probably reflects a political affiliation separate from an actual topographical connection. There are other archaeological sites within the Yehud Shephelah; however, these sites do not reveal Persian period material culture related to ritual and religion.

2.2.3 Judah and the Southern Levant under Persian Rule

The reconstruction of the Persian Empire provides challenges to historians due to the disparate sources and multiple languages used to gather this information. Still, classical writers like Herodotus, the Tanak, Old Persian royal inscriptions, Babylonian, Egyptian, Aramaic, and Elamite documents, and archaeology provide historians with sufficient data to understand this period.[32]

The southern Levant was situated somewhat in the middle of world empires prior to the Persian period. As figure 2 shows below in the sixth century BCE Babylonia controlled all of the southern Levant and a great portion of the land north, west, and south of this region. Powerful neighbors such as Egypt to the south, and Lydia and Media to the north surrounded Babylon. During this era Persia served a vassal territory of the Medes.

---

[31] Aharoni, *The Land of the Bible*, 26.
[32] Amélie Kuhrt, "The Persian Empire, c. 550–330 BC," in *Art et civilisation de l'Orient hellénisé: Rencontres et échanges culturels d'Alexandre aux Sassanides. Hommage à Daniel Schlumberger*, ed. Pierre Leriche (Paris: Picard, 2014), 51–52.

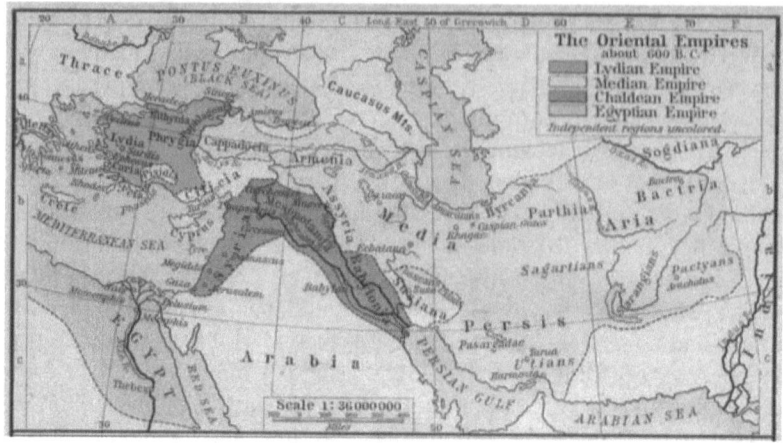

Figure 2. World powers during the sixth century BCE.

Source: Shepherd, *Persian Empire about 600 B.C.*, 1923. Courtesy of the University of Texas Libraries, University of Texas at Austin. Historical maps of the Middle East in PCL Map Collection.

Cyrus II, the Great, defeated Astyages in 550 BCE, probably on the plain of Pasargadae, and in large part due to the internal Median support that he received from their nobility. This key historical event contributed to Persian dominion over Median territories.[33] It seemed that religious and political propaganda might have had some influence: "Astyages held to the Old Iranian faith of his forefathers, whereas Cyrus [II] put himself forward as a champion of Zoroastrianism, and so attracted support from adherents of the eastern religion among Medes as well as Persians."[34]

After this victory, he dedicated two years to gaining control over the kingdoms of the Iranian plateau, and in 546 BCE he turned his attention towards the west as he conquered Lydia and most of Ionia.[35] Between 545 and 539 BCE

---

[33] Pierre Briant, *From Cyrus to Alexander: A History of the Persian Empire* (Winona Lake, IN: Eisenbrauns, 2002), 31.

[34] Mary Boyce, *Under the Achaemenians*, vol. 2 of *A History of Zoroastrianism* (Leiden: Brill, 1982), 43.

[35] Ibid., 49.

he came back east and expanded towards the Indian borderlands.[36] In 539 BCE the armies of Cyrus II conquered Babylon, and with this event, territories that were under Babylonian control became part of the new Persian Empire.[37] The last ten years of Cyrus II as king of Persia lack historical evidence, although it appears that Cyrus died while on a mission to Central Asia, shortly after he appointed Cambyses, his oldest son, as successor to the throne.[38] Further expansions increased the Persian presence in the area, and soon most of the Near East was under Persian control, as seen in figure 3. Cambyses assumed power as king without difficulty and traveled to Egypt between 525 and 522 BCE on a military campaign to expand and ensure better control of this Persian kingdom territory.[39] He left Egypt in the spring of 522 BCE to return to Persia to appease a rebellion that had emerged there led by his younger brother Bardiya, but was wounded while crossing Syria and died of gangrene complications in the thigh in the summer of 522 BCE.[40] Bardiya ruled briefly in 522 BCE, and was followed by Darius the Great, who reigned from 522 to 486 BCE. After Darius came, Xerxes who ruled from 486 to 465 BCE, followed by Artaxerxes I from 465 to 424 BCE. These kings were followed by Darius II, Artaxerxes II, Artaxerses III, and Darius III. During the reign of the last Persian kings, the empire continued to have challenges in maintaining control over such a vast area, but eventually most rebellions were controlled to the point of ensuring Persian dominion.

---

[36] Ibid., 50.
[37] Winn Leith, "Israel among the Nations," 371.
[38] Briant, *From Cyrus to Alexander*, 49.
[39] Ibid., 50–51.
[40] Ibid., 61.

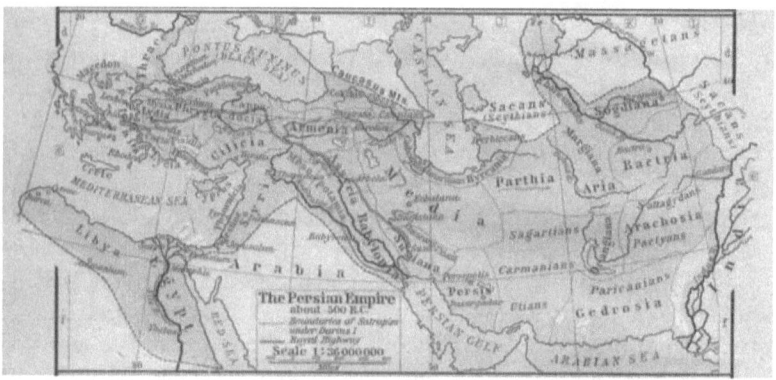

Figure 3. The extent of the Persian Empire.

Source: Shepherd, *Persian Empire about 600 B.C.*, 1923. Courtesy of the University of Texas Libraries, University of Texas at Austin. Historical maps PCL Map Collection.

The nature and structure of the Persian administration likely followed a similar method of organization to that of the Babylonian Empire.[41] According to Herodotus, Darius divided the empire into twenty provinces, which the Persians called satrapies.[42] Each province encompassed a large geographical territory, and always a Persian or Iranian noble resident, who acted as a satrap or governor, led the satrapal capital.[43] Kuhrt describes the role of these centers as follows: "The satrapal capital functioned as the administrative centre of the governor. It is here that tax was collected and stored (or sent on), satrapal archives were kept, petitions sent, and royal orders and edicts received. Each satrapal capital contained a palace, used by the satrap himself and also maintained for the king on visits."[44] It is likely that Mispah, a settlement associated with Tell en-Naṣbeh during this period, continued to be the largest administrative center in the Judean region from Babylonian rule through the early Persian period.[45] This position elevated the importance of Tell en-Naṣbeh as a Persian period settlement, and merits the more detailed discussion that follows in the next chapter. Yehud comprised a subprovince in the fifth Persian satrapy referred to as Abar Nahara or Beyond the River. Persian administration gave local satraps vast control of

---

[41] Winn Leith, "Israel among the Nations," 382.
[42] J. M. Cook, *The Persian Empire* (New York: Schocken Books, 1983), 77.
[43] Kuhrt, "Art et civilisation de l'Orient hellénisé," 53.
[44] Ibid.
[45] Brody, "Mizpah, Mizpeh," *NIDB* 4:116–17.

military affairs for war and/or public works, as well as the administrative and financial freedom to ensure the province's well-being and productivity.[46] This effective system of administration provided for regional variations to meet the diversity found in political units, as seen in the accommodation of sacred laws for the Jewish community in the province of Yehud, and yet it kept provinces loyal to a centralized form of government.[47] These Persian leaders and nobles intermarried with the local elites and participated at their rituals and religious practices as an effective way to integrate the empire's agendas.[48]

The higher ranking officials and nobles were not the only social strata to capitalize on Persian dominion, as the lower classes of local people, soldiers, and deportees gained land-parcels in exchange for an obligation to serve a specified military function in the army as the need required it.[49] This became an effective way to gain loyal troops at a local level, troops that could be activated at short notice.

2.2.4 Persian Influence on Religion

Persian religious practices manifested themselves during the Persian's time in power.[50] The Persians continued the Zoroastrian tradition, founded by the prophet Zoroaster in the Bronze Age.[51] This tradition traced back to Bactria, a region in the east located south of the Hindu Kush Mountains and just north of the Indus Valley, and this location was considered an ancient center for the faith.[52] It moved west via the camel caravan that traveled west to Raga through the Khorasan Highway, as part of trade and economic activities in the region.[53] Median sources are thought to have contributed to the adoption of

---

[46] Kuhrt, "Art et civilisation de l'Orient hellénisé," 53.
[47] Ibid., 54.
[48] Ibid.
[49] Ibid., 55.
[50] Even though the focus of the discussion in this section centers on Zoroastrianism and its possible influence or relationship to strands of early Judaism, it merits recognizing that people present in the southern Levant during this time practiced various religious expressions beyond Zoroastrianism and Judaism.
[51] Boyce, "Under the Achaemenians," 1–13. She presents the difficulties for dating Zoroaster with precision, but suggests a time prior to 1200 BCE; see p. 3. For recent coverage on Zoroastrianism and its influence on Judaism, see Jason M. Silverman, "Persian Influence on Jewish Apocalyptic," *PIBA* 32 (2009): 49–60. Silverman, "Iranian-Judean Interaction in the Achaemenid Period."
[52] Boyce, "Under the Achaemenians," 7–8.
[53] Ibid.

Zoroastrianism into the Achaemenian family.[54] The first direct proof of the religion is found within the Achaemenian family in the early sixth century BCE, as names of the royal family incorporate the nomenclature of the Zoroastrian moral beings or deities.[55] The great divinity, *Khšathra Vairya*, is the guardian of warriors, lord of the sky, and men in general, while his partner, *Spenta Ārmaiti*, is the protector of "lowly earth" and women.[56] In addition to these two important deities, *Ahuramazda*, who was the "Lord of Wisdom" selected priests of worthy wisdom and imparted them with his holy spirit, *Spenta Mainyu*.[57] *Ameša Spenta Ameretāt* symbolized immortality and the lord of the creation of plants, represented by a flower or rosette.[58] This symbol appeared in many aspects of daily living in Zoroastrian traditions as a reminder of the duty to live a life that would lead to immortality.[59] Boyce understands the preservation of the faith for thirty plus centuries as being connected to the following:

> Zoroaster, himself a priest, gave his followers simple, impressive, repetitive observances to maintain: the daily 'kusti' prayers to be said by each, and the seven yearly feasts to bring every local community together fraternally. The observances imprinted his doctrines on their minds; and these doctrines, themselves positive and hopeful, were ones which could give a purpose and cosmic significance even to humble acts of daily life.[60]

In Zoroastrianism, priests or *magu* dress in distinguishable clothing with white garments that are simple in nature, such as a simple shirt and close-fitting pants, to prevent them from brushing against sanctified ritual items as they preside over the ceremonies.[61] Access to the priesthood comes through heredity, transferring from father to son.[62] The worshipping activities take place in open

---

[54] Ibid., 42.
[55] Ibid., 41–42.
[56] Ibid., 3.
[57] Ibid.
[58] Ibid., 57.
[59] Ibid.
[60] Ibid., 4. Pierre Briant suggests that the "Persian religious beliefs and practices at the time of Cyrus and Cambyses is extraordinarily thin and contradictory." See Briant, *From Cyrus to Alexander*, 93. He calls into question the religion(s) practiced during the early part of the sixth century due to the lack of sources, although at the same time acknowledges the value of the Avesta, the sacred books of the Iranian tradition. For a position supporting Persian religious practices, see studies by Silverman and Boyce.
[61] Boyce, "Under the Achaemenians," 20.
[62] Ibid., 21.

spaces, typically high places, at the hearth-fire, near springs of water, and without temples, images, or altars.[63] I discuss in chapter 3 artifacts that were involved in fire rituals. It also appears that Zoroaster initiated the practice of celebrating festivals closely connected to pastoral and seasonal feasts in honor of all the gods.[64] Archaeological evidence from the eighth century BCE shows that Medians and western Iranians observed funerary rites, which included inhumation, or the burial of the body.[65] Recovered grave goods in the form of pottery, mostly jar, cups, pots, and vases, highlighted their belief in the afterlife, and the importance that Medians and western Iranians placed on taking care of the dead.[66] The religion also included purity laws, which prevented contamination of individuals with dead bodies, although Zoroastrianism considered stone to be an impermeable, solid barrier that could separate pure and impure.[67] The number three represented a Zoroastrian sacred number and it appeared at various places, such as steps to altars, tombs, as a key architectural feature in the design of divisions and construction details.[68]

It may be difficult to differentiate at times between Zoroastrianism and Israelite religion. It is likely that Zoroastrianism influenced Judaism during this period. In discussing these issues it is important to identify the background and influences that affected the Persian religion in the early days, as these factors contributed to its development into its final form. Mesopotamia, and in particular Babylonia, exerted influence over the Persian and Iranian Zoroastrian tradition as seen in the assimilation of the two alien cults of *Nabû* and *Ishtar*.[69] Some of these influences surfaced in their rituals and celebration of festivals, such as the spring and fall celebrations. It also appears that Persians influenced Mesopotamian cultures with their own rites, as seen in the ceremonial rite of the procession of white horses pulling an empty chariot with the invisible deity present in the chariot.[70]

The influence of Zoroastrianism on Judaism is disputed. Zoroastrianism differs from Judaism in its worship of many moral beings or deities. Boyce suggests that Zoroastrian influence appeared in the Near East starting in the

---

[63] Ibid., 21–22.
[64] Ibid., 23.
[65] Ibid., 25.
[66] Ibid., 26.
[67] Winn Leith, "Israel among the Nations," 370. Also see Boyce, "Under the Achaemenians," 56.
[68] Boyce, "Under the Achaemenians," 54, 58.
[69] Ibid., 33.
[70] Ibid., 36.

sixth century BCE, and she credits the remote satrapies in Asia, Babylonia, Israel, and Egypt for producing the evidence to support Zoroastrianism's presence.[71] Commenting on Zoroastrian's impact, she states: "as the religion of a great empire, Zoroastrianism exerted its widest influence, notably upon the Jews, contributing thus to shaping the beliefs and hopes of a large part of mankind."[72] Jason M. Silverman argues for a definite impact and notes that, "from a sociological-historical point of view it is unlikely that the Judaeans could have lived under Persian rule for roughly two centuries without having been influenced at all.... The outstanding questions, then, are the identification, type, and importance of any influence, and whether or not the available evidence is sufficient for demonstration."[73] Winn Leith opposes this view and argues that Judaism during the Persian period did not show strong influences from Zoroastrianism.[74] Boyce suggests that the Persians did not impose their religion on the people that they ruled, and "there appears to have been no official proselytizing, individuals (like the earlier propagandists for Cyrus) evidently spoke ardently about their faith."[75] However, Silverman notes that past scholarship was misguided in this area, and convincingly argues that these questions call for a more comprehensive examination which goes beyond Zoroastrian texts or tradition, and looks to "other Iranian religious traditions (perhaps 'unorthodox' traditions), Imperial ideology and propaganda, and cultural influences of a more general nature."[76] Furthermore, he encourages investigations beyond the Persians to other Iranian groups that were present in the area.[77] This point is important when considering how these influences may have manifested themselves in political rites and rituals at the family and household level.

Silverman identifies several avenues by which interaction occurred and references the work of John Hinnells as an important source of ideas.[78] Hinnells identifies "two basic types of influence, each with their own variations. The first type is the conscious imitation or borrowing of elements from another

---

[71] Ibid., xii.

[72] Ibid.

[73] Silverman, "Persian Influence on Jewish Apocalyptic," 52–53. Also, Silverman, "Iranian-Judean Interaction in the Achaemenid Period."

[74] Winn Leith, "Israel among the Nations," 370.

[75] Boyce, "Under the Achaemenians," 66.

[76] Silverman, "Persian Influence on Jewish Apocalyptic," 53.

[77] Ibid.

[78] Ibid., 57–59. Also, Silverman, "Iranian-Judean Interaction in the Achaemenid Period," 134.

tradition.... The second type of influence is the conscious rejection of another tradition." [79] Silverman points out that Iranian-Judaean interaction was significant not only at the official administrative level, but also in the daily aspect of daily living which suggested that the family and household level was a likely source of this interaction and included religious practices.[80] In addition to these two "conscious" influences, it seems likely that there was also an influence at the subconscious level. Even though Silverman does not address this issue directly, his observations and conclusions incorporate the idea that there was influence regardless. In another study related to Judaism, the authors acknowledge unconscious influences into Judaism and identify it as an intermingled component of the conscious influences: "Quite often a conscious rejection may go hand in hand with unconscious appropriation and transformation."[81] These ideas highlight the importance of carefully evaluating possible influences at different levels of social interactions, such as the administrative or official level of the Persian government, as well as at the household level.

2.2.5 Language

Ezra-Nehemiah portrays a strong condemnation towards Israelites using languages other than Hebrew. Nehemiah 13:24–25 narrates the negative view towards the language of Ashdod and the other foreign languages when it describes the inability of the Israelites to speak the language of Judah. In this case, Nehemiah curses and reprimands them for this action and for intermarriage. Ashdod is on the coast and during the Persian period this area shows material culture that suggests Philistine as well as Phoenician occupation. Lawrence Stager argues for a strong Phoenician presence, since he believes "the excavations at these two sites [referring to Ashkelon and Ashdod] show that the Phoenicians, not the Philistines, dominated their cultures. From the postexilic period on, there is not a trace of Philistines anywhere."[82] There is little known

---

[79] Silverman, "Iranian-Judean Interaction in the Achaemenid Period," 134.
[80] Ibid., 133, 134.
[81] Marcel Poorthuis, Joshua Schwartz, and Joseph Turner, *Interaction between Judaism and Christianity in History, Religion, Art and Literature*, Jewish and Christian Perspectives Series (Leiden: Brill, 2009), 1.
[82] Lawrence Stager, "Biblical Philistines: A Hellenistic Literary Creation?," in *"I Will Speak the Riddles of Ancient Times": Archaeological and Historical Studies in Honor of Amihai Mazar on the Occasion of His Sixtieth Birthday*, ed. Aren M. Maeir, Pierre de Miroschedji, and Amihay Mazar (Winona Lake, IN: Eisenbrauns, 2006), 383.

currently about the Philistine language, although it appears that the peoples living in the region of Philistia adopted the Aramaic language in ca. 300 BCE.

Language may constitute an important determinant in an ethnic group, and it may become a distinguishing mark within a religious community.[83] This factor was more significant in ancient times when language unified or separated groups and people. The text of Ezra-Nehemiah represents the socio-cultural existence of the Hebrew and the Aramaic languages in the southern Levant. As Polak notes, "bilingualism is not a matter of 'languages in contact' but of communities in contact and, thus, of political and social structure."[84] Aramaic, a Northwest Semitic language dating back to at least the beginning of the first millennium BCE, became the official and predominant language of the Persian Empire. Its usage grew with the empire, developing into the language of international trade, legal affairs, administration, and commerce.[85]

Even though Aramaic dominated the legal, administrative, and commercial area, Hebrew retained its preferential status for religious life and religious literary production.[86] Research points to Hebrew also being used as a language for communicating between family and friends.[87] Polak examines textual sources and determines the existence of a "Hebrew vernacular" during the Persian period.[88] Judeans appear to have continued to use Hebrew colloquially more than populations in the north, such as Galilee and Samaria.[89] Ingo Kottsieper and William Schniedewind challenge these notions based on biblical and epigraphic information, and argue that Aramaic replaced Hebrew for the

---

[83] Frank H. Polak, "Sociolinguistics and the Judean Speech Community in the Achaemenid Empire," in *Judah and the Judeans in the Persian Period*, ed. Oded Lipschits and Manfred Oeming (Winona Lake, IN: Eisenbrauns, 2006), 589–90.

[84] Ibid., 591.

[85] Winn Leith, "Israel among the Nations," 370. Also, Michael Guinan, "Aramaic, Aramaism," *NIDB* 1:228–31. Polak, "Sociolinguistics and the Judean Speech Community," 592. William Schniedewind, "Aramaic, the Death of Written Hebrew, and Language Shift in the Persian Period," in *Margins of Writing, Origins of Cultures*, ed. Seth L. Sanders, OIS 2 (Chicago: University of Chicago Press, 2006), 138.

[86] Ángel Sáenz-Badillos, *Historia de la Lengua Hebrea* (Sabadell: AUSA, 1988), 121. Also Polak, "Sociolinguistics and the Judean Speech Community," 614.

[87] Polak, "Sociolinguistics and the Judean Speech Community," 606. Also, Schniedewind, "Aramaic, the Death of Written Hebrew," 139. This last author supports a different position.

[88] Polak, "Sociolinguistics and the Judean Speech Community," 606.

[89] Sáenz-Badillos, *Historia de la Lengua Hebrea*, 121–22.

most part in Judah as the commonly spoken language.[90] In light of the work of Sáenz-Badillos and Polak, the existence and utilization of Hebrew in some religious and family contexts is well supported, even though Aramaic became the language of preference for official communication.

2.2.6 Demographic Changes: Social and Ethnic Groups

Nehemiah 7:66–68 provides estimates for the number of Israelites returnees. The text indicates 49,942, a number 45 people higher than that given in Ezra 2:64. Population results based on surveys and excavations illustrate possible settlement patterns for these returnees that start to inhabit the land outside of Jerusalem. The text of Nehemiah may present total numbers, but not necessarily a representation of a single return. Leen and Kathleen Ritmeyer suggest that Ezra-Nehemiah covers three separate trips of exiles; the first trip in 538–515 BCE led by Joshua and Zerubbabel in Ezra 1–6, the second trip in 458 BCE in Ezra 7–10, and the third trip in 444 BCE with Nehemiah from Neh 1–12.[91] The source and accuracy of the number of returnees in Ezra-Nehemiah has been a topic of extensive discussions, and the general consensus seems to be that "the list of returnees to Zion is a literary construction based on various lists, perhaps a list derived from a census of all residents of the province at various intervals."[92] Most scholars have difficulty placing the details of the list on a historical reconstruction.[93]

The southern Levant included various cultures during the Persian period. It appears that this region was the home of diverse groups, many of which were displaced, disrupted, and exiled by the Babylonians in the prior historical period. These included Philistines, Judahites, Samarians, Moabites, Ammonites, Edomites, Arabs, and Phoenicians.[94] Some Greek population and culture was integrated into the Phoenician civilization in the coastal areas, and therefore,

---

[90] Ingo Kottsieper, "And They Did Not Care to Speak Yehudit," in *Judah and the Judeans in the Fourth Century B.C.E.*, ed. Oded Lipschits, Gary N Knoppers, and Rainer Albertz (Winona Lake, IN: Eisenbrauns, 2007), 96–97. Also, Schniedewind, "Aramaic, the Death of Written Hebrew," 139–43.

[91] Leen and Kathleen Ritmeyer, *Jerusalem in the Time of Nehemiah* (Jerusalem: Carta, 2005), 15.

[92] Oded Lipschits, *The Fall and Rise of Jerusalem: Judah under Babylonian Rule* (Winona Lake, IN: Eisenbrauns, 2005), 160. Lipschits provides a detailed examination of the arguments.

[93] Ibid., 160 fn. 92.

[94] Winn Leith, "Israel among the Nations," 381.

indirectly Greek life also influenced part of the southern Levant.[95] Demographic studies based on archaeological surveys and excavations in table 1 show population estimates for Judah and Jerusalem which provide guidelines as to the number of inhabitants before and during the Persian period.

TABLE 1 Population estimates for Judah and Jerusalem

Location	Preexilic	Persian I Period (539–450 BCE)	Persian II Period (450–332 BCE)
Judah	32,250	10,850	17,000
Jerusalem	n/a	475–500	1,750

Note: n/a = not applicable.

Source: Data gathered from Winn Leith, *Israel among the Nations: The Persian Period*, 1998, 384.

The numbers show that Judah suffered a decline in population due to the previous Babylonian exile and the military devastation of the area. It is also possible that the regional and local economic situation improved over the length of the Persian period and this assisted in the increase of population in the area. This number increases later in the Persian II Period as Judah began to occupy a more strategic position in the region's economy and more exiles entered the land. Jerusalem's numbers illustrate a similar position.[96]

---

[95] Ibid.

[96] Lipschits's estimates for Jerusalem place the number of inhabitants during Persian I Period at 1,200–1,500. He criticizes Israel Finkelstein and other scholars' previous low population estimates for Jerusalem. Lipschits suggests that Jerusalem was bigger than the 20–24 dunams claimed by Finkelstein, and that in all likelihood it was closer in size to 60 dunams. Using this larger figure for the area, with the estimate of 20 to 25 persons per dunam gives a range of 1,200 to 1,500 total for the city. A dunam represents a portion of land equivalent to about 900 square meters. It comes from the times of the Ottoman Turkish period when it was associated with the amount of land that could be plowed in one day. See Oded Lipschits, "Persian Period Finds From Jerusalem: Facts and Interpretations," *JHebS* 9 (2010): 18.

2.2.7 Identity Formation

Given our present interests, it is essential to identify who is specifically signified by the name "Israel" in the book of Ezra. A review of the text suggests that there are two groups that seem to fit this term. First, there are those returnees that come back from the exile with a proven lineage. Ezra 2:70–3:1 identifies the exiles that settled in the land. Ezra 6:21 points to the exiles and those who joined them. Nehemiah 9:2 mentions the stock or seed of Israel. The second group incorporates the people who join the exiles by separating themselves from the rest. These are mentioned in Ezra 6:21 and Neh 10:29.

Who, on the other hand, is the other or enemy in Ezra-Nehemiah? In answering this question it is important to keep in mind that the text of Ezra-Nehemiah addresses theological conflicts and self-definitions in ways that create new identities. As such, references to people or ethnic groups contain motivations which need to be examined carefully.[97] Ezra 3:3 and 4:4 identify these inhabitants as the people of the land, and Ezra 4:1 calls them the adversaries of Judah and Benjamin. Ezra 4:1–5 could refer to several groups of ethnic people, such as foreigners, those in mixed marriages, returnees with doubtful lineage, Israelites that remained in the land, or a combination of all of these options.[98] The text of Nehemiah seems to be more specific in naming these other or enemies. Nehemiah 2:19 and Neh 3:33–35 identify Sanballat, the Horonite and Tobiah, the Ammonite servant, and Geshen, the Arab. Nehemiah 4:1–2 includes Sanballat, Tobiah, the Arabs, the Ammonites, and the Ashdodites. Nehemiah 5:1 is more general and refers to the people of the land. In terms of group identity, it appears that the text of Ezra-Nehemiah sets boundaries and considers as other or enemies those Israelites that were not part of the returnees. To these groups belong the lower classes that Nebuchanedzzar left behind in the land, in addition to people of other nations, some of which included those that were brought to Palestine as a result of the Assyrian resettlements. The term Arabs makes reference to people in the Arabian Peninsula, some of whom migrated as pastoral-nomads to the Levant in the Persian period. Ammonites settled east of the Jordan River in the early Iron Age, developing their own eponymous kingdom in the Iron Age II. During the Persian period, Ammon was considered part of the district of the fifth satrapy, Beyond-the-River.[99] To this group Nehemiah also adds the Samaritans, whom he considers to be gentiles and

---

[97] See Japhet, *From the Rivers of Babylon to the Highlands of Judah*, Chapter 5.
[98] Winn Leith, 398.
[99] Jean-Michel De Tarragon, "Ammon (Person)," *ABD* 1:195.

spiteful enemies of the true Israel, despite their Jewish background.[100] I suggest that some of these antagonistic views may be the result of competitive issues related to the building of the Samaritan Temple in Mt. Gerizim in the mid-fifth century BCE.

2.3 Analysis of Ezra

In light of the discussion of language, external religious influences and other contextual elements, I now move on to consider ritual in Ezra in order to evaluate what ritual evidence may be gathered from this text. Ezra 1:1 starts with a reference to the proclamation made by King Cyrus of Persia after "the LORD roused" his spirit to begin the building of the temple in Jerusalem.[101] The text cites the actual proclamation from Ezra 1:2–4. This instance may be a political rite meant to establish credibility in selecting Jerusalem as the official settlement for the construction of the temple, and also to reestablish, with imperial endorsement, the worship of the God of Israel. The proclamation repeats and refers to Jerusalem three times in two verses. Persian official protocols started the dissemination of proclamations, first in oral form, and then in writing utilizing Aramaic.[102] There are religious connections in this proclamation and the interrelationships that existed between imperial acts and rituals.[103] This passage represents one of the two versions of the Cyrus edict found in Ezra, the other being in Aramaic in Ezra 7:3–5.[104] There is a possible correlation between this last one to the Jewish version circulating in communities at this time.[105] Myers suggests that Cyrus' decree publicly read in

---

[100] Yitzhak Magen, "Bells, Pendants, Snakes, and Stones: A Samaritan Temple to the Lord on Mt. Gerizim," *BAR* 36.6 (2010): 30. Also Winn Leith, "Israel among the Nations," 385.

[101] Adele Berlin et al., *The Jewish Study Bible* (Oxford: Oxford University Press, 2004). All biblical references in this section utilize this version unless otherwise noted.

[102] Blenkinsopp, *Ezra-Nehemiah: A Commentary*, 75. Also, Andrés Fernández S.J., *Comentario a los Libros de Esdras y Nehemías* (Madrid: Consejo Superior de Investigaciones Científicas, 1950), 48–49.

[103] Davies, *Ezra and Nehemiah*, 6.

[104] Myers, *Ezra Nehemiah*, 5. Schoville, *Ezra-Nehemiah*, 41. Also, Samuel Pagán, *Esdras, Nehemías y Ester*, Comentario Bíblico Hispanoamericano (Miami, FL: Editorial Caribe, 1992), 52.

[105] Myers, *Ezra Nehemiah*, 5.

these communities and then posted for all to read.[106] Given the level of literacy during this time, it is most likely that the decree was heard rather than read.

Ezra 1:4 and 1:6 mention freewill offerings, in relationship to "the House of God." These were voluntary offerings which were made spontaneously.[107] This kind of offering may be classified as a rite of exchange and communion, since it is made as part of the relationship that existed between God and the sons of Israel. Ezra 2:68–70 also refers to freewill offerings made "to erect the House of God" by "the chiefs of the clans."

Ezra 3:2 mentions the assembly of the Israelites to build "the altar of the God of Israel to offer burnt offerings," as prescribed in the Torah of Moses, and Ezra 3:6 also establishes the continued tribute of burnt offerings. The Hebrew text has *'ōlōt*, which are "sacrifices wholly burned, comprising domestic animals and occasionally birds."[108] Steinmann notes that the burnt offering "consisted of the evening and morning sacrifices that ensured that there would be part of a sacrificial lamb on the altar at all times. It also included offerings of flour, oil, and wine."[109] These offerings may be classified as rites of exchange and communion.

Ezra 3:4 shows how the Israelites "celebrated the festival of Tabernacles as is written," in conjunction with its daily burnt offerings for the duration of the festival. These were in addition to the regular burnt offerings. The sacrifices for the seven-day festival and the reasoning behind the comment "as is written" refer to the legislation available in Lev 23:34, 39 and Num 29:12–38.[110] The text may refer to this festival lasting seven days, but there is also mention of an eighth day.[111] Also of interest is the integration within the Tabernacles festival offerings of a sin offering of a male goat done daily during the seven-day period. Tabernacles may be classified under the category of feast, fasting, and festivals, as well as a calendrical rite due to its celebration at the specific date of the fifteenth day of the seventh month. The text in Ezra 3:5 also mentions "offerings for the new moons and for all the sacred fixed times of the LORD." These offerings would also fall under calendrical rites.

---

[106] Ibid., 6.
[107] Ludwig Koehler, Walter Baumgartner, M. E. J. Richardson, and Johann Jakob Stamm, *HALOT*.
[108] Ibid.
[109] Steinmann, *Ezra and Nehemiah*, 208.
[110] James C. VanderKam, "Calendars: Ancient Israelite and Early Jewish," *ABD* 1:816. Also, Blenkinsopp, *Ezra-Nehemiah: A Commentary*, 98.
[111] VanderKam, "Calendars," *ABD* 1:816.

Ezra 3:10–11 narrates the assembly of priests, Levites, and all the people to celebrate the construction of the foundation of the Temple of the LORD with singing, praising, and weeping. The mention of "all the people" shows how families and households participated in rituals at various levels of their social life, some of which included more public ceremonies. The priests and Levites wore their vestments and celebrated with musical instruments. These activities may be feasting rites, or may also symbolize aspects of a political rite. Blenkinsopp identifies a close connection to ritual with the re-establishing of the temple on ground used for the First Temple. He notes, "the ceremony in question was known in ancient Mesopotamia as the kalu ritual (*kalû* = ritual singers), implying a liturgy of hymn-singing and inevitably recalling the situation as described in Ezra 3."[112] There may be support for a political rite in Ezra 4:1–2, which presents the confrontation with the adversaries of Judah and Benjamin over the building of the temple in Jerusalem and the worshiping of the God of Israel. This ritual may be publicly acknowledging the reinstatement of the Israelite worship system.

Ezra 4:23 mentions the occurrence when "the text of the letter of King Artaxerxes was read." The act and the rites accompanying the reading of an official Persian imperial letter may have presented the opportunity to construct, display, and promote power by the ruling officials. As such, these instances may be classified as political rites.

Ezra 6:16–17 indicates that, "the Israelites, the priests, and the Levites, and all the other exiles celebrated the dedication of the House of God" by sacrificing various animals as a "purification offering for all of Israel." The offering of the twelve goats as expiation for all of Israel is based on priestly ritual from Lev 4:22–26; 9:3, and Ezek 43:18–27; and the sin offering for the leaders is from Num 7.[113] These offerings may be classified as rites of affliction by which the community seeks to purify and dedicate something or someone.

Ezra 6:19–22 incorporates several rites into one passage. First, Ezra 6:19 mentions the celebration of Passover "on the fourteenth day of the first month." For Israelites, this festival marks critical points in their history. Blenkinsopp, highlighting its importance within this narrative and Chronicle's, notes "[in] the context of C's [Chronicle's] history as a whole, which must always be borne in mind, this is the third new beginning marked by the celebration of this festival with the participation of all the people ... the festival marked the climax of

---

[112] Blenkinsopp, *Ezra-Nehemiah: A Commentary*, 104.
[113] Ibid., 130.

religious renewal including the restoration of temple worship."[114] This celebration may be classified as a calendrical rite due to its associations with a specific day of the year. It is also feasible to see this ritual as a rite of exchange and communion, if one considers it within the context of the covenant, and the renewed commitment to follow God's divine plan. Verse 20 notes that "the priests and Levites had purified themselves to a man," as well as others who were to participate in the Passover's activities. These purifications may be classified as rites of affliction. Verse 22 continues with the Feast of Unleavened Bread, which lasted for seven days. This celebration is both a calendrical rite and a feasting rite.

Ezra 7:11 cites "the text of the letter which King Artaxerxes gave to Ezra," and verses 12–26 narrates such communication. Again, official diplomatic letters may be classified as political rites if one assumes that they incorporate symbols and other rituals in favor of promoting those in positions of power. Verse 14 hints at such motives: "For you are commissioned by the king and his seven advisers to regulate Judah and Jerusalem according to the law of your God." Here too the text several times specifies the House of God being in Jerusalem.

Ezra 8:21–23 mentions the fast that Ezra proclaimed as a petition for a safe journey from the Ahava River to Jerusalem. These actions may be both a rite of exchange and communion as well as a fasting rite. Ezra and his companions fasted to beseech God, and to receive consideration in the form of protection during their passage to Jerusalem. The connection with ritual is assumed, as Blenkinsopp notes, "[fasting] often acts as a reinforcement of prayer, not infrequently involving confession of sin…. The very ancient idea of fasting as a form of mortification, in the etymological sense of bringing oneself to the point of death in order to bring into play the saving power of God, is also present here in connection with self-abasement."[115] Ezra 8:35 indicates the burnt offerings made once the exiles got to Jerusalem as a purification offering. These may be classified as a rite of affliction.

Ezra 9:3–10:1 narrates the moment when Ezra became aware of the intermarriage that had taken place among the priests, Levites, and the people of Israel, and how he responded in sorrow and distress. The passage provides a prayer and confession for the maladies and iniquities committed by Israel. The passage is full of symbolic representations, which are associated with mourning and deep sorrow. These are outward signs shown with the ripping of clothes, shaving of the beard or head's hair, sitting on the floor or on ashes, and not

---

[114] Ibid., 132.
[115] Ibid., 168.

eating or drinking. Blenkinsopp recognizes these rituals as representing a public relation effort on the part of Ezra to draw attention to support his views.[116] This section may be classified as a rite of affliction. Ezra 10:5–6 contains Ezra's decision "to put the officers of the priests and the Levites and all Israel under oath," and his not eating or drinking following this announcement. Even though these actions illustrate a fast, the underlying motive for the fast may be more closely associated with the purification of the people for their sins related to their intermarriage practices. As such, it is more likely to be classified as a rite of affliction than as a fasting rite.

Ezra 10:7–11 mentions Ezra's proclamation and command for all the people to assemble. At the meeting they confess their guilt and agree to purify themselves through separation from foreign people. These include those who had been involved in intermarriages outside of Israel. The assembly may be seen as a feasting, fasting, festival type of rite portraying religio-cultural sentiments. Verse 19 indicates the people's acknowledgement of the guilt and the offering of animals as expiation. This last action may be classified as a rite of affliction. Refer to table 2 for a summary of the types of rites analyzed above.

---

[116] Ibid., 177.

TABLE 2 Ritual Typologies in Ezra

Reference	Event	Type of ritual
Ezra 1:1	King Cyrus' proclamation	Political
Ezra 1:4, 6; 2:68–70	Freewill offerings for "the House of God"	Exchange and communion
Ezra 3:3	Establishment of daily burnt/whole offering	Exchange and communion
Ezra 3:4	Celebration of the Festival of Tabernacles/Booth	Feast, fasting, and festival Calendrical
Ezra 3:5	Offerings of new moons	Calendrical
Ezra 3:10–11	Assembly to celebrate construction of Temple foundations	Feast, fasting, and festival Political
Ezra 4:23	Reading of letter of King Artaxerxes	Political
Ezra 6:16–17	Dedication of the House of God and the purification as expiation for all of Israel	Affliction
Ezra 6:19–22	1. Celebration of Passover 2. Purification ceremonies 3. Feast of Unleavened Bread	1. Calendrical 2. Affliction 3. Calendrical and/or feast, fasting, and festival
Ezra 7:11, 12–26	King Artaxerxes' letter	Political
Ezra 8:21–23	Ezra's fast for safe journey to Jerusalem	Exchange and communion
Ezra 8:35	Burnt/whole offerings as purification offerings	Affliction
Ezra 9:3–10:1	Ezra's mourning and outward physical expressions of sorrow for intermarriages	Affliction
Ezra 10:7–11	1. Ezra's proclamation for people to assemble. 2. Guilt offerings associated with expiation.	1. Assembly: feasting, fasting, festival. 2. Guilt offering: affliction

The analysis of Ezra shows at least seventeen occurrences of ritual practices, as outlined in table 2. Ezra contains repeated instances of rituals that cover five of the six ritual typologies; only the rite of passage is absent. Ezra shows a wide distribution of ritual considering the relatively short, ten-chapter length of the text.

The placement of these rituals in the text possibly suggests an intentional pattern in support of the reinstatement of centralized worship of the God of Israel. The first is a political rite in Ezra 1:1 with King Cyrus's proclamation. As defined by Bell earlier, these rites "construct, display, and promote the power of political institutions," and in Ezra the proclamation may very well be acting in such manner.[117] I find support for this view of political rites in Renfrew's comments: "a ritual does not only establish social convention, it establishes acceptance.... Ritual can play a crucial role in establishing and maintaining many aspects of the social order."[118] Rites of exchange and communion follow in Ezra 1:4, 1:6; 2:68–70; and 3:3. These rites reestablish the foundational offerings for the worship of God by instituting the freewill offerings and the daily burnt or whole offerings.

In addition to placement, I suggest that the large number and wide distribution of rites in Ezra show how key components of early Judaism resurfaced in the book, in what appears to be a strong support of the book's theme of the reestablishment of the people of Israel in the land during the postexilic times. Rites such as the Festival of Tabernacles, the celebration of Passover, the Feast of Unleavened Bread, and various rededication rituals provide a well-represented repertoire of Judaism's rituals. These are some of the most foundational and important rites of the religion and Ezra contains all of these. The rites of affliction presented in the text provide an opportunity for purification and the recommitment of the people to the God of Israel. The appearance of calendrical rites in a sense serves to reenact and remember past relationships that Israel had with God. It also places the history of the renewed Israel within the previous relational context keeping in mind their covenantal ties. In summary, rites in Ezra provide a framework that supports some of the book's principal messages.

---

[117] Bell, *Ritual: Perspectives and Dimensions*, 128.
[118] Renfrew, "The Archaeology of Ritual, Cult, and of Religion," 119.

2.4 Review of Other Persian Period Biblical Texts

Are the findings discussed above unique to Ezra-Nehemiah? What contributions do other biblical texts dated to the Persian period make to family or household ritual and religion? I will address these questions by looking at the comprehensive work of Rainer Albertz, in which he analyzes the biblical texts that relate to Israelite family and household religion during the Persian period.[119] In this study he concludes that there was a convergence of the religious strata and a split in personal piety.[120] He recognizes two "class-specific types of personal piety: the theologized wisdom of the pious upper class and the piety of the poor in lower-class circles with a religious orientation."[121] For the first type Albertz lists Job and Prov 1–9 as evidence. He also suggests that there was a social and theological crisis during this time.[122] Albertz conducts a detailed analysis of Job and highlights the importance of the dialogue between Job and his friends. For the second type he attributes Pss 9–10, 35, 69, 70, 109, 140 to the religious circles of the lower class, and Pss 12, 14, 75, 82 for prophetic liturgies.[123] A detailed analysis of these texts, such as the one that I conducted for Ezra-Nehemiah would be beyond the scope of this study. However, my review of Albertz's work covering the above mentioned biblical texts indicates that these texts do not provide sufficient details to develop a comprehensive understanding of family and household ritual and religion during the Persian period. Furthermore, it would be advantageous to explore the material culture to gather data that is absent from the text.[124]

This chapter provides contextual background of the Persian period in the southern Levant, and analyzes Ezra in detail as a representative sample of a biblical text from this time. After a review of a representative sample of

---

[119] Albertz, "From the Exile to the Maccabees." In this early work Albertz references the term personal piety in connection with family and household ritual and religion.

[120] Ibid., 508.

[121] Ibid.

[122] Ibid.

[123] Ibid., 519.

[124] Albertz shares a similar view with regards to the need to examine other sources. In 2012 he published a study that incorporates among other sources the archaeology of ritual and religion in his coverage of household and family ritual. Addressing the validity of the study, he writes, "there has yet to appear a single, comprehensive description of Israelite family and household religion in all of its aspects and dimensions and comparing it with the family religions of the broader Syro-Levantine environment." See Albertz and Schmitt, *Family and Household Religion in Ancient Israel and Levant*, 15, 17.

commentaries on Ezra-Nehemiah as well as Albertz's detailed study on Persian period Israelite religion, I conclude that there is an overall lack of scholarly dialogue and minimal coverage on rituals and religious practices in these texts. The same can be said for the lack of information on family and household rituals or religious practices. The few references to family or household practices in Ezra are all located around official ceremonies related to the reestablishment of a temple in Jerusalem. This leaves a large gap regarding family practices outside of Jerusalem, let alone the possibility of rituals or religion taking place in the houses in which most Judeans resided. These findings support the need for a household archaeological approach to the ritual and religion of Persian period Yehud.

3. PERSIAN PERIOD RITUAL ARTIFACTS FROM TELL EN-NAṢBEH HOUSEHOLDS

In this chapter I investigate the archaeology of ritual and religion in Persian period southern Levant and how this provides insights into identifying this type of material at Tell en-Naṣbeh. I present my investigation of Persian period ritual artifacts from the Tell en-Naṣbeh collection at the Badè Museum of Biblical Archaeology in Berkeley, and with the help of those findings, identify locations at Tell en-Naṣbeh where family and household ritual and religious practices might have taken place.

3.1 Significance of Tell en-Naṣbeh

Tell en-Naṣbeh constituted an important and strategic settlement in Judah. Occupation covered from the Late Chalcolithic period to the Roman period, with some later extramural tombs dating to the Byzantine period.[1] The road that ran north-south connecting Jerusalem with the hill country passed right by this location, making Tell en-Naṣbeh an important stopping point.[2] There have been scholarly discussions on whether this settlement should be associated with biblical Mispah. The majority of scholars tend to support this identification. Aaron Brody examined the data and provided an insightful interpretation of the location with the conclusion that this settlement was likely Mispah of Benjamin prior to the Hellenistic period.[3] He attributes the connection between Naṣbeh and Mispah to the impressive Iron II-period wall that surrounds the ancient city.[4] Zorn views this elaborate wall as an important component, as it served to

---

[1] Jeffrey R. Zorn, "Nasbeh, Tell en-," *NEAEHL* 3:1098. There are tombs and a church floor that date to the Roman and Byzantine periods.

[2] Ibid., 1098.

[3] Ibid. Also, Brody, "Mizpah, Mizpeh," *NIDB* 4:117. Brody suggests a possibility of Nebi Samwil being the settlement of Hellenistic period Mispah mentioned in 1 Maccabees.

[4] Brody, "Mizpah, Mizpeh," *NIDB* 4:117.

position Mispah as Judah's northernmost border military installation.⁵ Silverman likewise supports the idea that the route that passed by Tell en-Naṣbeh was strategic, and recognizes the importance of fortifications in the Persian period as a conduit and way station for royal and administrative personnel, as well as the royal mail.⁶ Mispah rose in importance after Jerusalem's destruction in 587 BCE when it became the regional capital for the province of Judah.⁷ Oded Lipschits suggests that Tell en-Naṣbeh was the main administrative center during the Babylonian period with its own local governor, but points to the palace at Ramat Raḥel as an indication that the latter rose in importance during Persian control, and considers Ramat Raḥel to have been the main administrative settlement during the Persian period.⁸ Lipschits bases these arguments on his interpretations of his excavations at Ramat Raḥel. He recognizes the presence of a magnificent palace-like structure and elaborates adjacent gardens as important indications that Persian officials resided here.⁹

The Tell en-Naṣbeh excavations of almost two-thirds of the whole site, excavations that took place from 1926 to 1935 led by the late William Badè, offer a unique view into a Judean fortified village. The site provides a fairly complete representation of the living conditions during both its Iron II and Babylonia-Persian period phases due to the large area that was excavated. I find that this contributes significantly to better understanding family and household ritual and religion, especially since the pillared house is the only building type at the site. In fact, as this study demonstrates, Tell en-Naṣbeh's Stratum 2 architecture and domestic material culture are unique in the southern Levant. And these provide an excellent context for the study of family and household rituals and/or religious practices because extensive excavations of structures

---

⁵ Zorn, "Nasbeh, Tell en-," *NEAEHL* 3:1098. Mispah diminished in importance with the shift of the location of the administrative center to Ramat Raḥel and Jerusalem during the Persian period. Brody also recognizes this fortification and the existence of water sources as evidence of its strategic role. Brody, "Mizpah, Mizpeh," *NIDB* 4:116.

⁶ Silverman, "Iranian-Judean Interaction in the Achaemenid Period," 158–59.

⁷ Brody, "Mizpah, Mizpeh," *NIDB* 4:116–17. Also, Jeffrey R. Zorn, "Tell en-Nasbeh and the Problem of the Material Culture of the Sixth Century," in *Judah and the Judeans in the Neo-Babylonian Period*, ed. Oded Lipschits and Joseph Blenkinsopp (Winona Lake, IN: Eisenbrauns, 2003), 413.

⁸ Oded Lipschits, Yuval Gadot, and D. Langgut, "The Riddle of Ramat Raḥel: The Archaeology of a Royal Persian Period Edifice," *Transeu* 41 (2012): 77.

⁹ Ibid.

from one stratum provide some of the most valuable mechanisms to investigate social aspects of a culture.[10]

As indicated in the Introduction, excavation reports and data from the early 1900s represent both challenges and benefits to the researcher.[11] Brody and Zorn identify several challenges that are applicable to archaeological expeditions from the 1920s to the 1930s, the time when William Badè excavated Tell en-Naṣbeh, and therefore these need to be mentioned:[12] first, the timing of the Great Depression and the effects that this event had on the expedition; second, the death of Badè, the director, that caused a break in leadership continuity; third, the lack of sufficient comparative material from other sites to aid in diagnosis and stratigraphy; and finally the challenge of Badè's methodology of excavation that was based on the previous model developed by Clarence Fisher, but with the additional limitation that "Badè did not differentiate between materials from room fills and in situ floor material.... This methodology could not help but mix material from later leveling fills with debris from floor surfaces and earlier sub-floor material."[13] Even with these limitations, there is much that Tell en-Naṣbeh can contribute to the study of both ritual and religion and of family and household archaeology.[14] In summary, the extensive excavations at Tell en-Naṣbeh and the large assembly of recovered artifacts offer a unique view and a significant contribution to better understand Judean rituals during the Babylonian occupation and the Persian period.

---

[10] Jeffrey R. Zorn, "This Old Site: Issues in the Reappraisal of Early Excavations," in *Archaeology's Publication Problem*, ed. J. Aviram and Hershel Shanks (Washington, DC: Biblical Archaeology Society, 1996), 63.

[11] Ibid., 59–61. Zorn identifies two benefits of reevaluating an older site compared with beginning a new excavation: reduced costs, and the availability of records and artifacts in museums and universities in the United States and Europe.

[12] Aaron J. Brody, "The Archaeology of the Extended Family: A Household Compound from Iron II Tell en-Nasbeh," in *Household Archaeology in Ancient Israel and Beyond*, ed. Assaf Yasur-Landau et al., Culture and History of the Ancient Near East, 50 (Leiden: Brill, 2011). Also, Zorn, "This Old Site," 60–61.

[13] Zorn, "This Old Site," 62.

[14] Brody provides a fine example of this with his analysis of the extended family at Tell en-Naṣbeh. See Brody, "Archaeology of the Extended Family." Zorn shares this positive outlook despite the challenges: "it is still possible to clarify not only the stratigraphy and architecture of a site, but also questions of social organization, economy and political organization, and foreign influences." See Zorn, "This Old Site," 67.

3.2 Persian Period Tell en-Naṣbeh

Prior to discussing the archaeology specific to Persian period Tell en-Naṣbeh, it is important to comment on particularities of the depositional record and material culture of the Persian period, as these have an effect on what has been recovered. Persian period material culture, and in particular architecture, poses challenges to archaeologists that investigate this period. At many sites Persian layers tend to be at the top, making them subject to erosion and damage.[15] In addition, sites that have had Hellenistic and Roman occupation often lack much of the Persian period architecture and structures, since later inhabitants damaged or utilized the materials from the Persian period for their own constructions.[16] The Babylonians and the Persians showed little interest in growing urban areas in the hill country.[17] Despite these challenges, archaeologists continue to excavate new or existing sites that contain Persian period material, and this is leading to a better understanding of this era.

The architectural remains at Tell en-Naṣbeh provide a mechanism to relate architecture and artifacts during the Persian period. Zorn's dissertation reevaluates the site's architecture and stratigraphy with the intention of reviewing the dating that the original excavators assigned the site.[18] Zorn attributes material culture from the Persian period to Stratum 2, which he dates to ca. 586 to 450?/400? BCE.[19] This range encompasses Babylonian to mid-Persian periods.

Persian period Tell en-Naṣbeh architectural remains survived at various states of preservation. Zorn's 1993 study contributes significantly to the identification of architecture at Tell en-Naṣbeh. Figure 4 shows the complete site map of Tell en-Naṣbeh with Zorn's identification of Stratum 2 architecture. He notes how over half of "Stratum 2 buildings are preserved only at foundation levels."[20] However, it was possible to distinguish this stratum from previous and

---

[15] Oded Lipschits, "Achaemenid Imperial Policy and the Status of Jerusalem," in *Judah and the Judeans in the Persian Period*, ed. Oded and Manfred Oeming Lipschits (Winona Lake, IN: Eisenbrauns, 2006), 28. Also Ephraim Stern, *Material Culture of the Land of the Bible in the Persian Period 538–332 B.C.* (Warminster, England: Aris & Phillips, 1982), vii.

[16] Lipschits, "Achaemenid Imperial Policy and the Status of Jerusalem," 28.

[17] Ibid., 28–29.

[18] Zorn, "Tell en-Nasbeh: A Re-evaluation."

[19] Ibid., 163. The interrogation marks denote approximate dating.

[20] Ibid., 167.

subsequent strata, due to differences in building construction techniques and the orientation of the buildings.[21]

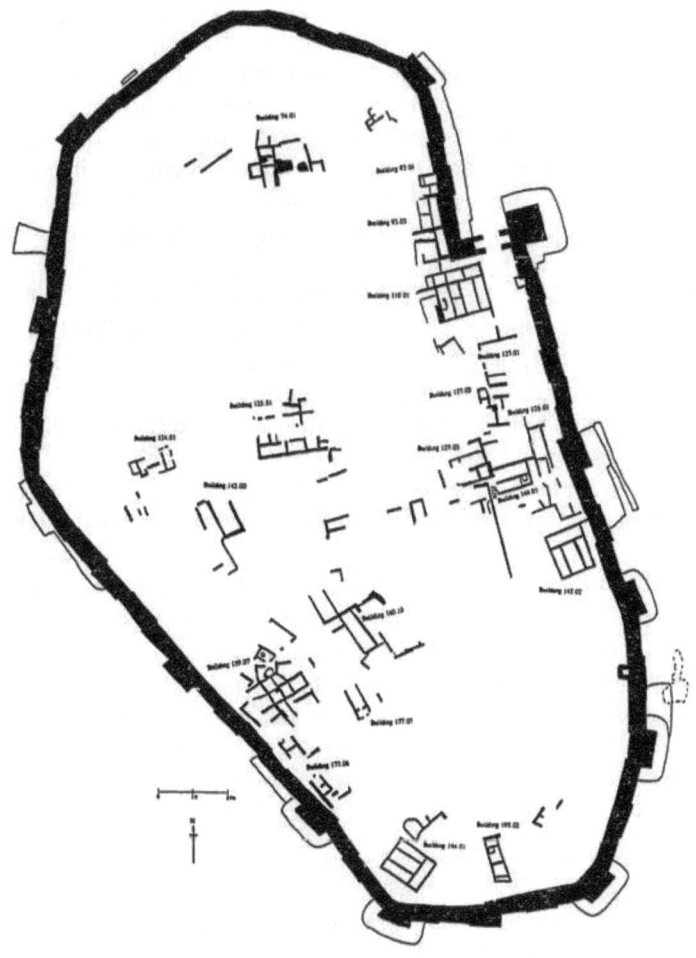

Figure 4. Tell en-Naṣbeh Stratum 2 architecture.

Source: Zorn, "Tell en-Nasbeh: A Re-evaluation," 966. Used by permission.

---

[21] Ibid.

Zorn identifies the following structural differences between Stratum 2 and Stratum 3: a more common use of stone paved floors in buildings, the use of more costly monolithic pillars in buildings, walls that were almost always two stones wide, the construction of larger four-room buildings that were "1.3 to 2.2 [times] larger than the largest Stratum 3 buildings," and "the larger size of 3-Room buildings" compared to Stratum 3.[22] Zorn reconstructs building floor plans and I include in appendix B those specific to Stratum 2. It appears that there was a deliberate leveling of Stratum 3 buildings and architecture in order to accommodate the larger and more elaborate Stratum 2 construction.[23] Development of the Stratum 2 building foundations at times used Stratum 3 building walls, and it appears that there was no gap in the occupation of Tell en-Naṣbeh between the Iron Age and the Persian period.[24] Like many contemporary sites, and as discussed above, Tell en-Naṣbeh's Stratum 2 suffered from erosion in some areas, specifically the SE and NW corners.[25] Yet, Zorn notes the following four areas as locations with significant remains of Stratum 2: (1) "from the outer gate to just S of the inner gate;" (2) "the N end of the town;" (3) "the center of the town;" and (4) "the SW corner to the S end."[26] Even with these remains and those of the four-room houses, there is insufficient evidence to suggest any type of pattern for TEN during Stratum 2 or a definitive citywide road system.[27]

To the extent that it pertains to this study, I utilize the archaeology of Stratum 2 Tell en-Naṣbeh as a representative layer for Persian period material culture, even though it may be difficult at times to isolate a pure Persian period date, since the stratum also covers the Babylonian period of 586–537 BCE. In addition, in order to assist in better identifying only Stratum 2 material, I use data from Zorn's architectural and stratigraphic analysis that can be pinpointed exclusively to Stratum 2 with certainty. He labels these remains with an exclamation point in his report.[28] The only exceptions to this approach are

---

[22] Ibid., 173, 170–85. Also, Zorn, "Tell en-Nasbeh and the Problem of the Material Culture of the Sixth Century," 428–29.

[23] Zorn, "Tell en-Nasbeh: A Re-evaluation," 163. Also, Zorn, "Tell en-Nasbeh and the Problem of the Material Culture of the Sixth Century," 420. Zorn associates this new building to "Gedaliah's transformation of Mispah from a fortified town on Judah's northern border into a new administrative center." See ibid., 419.

[24] Zorn, "Tell en-Nasbeh: A Re-evaluation," 163–64.

[25] Ibid., 176.

[26] Ibid., 177.

[27] Ibid., 179.

[28] Ibid., 164.

Building 93.01 and Rooms 373, 374, and 377, which are located around the outer gate. These may date prior to Stratum 2, but there is certainty that they continued to be in use during the Persian period. I present in table 3 a list of Stratum 2 building remains adapted from Zorn's analysis.[29] The excavation and recording methods used at the time of Tell en-Naṣbeh expedition, resulted in challenges when trying to associate strata with most of the artifacts found at Persian period Tell en-Naṣbeh.[30] However, there were two houses, Building 110.01 and 125.01, where in situ artifacts were found, and these buildings provide strong context for analysis.[31]

---

[29] For a list of Stratum 2 building materials which include data which may extend prior and past Stratum 2 see table B.4.1 in ibid., 165.

[30] For a detailed discussion of these see Zorn, "Tell en-Nasbeh and the Problem of the Material Culture of the Sixth Century," 414–17.

[31] Ibid., 416.

TABLE 3 Tell en-Naṣbeh Stratum 2 architectural remains

Building[1]	Room	Type
Building 74.01	149, 187–196, 198	Palace?
Building 93.01	273a, 273b, 273c, 274–276	Outer Gate
Building 93.03	365–370	4-Room
Building 93.04	363, 364	Fragment
Building 110.01	266b, 267–269, 375, 376, 378, 379, 380a, 380b, 400	4-Room
Building 125.01	470(?), 472, 473, 477, 637(?), 638, 641, 643, 647, 659	4-Room
Building 127.01	97, 106, 108	4-Room?
Building 127.03	333–336	4-Room
Building 144.01	318(?), 324–327, 331, 332	3-Room?
Building 145.02	220(?), 224–227	4-Room
Building 160.10	463, 468, 565, 567, 569, 574	Storehouse?
Building 194.01	20–26	4-Room
Building 195.02	29–31	?
Enclosure Wall	284	Enclosure?
Rooms over Inner Gate Complex	222, 223, 228, 229, 231, 319	?
Outer Gate Road?	373, 374, 377	Access Road?

Note: Zorn refers to four-room as 4-Room. I use the former throughout this study unless I quote or directly use Zorn's term. I have left out from table 3 "Features" for "Bins" and "Cisterns," since these tend to represent contents of unknown stratigraphy and are few in number. The column "Type" represents Zorn's architectural interpretation of the structure.

[1] I incorporate an explanation of the numbering system used by Zorn: "The numbering system for buildings at Tell en-Nasbeh is based first on the section of 1:100 site plan in which the majority of the building is found and second on the order of discussion of the building in the author's [Zorn] dissertation." See Zorn, *Tell en-Nasbeh and the Problem of the Material Culture of the Sixth Century*, 2003, 416.

Source: Adapted from Zorn, "Tell en-Nasbeh: A Re-evaluation," 165. Used by permission.

3.3 Archaeology Related to Ritual and Religion

Various publications cover important elements of the archaeology of ritual and religion during the Persian period. The first general studies of the material culture of the Persian period appeared in the 1960s to 1970s. Excavation reports prior to this time dealt with Persian period strata, but there was no comprehensive study that presented an overview of the period.[32]

The first comprehensive study of the archaeology of the Persian period was produced in Hebrew in 1973 by Ephraim Stern, and was translated into English with the title, *The Material Culture of the Land of the Bible in the Persian Period 538–332 B.C.*[33] I review below some of the important ideas that he presents and propose revisions based on my observations from working with the material culture at TEN. I argue that some of the assertions made by Stern are not sustainable based on the evidence present at TEN.

In his study, Stern comments that the two most common cultic objects for the period were figurines and incense altars. And he argues that Jews and Samaritans did not use these items. As he notes,

> This cult was confined to a single section of the population of Palestine since the two main groups—the Jews and Samaritans—did not utilize such objects in their rites and whenever they did appear among these peoples, they were in direct opposition to their religious precepts.... In the majority of cases the excavators even explicitly attributed them to the Phoenicians or Arabs.[34]

Stern argues that the incense altars from the Persian period were the result of a foreign cult, though he offers no evidence to support this claim in this work, and it seems that he bases his argument on assumptions.[35] He concludes that the material culture of Palestine exhibited no influences of the ruling Persians, except for economic life and taxation.[36] Even though I do not agree with all of his claims and much information has been added to the field since 1982, Stern

---

[32] Paul Lapp perceives this need when he writes a short but helpful analysis of Persian period pottery to develop an understanding of the forms in this period. In this study, he brings together data from multiple sites, utilizing comparative methods of analysis. The study is primarily typological and chronological, and does not attempt to analyze form, function, or possible religious interpretations of the items. See Paul W. Lapp, "The Pottery of Palestine in the Persian Period," in *Archäologie und Altes Testament: Festschrift für Kurt Galling*, ed. Arnulf Kuschke and Ernst Kutsch (Tübingen: Mohr Siebeck, 1970), 179.

[33] Stern, *Material Culture of the Land of the Bible*. The English translation published in 1982 benefited from an update to the bibliography and from newer archaeological data based on excavation reports through 1978.

[34] Ibid., 158.
[35] Ibid., 182.
[36] Ibid., 237.

provides a comprehensive and valuable overview of the study of the material culture of the Persian period in Palestine.[37]

Stern also makes a difference between Assyrian and Persian periods: "in all the territories of Judah and Samaria, there is not a single piece of evidence for any pagan cults!"[38] It is difficult to support or refute this claim. However, it seems that this statement may need to be revised based on the findings of ritual and religious artifacts that have been found, some of them even from Tell en-Naṣbeh. I have summarized Stern's categories and typologies from both the 1982 and 2001 sources in table 4 and table 5, along with my own suggestions for revisions, which I discuss below. I am suggesting these typologies based on my experience in working with the material culture from Tell en-Naṣbeh. I consider this to be a work-in-progress that needs further development by testing it with material from other sites. I recognize the fact that I am including in table 5 artifacts that may be in domestic settings but may not be functioning as ritual objects consistently. For example, bowls, cooking pots, et cetera. My intent is to include these so I can gather statistical information at each locus in order to determine if they were used in conjunction with other ritual items.[39]

---

[37] In 2001 Stern updates this study as part of an even larger series devoted to the archaeology of Palestine. For the update Stern notes, "while during the Assyrian period, Phoenician, Philistine, Judaean, Edomite, and Ammonite cults are distinguishable because each ethnos had its own specific cult objects, during the Persian period this is no longer true." See Ephraim Stern, *The Assyrian, Babylonian, and Persian Periods (732–332 B.C.E.)*, vol. 2 of *Archaeology of the Land of the Bible* (New York: Doubleday, 2001), 478–79.

[38] Ibid., 479.

[39] For a similar approach see P. M. Michèle Daviau, "Family Religion: Evidence for the Paraphernalia of the Domestic Cult," in *The World of the Aramaeans*, ed. John William Wevers, Michael Weigl, and Paul-Eugène Dion, JSOTSup 325 (Sheffield: Sheffield Academic, 2001). I do not include the categories suggested by Albertz and Schmitt that are discussed below since their study focuses on the Iron Age. I provide alternative views below.

TABLE 4 Typologies possibly related to ritual loci

Balcells 2015	Stern 2001	Stern 1982
1. Ritual Loci: Architecture		

1.1 Monuments:
    1.1.1 City gates
    1.1.2 Other architecture
	City gates are mentioned under the "Fortifications" section in Chapter 2 Architecture. No ritual discussions	City gates are mentioned under the "Fortifications" section in Chapter 2 Architecture. No ritual discussions

1.2 Temples: use Stern's typology but group under Architecture
    1.2.1 Large
    1.2.2 Medium
    1.2.3 Small
	Temples: listed in Chapter 4 Temples and Cult Objects Change in typology to three types based on size:
	  1. Large, central, city temples
	  2. Medium-sized sanctuaries
	  3. Small (~ 1 sq. m) chapels
		Temples: covered in Chapter 2 Architecture. Two types:
		  1. Long
		  2. Broad

1.3 Houses and other household areas:	"Residential Structures" mentioned under Chapter 2 Architecture. No ritual discussion	"Domestic Architecture" listed under Chapter 2 Architecture. No ritual discussion. Two types:
		  1. Open court building
		  2. "Lachish Residency"

2. Ritual Loci: Natural Landscape	No ritual discussions	No ritual discussions
2.1 Ritualized open spaces and caves	No ritual discussions	No ritual discussions

3. Ritual Loci: Burials
Details in this area need further research
	Classified into "eastern" and "western" types based on structure and contents. Listed under Chapter 3 Burial. No ritual discussions. Three Types:
	  1. Cist graves
	  2. Shaft tombs
	  3. Pit graves
		Listed under Chapter 3 Burial. No ritual discussions. Typology based on structure and contents Three types:
		  1. Transitional
		  2. Cist graves
		  3. Shaft tombs

TABLE 5 Typologies possibly related to ritual artifacts

Balcells 2015	Stern 2001	Stern 1982
1. Ritual artifacts:		
1.1 Altars and stands	Cultic Incense Vessels: listed in Chapter 4. Two types: 1. Bronze 2. Clay or limestone	Incense Altars: assigned to "foreign cult." Classified as: 1. Type A 2. Type B
1.2 Figurines and statuettes.[40] 1.2.1 Anthropomorphic 1.2.1.1 Females 1.2.1.1.1 Nude women 1.2.1.1.2 Judean Pillar Figurine 1.2.1.1.3 Woman and child 1.2.1.2 Males 1.2.1.2.1 Bearded men 1.2.1.2.2 Rider figurine 1.2.2 Zoomorphic	Listed in Chapter 4. Two types based on clothing style of men and women: 1. Eastern: subdivided into Phoenician, Egyptian, Persian, Babylonian, nude females 2. Western: Greek style	Divided as follows: 1. Stone statuettes 2. Terracotta figurines 2.1 East 2.2 West 3. Bronze figurines
1.3 Bowls, cooking pots, kraters, saucers, cups, and chalices	Listed in Chapter 5 and some in Chapter 6	Listed in Chapter 4. Not treated as ritually related
1.4 Jugs, juglets, jars, bottles	Discussed in Chapter 6.	Listed in Chapter 5 in the section titled "Jewelry"
1.5 Lamps. Use Stern's typology	Listed in Chapter 5. Not treated as ritual	Listed in Chapter 4. Two types: 1. Open with 3 subtypes 2. Closed with 2 subtypes
1.6 Masks	Listed in Chapter 4	Not treated as ritual
1.7 Rattles	Not treated as ritual	Not treated as ritual
1.8 Zoomorphic vessels	Some cultic items in Chapter 4.	Listed in Chapter 4
1.9 Beads, amulets, pendants, bones, and other small items	Discussed in Chapter 6	Listed in Chapter 5 in the section titled "Jewelry"

---

[40] I use the broad categories of anthropomorphic and zoomorphic and then base my subcategories on Izak Cornelius's figurine typology discussed below.

Further support for the need to re-evaluate Stern's thesis comes from the publication of an edited volume on the archaeology of the Persian period in Palestine.[41] The book focused on examining Ephraim Stern's hypothesis "that Judah witnessed a 'religious revolution' between the Neo-Babylonian and the Persian period with the end result of 'an imageless monotheism.'"[42] The authors conclude that there was continuity and discontinuity at various levels, and suggested that Stern's thesis cannot be substantiated.[43] There are other studies that deal with family and household ritual or religious practices for the Iron Age that I have incorporated in my approach of this study.[44]

The assemblages that have been recovered from Persian period sites give us an indication of the material culture that may be related to ritual and religion. I list and describe below the artifacts that traditionally have been associated with ritual and religion, along with my own suggestions for categories for the archaeology of ritual and religion for the Persian period, which I listed in table 4 and table 5 above. In these tables I organize material culture based on two categories. First, there are loci of ritual activities, such as architecture, natural

---

[41] Christian Frevel, Katharina Pyschny, and Izak Cornelius, eds., *A "Religious Revolution" in Yehud?: The Material Culture of the Persian Period as a Test Case*, OBO 267 (Fribourg, Switzerland: Academic Press Fribourg; Göttingen: Vandenhoeck & Ruprecht: 2014).

[42] Ibid., iii.

[43] Ibid.

[44] John S. Holladay researches the religion in Israel and Judah from a strict archaeological perspective. He makes significant progress in highlighting the need to use categories to identify religious and non-religious artifacts based on known contexts for ritual and sacred areas. See John S. Jr. Holladay, "Religion in Israel and Judah under the Monarchy: An Explicitly Archaeological Approach," in *Ancient Israelite Religion: Essays in Honor of Frank Moore Cross*, ed. Patrick D. Miller, Paul D. Hanson, and S. Dean McBride (Philadelphia, PA: Fortress, 1987), 251. P. M. Michèle Daviau utilizes the excavation data from her project at the Jordanian site of Jawa to explore family religion. Her study develops a list of artifacts that she found in loci associated with rituals, and from this she suggests common artifacts that may possibly be indicators of domestic ritual. Her observations on the types of artifacts that may be involved and/or related to ritual are in line with my investigation at TEN. See Daviau, "Family Religion," 221. Aaron Brody develops a study specific to household archaeology at Tell en-Naṣbeh. Brody's tabulation of pottery distribution by room number provides a framework to investigate the massive amount of data that is available at Tell en-Naṣbeh. See Brody, "Those Who Add House to House," 45, 49. Rainer Albertz and Rüdiger Schmitt recent study of family and household religion divides assemblages into categories A, B, and C and assigns items to each of these categories based on the level of certainty related to ritual function. See Albertz and Schmitt, *Family and Household Religion in Ancient Israel and Levant*, 59.

landscapes, and burials. Second, there are artifacts that are associated with ritual function, such as altars, stands, et cetera. I separate and organize material culture this way to emphasize the need to keep ritual loci and ritual artifacts as two separate categories. It seems prudent to recognize that these loci may serve as a site for ritual even though ritual artifacts are not always discovered in these areas. Likewise, a ritual artifact may be located in situ at a location, but that does not always assume that the location has a ritual connection or use. I argue that by recognizing the possibilities of each artifact and locus individually, it may be possible to not exclude possible uses and meanings of each and thus keep options open. At the same time I support the idea discussed above for determining meaning from the material culture encountered in a specific context. To me, these various possibilities are not mutually exclusive. Thus, I first introduce and examine in this chapter ritual artifacts following the categories and the order from the table above. Then, in the next chapter I discuss loci that I suggest are associated with ritual. Some of these loci contained ritual artifacts and others did not. However, these loci could have played an important role in ritual and/or religious practices at Tell en-Naṣbeh.

In the end I continue to question how pervasive the activities of ritual and religion might have been in daily life.[45] Such a perspective could potentially present an opportunity to see routine living spaces and objects also serving a function within a religious context. In this, I am following Joyce's synthesis of Bell's and Bradley's approaches on how to identify material culture linked with ritual and religion, when there is activity or ritualization of artifacts:

> It is the stylization of action that singles out ritual practice from other forms of daily practice.... In part, the stylization of ritual practices is mediated by the use of distinctive things. It is this capacity for the substance of things to embody and in fact create distinctions in experience that is the second contribution of the archaeology of religion that we need to consider in more depth.[46]

---

[45] I am also cautious to draw quick conclusions based on the lack of evidence. Most archaeological excavations tend to focus on smaller portions of a site, potentially missing available data. As previously indicated, Tell en-Naṣbeh offers a unique situation as more than 65 percent of the site was excavated.

[46] Joyce, "What Should an Archaeology of Religion Look Like to a Blind Archaeologist?," 182, 186.

Joyce's conclusions about contextual comparative approaches are insightful.[47] Her comments demonstrate the need for an open mind when investigating this topic. At the same time, I appreciate Renfrew's warning against seeing religious connections in every ritual.[48] All these ideas point to the fact that we need to be cautious in our research approaches to ritual and ritual contexts.

Based on my outline in table 4 and table 5, I suggest the following as elements of material culture and special loci related to ritual and religion, even though the list is not exhaustive of all possibilities: monuments including city gates or other architecture, temples, houses, shrines, ritualized open spaces, caves, burial sites and their contents, altars and stands, figurines and other statuettes, bowls, cooking pots, kraters, saucers, cups, chalices, jugs, juglets, flasks, jars, bottles, lamps, masks, rattles, specialized ritual artifacts, beads, amulets, pendants, bones, and other small personal items. I emphasize the term related because some of these artifacts form part of daily ware or functions, and their existence does not constitute the presence of ritual. They need to be examined in context and together with other considerations. It is interesting to note that burial per se could be associated with ritual and/or religion in two ways. First, it may be seen as a locality where these activities take place, and as such form part of sacred space. Second, burial may also contain special artifacts, such as figurines, amulets, et cetera as part of its practice. Funerals and burials are part of specialized kinds of ritual, and as such will not be examined in this study. They deserve a focused study such as the ones done by Samuel R. Wolff and Elizabeth Bloch-Smith.[49]

As I explore the possible elements of ritual and religion in the following sections, we should keep in mind the importance and need in present and future

---

[47] Ibid., 182. For a discussion on how archaeologists should establish a system of relationships between objects and cultural/symbolic functions, see Llinares García, *Los Lenguajes del Silencio*, 153.

[48] Renfrew, "The Archaeology of Ritual, Cult, and of Religion," 120. His comments apply to rituals that are not religious in nature, and tend to fall in the secular realm.

[49] Samuel R. Wolff, "Mortuary Practices in the Persian Period of the Levant," *NEA* 65.2 (2002). Also, Elizabeth Bloch-Smith, *Judahite Burial Practices and Beliefs about the Dead*, JSOTSup 123 (Sheffield: JSOT Press, 1992). Albertz comments on their unique nature: "burials have their own specific problems, because they often have been used over long periods of time, and objects found together may have belonged to different burials." See Albertz and Schmitt, *Family and Household Religion in Ancient Israel and Levant*, 59. I also share John S. Holladay's observations for this type of research in Holladay, "Religion in Israel and Judah under the Monarchy," 282, fn.3.

research not only to identify these but also to think about the meaning that they convey as agents and carriers.[50] Perhaps one of the greatest values that I see in suggesting these new or expanded categories comes from opening our minds to new horizons of where and how ancient people, particularly ordinary men, women, and children, might have engaged in rituals or religious activities.

3.3.1 Ritual Artifacts

The writers of the Tell en-Naṣbeh excavation report dedicate a chapter to material culture that they consider to be "cultic."[51] This final report does not cover all of the findings from the excavations, although it discusses what they considered to be significant. The chapter categorizes artifacts as follows: (1) cylindrical pottery stands with vents; (2) flat-topped stands; (3) chalices; (4) censers and altars; (5) baetyl; (6) votive offerings; (7) Astarte figurines; (8) mold for a figurine; (9) animal and serpent figurines; and (10) rattles, amulets, and tools of magic. I incorporate a discussion of Stratum 2 artifacts from these nine sections in each of the respective categories from table 5. The study contains site-wide maps of the distribution of some of these cultic items, as well as other artifacts that may be related to ritual and occupation of the settlement. These maps are included in figure 5. As part of my investigation I reviewed this chapter and identified those artifacts that can be associated with architecture or loci dating to Stratum 2.[52] In addition my study included a review of the Tell en-Naṣbeh collection records in millimeter cards to identify artifacts in architecture from Stratum 2 that may be associated with ritual and/or religious practices.[53]

---

[50] As Insoll writes: "It is thus apparent that there is a shift from the cataloguing of the residues of the archaeology of ritual and religions to thinking about what they encode—actively rather than as static residues—and how this is achieved materially through engaging with materiality." See Timothy Insoll, "Introduction: Ritual and Religion in Archaeological Perspective," in *The Oxford Handbook of the Archaeology of Ritual and Religion*, ed. Timothy Insoll (Oxford: Oxford University Press, 2011), 3–4.

[51] See Chapter XIX in McCown et al., "Archaeological and Historical Results."

[52] I utilized the architecture selected earlier in table 3.

[53] I have included pictures of some of these artifacts in this study. These pictures are low resolution renditions of Reflectance Transformation Imaging (RTI) photographs in high resolution format.

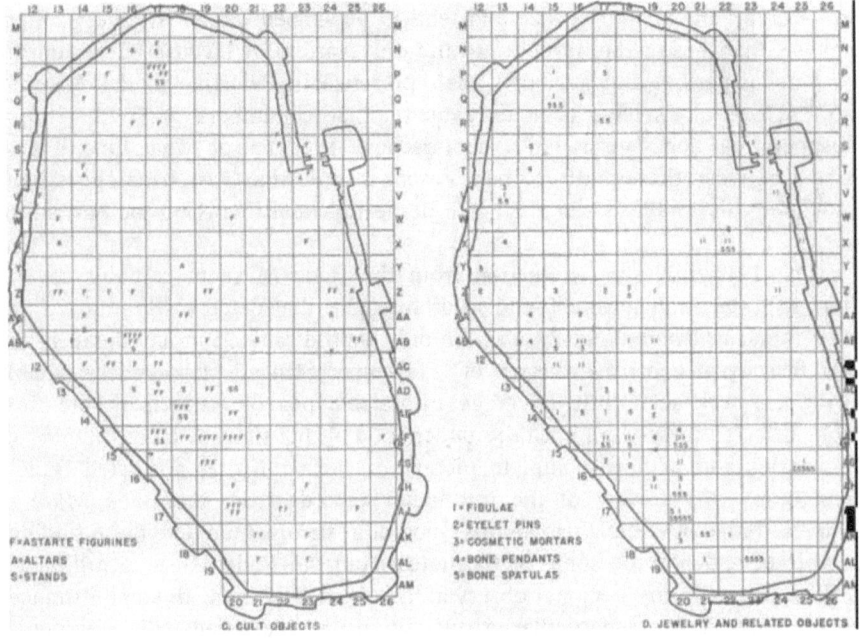

Figure 5. Excavator's distribution of possible ritual artifacts.

Source: Adapted by author from McCown et al., *Archaeological and Historical Results*, fig. 50. Used by permission of the Badè Museum, Pacific School of Religion.

3.3.1.1 Altars and Stands

Archaeologists and biblical scholars who study rituals and religion include altars and stands as an important component of this type of material culture. In his 2001 study, Stern used a new typology of incense vessels, which classified them into bronze vessels and clay or limestone altars.[54] As far as I have been able to discern, there have been no bronze incense vessels excavated in the Yehud Shephelah, although evidence exists from Tell es-Sultân (Jericho) and Tell Balaṭah (Shechem).[55] Clay or limestone altars are more common. These Persian period altars reflect a stylistic change from the Iron Age predecessors, as the

---

[54] Stern, "The Assyrian, Babylonian, and Persian Periods (732–332 B.C.E.)," 510–13.

[55] Ibid., 510.

Persian type are smaller in size and tend to be shaped like small chests. Stern suggests that these altars turned into the only variety of incense burner during the Persian period, and attributes their presence in Palestine to the Assyrian cult.[56] These altars have been excavated in large numbers in South Arabia, Mesopotamia, and Cyprus, and scholars have tried to see what link, if any, existed between these and the ones present in Palestine.[57] Archaeologists have associated this smaller sized altar with domestic ritual involving the burning of incense.[58]

The Tell en-Naṣbeh collection from the Badè Museum contains several altars and stands that were found in architecture that dated to Stratum 2. The stand found in Room 324 x27 was the only item discussed in any detail in the 1947 final report under the category of "Flat-topped Stands."[59] It is understandable why there was such little coverage of these types of artifacts in the final publication, as these were not fully understood at that time. A larger number of discoveries and a more complete picture of their function postdated Badè's excavations. My review of the millimeter records from the Badè Museum uncovered nine possible altars and five potential stands. I tabulate these findings in table 6, and provide some of the notes from the Badè Museum millimeter cards, along with my personal observations on each artifact. In some instances when I suggest that a particular artifact should be identified with a particular type, I provide some possible comparisons from other sites and/or other authors' research. It is interesting to note the recurrence of basalt stone in some of these altars and the possible connection with assemblages from other excavations. For example, Daviau identifies rectangular trays and mortars made of basalt in temple contexts and suggests that excavated basalt trays and mortars at Jawa could have a domestic ritual function.[60] I would suggest that basalt could have been used in some ritual artifacts as a contrasting stone with white stone, such as limestone.[61]

Persian period fire-holders provide another fruitful area of investigation. I describe these types of artifacts under lamps because of their possible closer

---

[56] Ibid., 513.
[57] Stern, *Material Culture of the Land of the Bible*, 182.
[58] Albertz and Schmitt, *Family and Household Religion in Ancient Israel and Levant*, 71.
[59] McCown et al., "Archaeological and Historical Results," 236.
[60] Daviau, "Family Religion," 220.
[61] This was brought to my attention while investigating plinths in Zoroastrian locations. It is likely that this contrast was also used with other ritual artifacts. See Boyce, "Under the Achaemenians," 53.

affiliation with these due to their function as fire carriers or holders. However, these artifacts did resemble an altar and some of the identifications at Tell en-Naṣbeh could have associated these artifacts with incense altars or stands. Boyce notes the specifics of how an artifact designed to hold fire could be confused with an altar:

> The term 'fire-altar' was applied to them by Western scholars; but the Zoroastrian fire-holder is not an altar in the sense of a 'raised structure with a plane surface, on which to place or sacrifice offerings to a deity,' but is simply a stand with hollow top, made to elevate fire for devotional purposes. Yet it is very likely that the inspiration for making such a stand came from the altars of other faiths.[62]

I suggest that these areas of Zoroastrian ritual manifestations provide important areas of research in order to determine possible Persian influence or presence. Altars and other stands need to be evaluated for fire rituals and other Zoroastrian religious practices.

---

[62] Ibid., 52.

TABLE 6 Altars and stands at Tell en-Naṣbeh

Type	TEN Rm, x number, and Badè Museum number[1]	Millimeter card notes	Comments
Altar	Rm 196, x2	Fragment of basalt stone vessel with legs. Diam.: ca. 116 mm, H.: 90 mm	Stern 1982, fig. 313, #21 incense altar. Also, Daviau, basalt trays.
Altar	Rm 228, x4	Object of black basalt. Diam.: 55 mm	Incense altar or mortar. See Daviau.
Altar	Rm 324, x27, B2013.1.89	White slip base (?)	McCown et al. Vol. 1, p. 236. Categorized as flat-topped. See figure 23 in appendix. C.
Altar	Rm 326, x4	Bath tub fragment (?) Finger-impressed ridge	Stern 1982, fig. 301 left incense altar.
Altar	Rm 370, x5	Basalt stone bowl fragment	Stern 1982 fig. 302 incense altar. Tray/ mortar in Daviau.
Altar	Rm 268, x8	Altar-stand (?) fragment	None.
Altar	Rm 378, x41 B2014.1.105	Incense altar fragment. Possible figurine attachment on corners	Publ. McCown et al., Vol. 1, p. 241. See figure 24 in appendix. C.
Altar	Rm 463, x19	Pedestal fragment of chalice H:30+ mm, Diam.: 60 mm + with depression in center	Incense altar or libation tray.
Altar	Rm 477, x20	Pedestal fragment; tubular votive stand?	Stern 1982, fig. 310, 5–12. Publ. McCown Vol. 1, p. 242.
Stand	Rm 276, x9	Ring stand fragment. Diam.: 280 mm	None.
Stand	Rm 327, x13	Basalt fragment bowl stand? or figurine fragment	Stern 1982, incense stand or altar. Daviau.
Stand	Rm 379, x3	Ring stand fragment. Diam.: ca. 160mm	None.
Stand	Rm 379, x15 (1707)	Stone fragment with incised decorations L:79 mm. Possibly part of cane or pole used in some ritual (?)	Decorations seem to complement those in incense altars from Stern 1982 pp. 188–91.
Stand	Rm 379, x25	Ring base fragment. Diam.: ca. 165 mm	None.

[1] Not all the artifacts have a museum number yet.
[2] A question mark (?) denotes uncertainty in identifying a particular artifact.

3.3.1.2 Figurines and Statuettes

Figurines and statuettes, made from terracotta, bronze, and other materials, also form an important component of the archaeology of ritual and religion, and as such scholars have provided various suggestions for typologies.[63] As indicated earlier, Stern's method of classification divided figurines into two groups: the eastern group and the western group.[64] Stern's distinction uses among its criteria the style of dress, with the eastern group representing Phoenicia, Egypt, Persia, Babylonia dressing, and nude females, and the western group including Greek attire.[65] Izak Cornelius utilizes gender as the first criteria for his typology and then subdivides them further.[66] The female type he separates into the following: (1) Nude women; (2) Judean Pillar Figurine; (3) Woman and child. The male type he divides as: (1) Bearded men; (2) Rider figurines, including horse riders or horsemen. I adapt some of Cornelius's method of classification to my proposal for these artifacts, since he makes a convincing argument showing that the Western type reflected more of a cultural influence from within the local area rather than an import from Greek sources.[67]

Stern discusses clay figurines and claims that, "none, as was already noted, have (sic) been found in Judah and Samaria."[68] He attributes most of the discoveries of figurines to favissae and notes how the Persian period figurines had a distinctive component in the way in which they were found—mostly in heterogeneous assemblages representing a mix of influences from Phoenicians, Persians, Canaanites, Cypriot, and Greeks.[69] My investigation of the collection

---

[63] Albertz and Schmitt provide a detailed discussion of the history of research with figurines. See Albertz and Schmitt, *Family and Household Religion in Ancient Israel and Levant*, 60–66. Darby also includes an extensive review of methodological considerations and interpretive trends for JPFs. See chapters 1 and 2 in Erin Darby, *Interpreting Judean Pillar Figurines: Gender and Empire in Judean Apotropaic Ritual*, FAT 2/69 (Tübingen: Mohr Siebeck, 2014).

[64] For a full discussion of styles for these groups, see Stern, "The Assyrian, Babylonian, and Persian Periods (732–332 B.C.E.)," 492–505. Ora Negbi also uses this method of categorization for her figurines in Tel Ṣippor. See Ora Negbi, *A Deposit of Terracottas and Statuettes from Tel Ṣippor*, 'Atiqot 6 (Jerusalem: The Department of Antiquities and Museums, The Israel Exploration Society, 1966). I was made aware of this by Cornelius's essay cited above. This site is also referred to as Tel Zippor or Tell et-Tuyur.

[65] Stern, "The Assyrian, Babylonian, and Persian Periods (732–332 B.C.E.)," 492.

[66] Izak Cornelius, "'East Meets West': Trends in Terracotta Figurines," in *A "Religious Revolution" in Yehud?: The Material Culture of the Persian Period as a Test Case*, ed. Christian Frevel, Katharina Pyschny, and Izak Cornelius, OBO 267 (Fribourg, Switzerland; Göttingen: Academic Press Fribourg; Vandenhoeck & Ruprecht, 2014), 70–78.

[67] Ibid., 80.

[68] Stern, "The Assyrian, Babylonian, and Persian Periods (732–332 B.C.E.)," 490.

[69] Ibid., 492.

at Tell en-Naṣbeh demonstrates the presence of figurines in Judah as indicated below in table 7. Cornelius criticizes Stern for making the above quoted argument as it does not reflect the material culture present at various sites.[70] Cornelius cites Schmitt's use of some of Tell en-Naṣbeh's figurines as evidence that these were present in Judah during the Persian period.[71] I suggest that some of these figurines were located within architecture associated with stratigraphy that did not date to Stratum 2, or the Persian period. I instead utilize some of the figurines in table 7 for closer association to the Persian period.

In terms of the importance of these artifacts with regards to the archaeology of ritual and religion for the family and household, I agree with Cornelius's suggestion that these figurines reflect popular iconography, and as I discuss below, these form part of the domestic setting.[72]

The female figurines have been studied more extensively and interpretations vary depending on the type. Within the female figurines the Judean Pillar Figurine forms an important type, although interpretations of these artifacts vary considerably. In a study on the JPFs, Raz Kletter notes the following:

> After reviewing more than a hundred years of research, it seems to me that there is no lack of suggestions and speculations in regard to the meaning and symbolism of the JPFs. What we still miss is an updated, systematic catalogue of figurines, and solid evidence for the preference of one specific explanation.[73]

---

[70] See for example, Cornelius, "'East Meets West': Trends in Terracotta Figurines," 68, 82.

[71] Ibid., 76–77.

[72] Cornelius's recent study of terracotta figurines suggests that these artifacts were cheap and widespread due to their ability to be mass produced via molds, a new development from the previous solid construction. See ibid., 67, 69. Daviau argues convincingly that figurines were not toys as had been suggested in the past. See Daviau, "Family Religion," 203. In addition Albertz and Schmitt attribute to these artifacts "primary importance in determining domestic cult activities." They assign different roles and functions to each type of figurine. The female terra-cotta figurines had multiple roles primarily in "domestic and funeral contexts" serving as 'votive objects' for petitions and thanksgiving. See Albertz and Schmitt, *Family and Household Religion in Ancient Israel and Levant*, 60, 65.

[73] Raz Kletter, *The Judean Pillar-Figurines and the Archeaology of Asherah*, British Archaeological Reports (BAR) International Series 636 (Oxford: John and Erica Hedges Ltd. and Archaeopress, 1996), 27.

Kletter suggests that scholars have explained JPFs in one of four ways: (1) toys; (2) mortal humans; (3) magical artifacts; and (4) cultic artifacts.[74] Darby indicates additional interpretations presented previously. From the work of Holladay discussed earlier, it seems conclusive that JPFs did not serve as toys and most of the contexts where they were found point to an interpretation that these were used in rituals. He suggests that these figurines served as protectors in the domestic setting especially in areas of female living.[75] Darby points out that the "common assumptions shared by the majority of interpreters stem from interpretations of the figurines' breasts and their concomitant implication for the function and owner of the figurines."[76] She criticizes the association of JPFs with Asherah which reflects a simple explanation of "'pillar figurine with breasts = female nurturing goddess = goddess in the Bible.'"[77] She ultimately interprets the function of JPFs as artifacts for protection and healing in rituals that took place mostly in the house involving "some type of formal officiant."[78] I support the overall interpretation that these figurines are part of the domestic setting and I discuss below within each context a more detailed interpretation.

The male figurines remain somewhat of an unknown as they have not been the subject of specialized studies due to their lower number compared to the female types. The male figurine subtype of the horse and rider has been identified with strength and power.[79] Animal figurines include multiple types.[80]

My review of the Badè Museum millimeter cards for architecture associated with Stratum 2 and the final excavation reports identified a total of fourteen figurines at Tell en-Naṣbeh, which are presented in table 7. Most of these figurines exist in fragments, except for the figurine in Room 369, x11, Badè Museum number B2012.1.140, as seen in figure 26 of appendix C, which is a complete figurine.

---

[74] Ibid. Kletter concludes that JPFs were a representation of the biblical Asherah in its simplest form used by the practitioners of the Yahwistic religion. See ibid., 80–81.

[75] Ibid., 81.

[76] Darby, *Interpreting Judean Pillar Figurines*, 34.

[77] Ibid., 38.

[78] Ibid., 401, 404.

[79] Cornelius, "'East Meets West': Trends in Terracotta Figurines," 31–32. Also, Albertz and Schmitt, *Family and Household Religion in Ancient Israel and Levant*, 65–66.

[80] Scholars have interpreted the animal figurines in various ways, although it seems that Albertz and Schmitt's conclusions of them being "votives connected to fertility and plentitude" seems reasonable given the lack of other convincing arguments. See Albertz and Schmitt, *Family and Household Religion in Ancient Israel and Levant*, 66.

TABLE 7 Figurines and statuettes at Tell en-Naṣbeh

Type[1]	TEN room, x number, and Badè Museum number[2]	Millimeter card notes[3]	Comments
AF	Rm 23, x12	Female body fragment (head missing) H:98+mm	Published in McCown et al., Vol. 1, Plate 86, #16 under "Pinched-faced Heads; Body Fragments"
F	Rm 23, x60	Body fragment	None
F	Rm 24, x28	Leg fragment L:63mm	None
ZF	Rm 108, x3 (568)[4]	Head of deity (bird shaped)	None
F	Rm 223, x12	Spout fragment or hollow leg of figurine	None
AF	Rm 273a, x1 B2012.1.82 (1698)	Figurine head, Astarte L:63mm	Published in McCown et al., Vol.1, Plate 85, #3 under "Astarte heads with molded faces." Kletter, Appendix 2, #165.
AF	Rm 274, x33	Head fragment	None
F	Rm 275, x16	Leg fragment	None
F	Rm 276, x2	Base fragment	None
AF	Rm 377, x11	Torso fragment	None
AF	Rm 366, x29 B2012.1.61	Base (hollow) fragment	Pillar base. See figure 25 in appendix C.
AF	Rm 366, x32	Body fragment	
AF	Rm 369, x11 B2012.1.140 (1608)	Female, pedestal base with prominent breasts. Pointed (pinched) face. Base diam.:44mm H:125mm	Whole figurine. Published in McCown et al., Vol. 1, Plate 86, #14 under "Pinched-faced Heads; Body Fragments." Kletter, Appendix 2, #126. See figure 26 in appendix C.
ZF	Rm 463, x20 B2013.1.19	Animal neck fragment	See figure 27 in appendix C.
ZF	Rm 463, x51 B2013.1.27	Animal limb fragment	None

[1] F= figurine; S= statuette; A= anthropomorphic; Z= zoomorphic
[2] Not all the artifacts have a museum number yet.
[3] A question mark (?) denotes uncertainty in identifying a particular artifact.
[4] Numbers in parenthesis represent older museum numbers.

3.3.1.3 Bowls, Cooking Pots, Kraters, Saucers, Cups, and Chalices

The presence of these types of artifacts in houses or household compounds serves to connect these objects with domestic functions. Brody and Daviau conducted studies at Tell en-Naṣbeh and Jawa, respectively, which demonstrate how this material culture forms part of the family and household setting.[81] At the same time, due to the multifunction capacity of these artifacts, it may be challenging to assign these exclusive roles of ritual and/or religious practices.[82] A representative example of this multifunction is seen in the incense or tripod cup that appears in ritual contexts as a possible burner of incense, although it is likely that this type of artifact also served other roles.[83] Typical ritual function for these artifacts include: votive offerings, libations, presentation of offerings, transportation of offerings, et cetera.

Tell en-Naṣbeh contained significant numbers of these types of assemblages. The totals for Stratum 2 architecture were: bowls, 189; cooking pots, 137; kraters, 14; baking-pans, 1; saucers and plates, 1; cups, 0; and chalices, 1. I list and tabulate each of these types below in the sections for Ritual Loci: Architecture to assist in determining their ritual function, if any within the family and household setting.

The review of the millimeter cards for Stratum 2 architecture identified some bowls and a chalice, which had interesting characteristics. Room 193, x1 is a fragment of a bowl with perforations 8mm in diameter in concentric circles, and 5mm apart. The size of the fragment does not permit one to make conclusive interpretations, but it may be that this type of artifact shared a function similar to the tripod-cups incense burners. Room 274, x34 is a stone rim and leg fragment of a basalt bowl that appears fitted for libations. Room 374, x8 is a similar stone bowl fragment made of basalt. Room 378, x37 is a chalice with a small piece missing with a diameter of 113mm and a height of 98mm

---

[81] Brody, "Those Who Add House to House." Also, Daviau, "Family Religion."

[82] I include these artifacts in my tabulations with the understanding that they may be serving multiple functions. Sensitive to this issue, Albertz and Schmitt categorize chalices, goblets, cups, saucers, and some bowls in their category B list. See Albertz and Schmitt, *Family and Household Religion in Ancient Israel and Levant*, 73.

[83] Tina Haettner Blomquist, *Gates and Gods: Cults in the City Gates of Iron Age Palestine; An Investigation of the Archaeological and Biblical Sources*, ConBot 46 (Stockholm: Almqvist & Wiksell, 1999), 32. For a description, see Ruth Amiran, *Ancient Pottery of the Holy Land: From Its Beginnings in the Neolithic Period to the End of the Iron Age* (New Brunswick, NJ: Rutgers University Press, 1970), 199, 201.

plus.[84] Daviau's study of domestic ritual assemblages is significant in providing support for the use of these artifacts in ritual as her investigation showed the presence of one chalice in every one of the main buildings where figurines were present.[85]

3.3.1.4 Jugs, Juglets, Jars, Bottles

These artifacts also appear in domestic settings and, like the ones previously discussed, may have performed multiple functions.[86] This material culture was well represented in Stratum 2 Tell en-Naṣbeh. The totals for Tell en-Naṣbeh were as follows: jugs, juglets, flasks, 49; jars, 277; and bottles, 4.

3.3.1.5 Lamps

Fire has long held a fascination for humans as seen in eschatology and rituals.[87] As a carrier and provider of fire, lamps have been an important component of the material culture of ancient Israel, and their role in ritual can be seen in Babylonia in conjunction with fire and the cult of the deified ancestors.[88] However, the connection with ritual and/or religious practices in Persian period Judah needs careful analysis. It is generally accepted that lamps are common in household settings due to their function of providing lighting.[89] As Daviau notes, "in the domestic context, lamps serve as primary evidence for roofed space and only secondarily as evidence of specialized activities."[90] Stern provides a typology for Persian period lamps that include the following: (1) open lamps with three subtypes based on size and outline; (2) closed lamps with two

---

[84] Albertz and Schmitt suggest that chalices may have been utilized as offering stands and incense burners. See Albertz and Schmitt, *Family and Household Religion in Ancient Israel and Levant*, 73.

[85] Daviau, "Family Religion," 208.

[86] Stern covers these artifacts and provides illustrations for the various types in his 1982 study. See Stern, *Material Culture of the Land of the Bible*. Also, Daviau includes these vessels in her domestic study of Jawa. See Daviau, "Family Religion."

[87] Anders Kaliff, "Fire," in *The Oxford Handbook of the Archaeology of Ritual and Religion*, ed. Timothy Insoll (Oxford: Oxford University Press, 2011), 51.

[88] Van der Toorn, *Family Religion in Babylonia, Syria, and Israel*, 129.

[89] Albertz and Schmitt, *Family and Household Religion in Ancient Israel and Levant*, 73.

[90] Daviau, "Family Religion," 211. Also, Brody, "Those Who Add House to House," 52.

subtypes based on stylistic influence, either Greek or Babylonian.[91] Boyce's claims pertaining to fire rituals in Zoroastrianism and how these might have been connected with lamps to highlight an area of family and household rituals merit further investigation.[92] She notes the importance and duty of prayer involving fire rituals for all Zoroastrians, and how in Pasargadae fire-holders played a critical role as a source of fire for the king and priests.[93] She writes:

> These fire-holders were carved of white stone, with the fine workmanship of the early Pasargadae period ... the fire-holders can be reconstructed as consisting of a three-stepped top and based, joined by a slender square shaft. The whole probably stood about 112 cm. (3 ft. 8 ins.) high; and in the top, harmoniously balanced by the solid base, a bowl was hollowed out 33 cm. (13 ins.) deep—deep enough, that is, to hold a thick bed of hot ash, such as is needed to sustain an ever-burning fire of wood.[94]

However, as fire-holders involved in Zoroastrian rituals, these artifacts maintained ritual purity by not being used for other practical uses, a critical component when investigating family and household rituals at archaeological sites.[95]

A review of the millimeter cards for Stratum 2 architecture revealed 50 lamps at Tell en-Naṣbeh. A large number of these were the high base saucer lamp. Most of these lamps were widely distributed throughout the various rooms with one or two lamps, except for Rooms 23 and 24, which had six and four lamps, respectively.

3.3.1.6 Masks

The Judean Hills and its surrounding deserts provided the context for the oldest masks known to us today, dating back to the Neolithic period.[96] These masks have been associated with rituals and religious practices involving rites of

---

[91] Stern, *Material Culture of the Land of the Bible*, 127–29.
[92] Boyce, "Under the Achaemenians," 51.
[93] Ibid., 51–52.
[94] Ibid.
[95] Ibid., 53.
[96] Debby Hershman, *Face to Face: The Oldest Masks in the World* (Jerusalem: Israel Museum, 2014), 8.

healing and magic.[97] My review of Stratum 2 architecture in the millimeter cards did not reveal any masks specifically associated with this stratum.[98]

3.3.1.7 Rattles

Discoveries of rattles have come mostly from burial contexts and until recently these artifacts have been linked with funerary rituals.[99] Tell en-Naṣbeh offers an important contribution to the archaeology of ritual and religious practices at the family and household level since the excavators recovered rattles in rooms that appear to be part of domestic contexts. These areas are discussed below under Ritual Loci: Architecture. These clay artifacts are shaped like a cylinder and contain pottery pellets or small stones in the interior. My evaluation of the Stratum 2 architecture millimeter cards identified one rattle fragment in Room 400, as seen in figure 28 in appendix C. The artifact is x19 and the Badè Museum number is B2012.1.132. The museum collection also includes a complete rattle from a different stratum. The Badè Museum's collection of rattles is an important source for the study of domestic assemblages.[100]

3.3.1.8 Zoomorphic Vessels

Zoomorphic vessels comprise a special type of artifact that occurs in smaller numbers, although their presence strongly suggests domestic ritual. Stern mentions zoomorphic vessels in Palestine and suggests that these imitated the Achaemenid metal rhyta.[101] Stern does not mention the artifacts from Tell en-Naṣbeh in his description of findings. Albertz and Schmitt note the wide

---

[97] Ibid.

[98] Tell en-Nasbeh's collection includes a mask fragment that was found in Room 478. This mask can be dated by parallels from other sites to the Persian period. However, Zorn dates this room to Stratum 3 and Stratum 2. Therefore the room and this mask were not evaluated in this study. Stern associates masks with the Apotropaic cult. See Stern, "The Assyrian, Babylonian, and Persian Periods (732–332 B.C.E.)," 507–08.

[99] Albertz and Schmitt highlight the collection's significance in Albertz and Schmitt, *Family and Household Religion in Ancient Israel and Levant*, 73.

[100] Ibid.

[101] Stern uses a two-fold typology to classify them. See Stern, *Material Culture of the Land of the Bible*, 131.

representation in Palestine during the Iron Age, and the occurrence of 30 of these artifacts at Tell en-Naṣbeh.[102] As for their attributes and use, they write:

> The zoomorphic vessels mostly resemble bovines and caprids and therefore share the same symbolic features of fertility and abundance with the related animal figurines. They were clearly a luxury item evidencing social prestige, because they were complicated to make and frequently decorated.... Their inherent religious symbolism suggests cultic purposes, such as in libation offerings, or as containers for drinks on special occasions.[103]

These authors also note that some excavations in Israel and within Judah have shown that these items were not in a clear ritual context, although these did indicate a domestic setting.[104] The Tell en-Naṣbeh final excavation report mentions the 30 "spout heads" in Appendix A List of Possible Cult Objects, but there was only mention of the vessel in Room 473 referred to below. Daviau does not include this type of category in her study, probably due to the lack of representation of such vessels at Jawa. Brody mentions the occurrence of one zoomorphic vessel fragment in his study of Iron Age Tell en-Naṣbeh.[105] My investigation of Stratum 2 architecture millimeter cards at Tell en-Naṣbeh revealed the presence of three zoomorphic vessels as described in table 8.

---

[102] Albertz and Schmitt, *Family and Household Religion in Ancient Israel and Levant*, 67.
[103] Ibid.
[104] Ibid.
[105] Brody, "Those Who Add House to House," 52.

TABLE 8 Zoomorphic vessels at Tell en-Naṣbeh

TEN Room, x number, and Badè Museum number[1]	Millimeter card notes[2]	Comments
Rm. 23, x59	Theriomorphic vessel fragment	None
Rm. 331, x8	Theriomorphic vessel cow head fragment	See figure 29 in appendix. C.
Rm. 473, x13 (2506)	Head and neck fragment. L:65mm	Published in McCown et al., Vol. 1, Plate 89, #1.

[1] Not all the artifacts have a museum number yet.
[2] A question mark (?) denotes uncertainty in identifying a particular artifact.

3.3.1.9 Beads, Amulets, Pendants, Bones, and Other Small Items

This group of artifacts encompasses smaller items, some of which form part of the jewelry, dressing, or adornment of ancient people. Brody notes the rarity of these items, and his study identifies small numbers of such artifacts in the Iron Age compound at Tell en-Naṣbeh.[106] These are challenging artifacts to recover from an excavation site.[107]

I group these artifacts into two groups, separating beads, amulets, pendants, and other small items from bones. I tabulate bones separately to allow for their potential categorization as being related to food consumption. My review of Stratum 2 architecture millimeter cards at Tell en-Naṣbeh show the following totals: amulets, pendants, and other small items, 53; bones, 12. There were multiple cases of bivalve white shells with perforations, bronze fibulas, and

---

[106] Ibid.

[107] As Albertz and Schmitt point out, these items have a tendency to travel easily across strata and from one context to another due to their size and the fact that as adornments they usually resided with a person or with a garment rather than with a specific setting in a house. They note the main function of amulets as "almost certainly associated with primary apotropaic magic," and as such they group these as part of their Category A. Sensitive to the issue that these items can function both in ritual and non-ritual contexts, they separate some of these artifacts into collectibles and assign these to their Category B. They use this group for "nonutilitarian or unusual objects, worked or unworked," such as shells and semiprecious stones, and consider these ritually affiliated if they were found with any Category A items. See Albertz and Schmitt, *Family and Household Religion in Ancient Israel and Levant*, 71, 73.

stone beads. The section below in Ritual Loci: Architecture, discusses bone distribution as a function of space use.

As seen from the vast amount and varied composition discussed in these previous sections of Ritual Artifacts, the Tell en-Naṣbeh Stratum 2 material culture serves as an important collection to study the archaeology of ritual and religious practices during the Persian period. In order to leverage this valuable resource and to present a summary of this information, I gather the data from the millimeter cards and tabulate it by building and room in relationship to the artifacts recovered from this architecture. I include this data for each individual building in the next section Ritual Loci: Architecture, and also include a more comprehensive table of all Stratum 2 architecture material culture in appendix A.

In summary, this chapter provides suggestions for the types of artifacts that may be associated with ritual and religious practices during the Persian period in the southern Levant. This data informs the review and analysis of Tell en-Naṣbeh available at the Badè Museum. The investigation presents and discusses various items of material culture that may be associated with ritual and/or religious practices. I present additional comments in the Conclusion.

4. PERSIAN PERIOD ARCHITECTURE AND NATURAL LANDSCAPE FROM TELL EN-NAṢBEH

In this chapter I investigate the architecture and natural landscape as loci for ritual and religion for Stratum 2 Tell en-Naṣbeh. I identify locations at Tell en-Naṣbeh where I suggest family and household ritual and religious practices might have taken place.

4.1 Ritual Loci: Architecture and Natural Landscape

The architecture of Persian period households comprises an important element of research for family/household ritual and religion. Stern, who has written extensively on the Persian period, authors a chapter on the architecture of the Persian period, although it does not provide details on household architecture.[1] In this study he examines construction elements such as walls with ashlar piers and fieldstone fills, proto-Aeolic capitals, Hathor capitals, recessed openings, decorated balustrades, crenellations, and paving of squares. He comments that these design and construction elements are based on Phoenician style and influence, which persisted and spread from the Iron Age to the beginning of the Hellenistic period from the coastal areas to Judah and Jordan.[2] I agree with his view that some of the architecture in Judah reflects Phoenician influence and later propose some ideas to assist in identifying rituals in different locations.

Scholars list temples, sanctuaries, shrines, and small household areas as possible places for ritual and/or religious practices, even though the definition and description of each of these may vary. The meaning and functionality of material culture within a particular context or location can change over time. As

---

[1] Ephraim Stern, "The Phoenician Architectural Elements in Palestine during the Late Iron Age and the Persian Period," in *The Architecture of Ancient Israel: from the Prehistoric to the Persian Periods*, ed. Aharon Kempinski and Ronny Reich (Jerusalem: Israel Publication Society, 1992).

[2] Ibid., 309.

Keane notes, "material forms do not only permit new inferences, but, as objects that endure across time, they can, in principle, acquire features unrelated to the intentions of previous users or the inferences to which they have given rise in the past. This is in part because as material things they are prone to enter into new contexts."[3] Given this, we must be careful to analyze material culture not based on its function in previous periods and contexts. The number and type of artifacts also matters. Albertz and Schmitt suggest that, "the designation of a locus as cultic generally requires the presence of more than one object."[4] While I agree that a higher number of cultic artifacts renders the likelihood of a loci's ritual function more perceptible, it seems prudent to be open to cultic designations based on a more comprehensive understanding of the loci or context.

I explore next some of these locations or spaces as possible contexts in which one may find ritual or religious materiality. Some of these may by themselves be ritual or religious, for example, a temple, while others may provide the location where ritual is performed, for example, a city gate. I structure and organize my analysis of these locations or spaces by following the sequential order from table 4 Ritual Loci: Architecture, and then Natural Landscape, to facilitate referencing the data. I integrate and discuss the information from the section "Ritual Artifacts" discussed above, as needed to support my overall thesis.

I divide and discuss the buildings for Stratum 2 according to my earlier analysis and with reference to Zorn's stratigraphic work.[5] For example, I suggest that Buildings 74.01 and 110.01 fit into the category of ritual architecture for monuments, and therefore I discuss them within this section. Other building discussions follow in the section for houses and other household areas.

Prior to examining the data from the Tell en-Naṣbeh millimeter cards and the final excavation reports, it is important to review the way in which the original excavation team kept records and briefly explain the process that they followed during their expedition.[6] As the team excavated an area, which encompassed a ten meter by ten meter square, they started to assign sequential x numbers to artifacts. When, and if, three walls were uncovered, they gave the

---

[3] Keane *apud* Insoll, "Introduction: Ritual and Religion in Archaeological Perspective," 2–3.

[4] Albertz and Schmitt, *Family and Household Religion in Ancient Israel and Levant*, 59.

[5] Zorn, "Tell en-Nasbeh: A Re-evaluation."

[6] For more details on the excavation methods and the process of recording artifacts, see Badè, *Manual of Excavation in the Near East*.

space within these walls a room number which matches the square number.[7] Once the room existed then the x numbers that were excavated within that space became associated with a room number. For example, the first artifact in Room 110 would be labeled Room 110 x1. If the excavators did not find three walls, the artifact then remained affiliated only with the square. This explains why there are artifacts with x numbers but no room number. The excavator team recorded these artifacts with x numbers in millimeter cards.

4.1.1 Monuments

Monuments lack coverage in most discussions of the archaeology of ritual and religion, yet it represents a valuable data source in better understanding this area. Today, when one thinks of monuments, one is bound to focus on large and impressive architectural structures. However, as Chris Scarre points out, the original meaning of monuments comes "from the Latin *monumentum* 'something that reminds' which is related to the verb *monere* 'to remind' or 'to warn.'"[8] He clarifies current perceptions: "'Monument' today carries a double meaning, evoking size and durability on the one hand, and commemoration or memorial on the other."[9] This sense of reminding applies to material culture large or small and is important to consider as one searches for ritual or religious practices in relationship with this type of evidence. It is possible for there to be overlaps in terms of the type of material culture when working with monuments. For example, it may be that a temple could be seen as a monument in addition to the religious affiliation to a particular site. Another example is a city gate that may perform a civil or social function, but at times it may be helpful to see this type as a monument that relates to political rituals. Equally important is the need to be sensitive to the context and the meaning that one assigns to monuments, since, as Scarre explains, "the messages themselves need not always be those intended by the originator of the monument, since later observers may interpret

---

[7] The site of Tell en-Naṣbeh was divided in whole with these ten by ten squares in a grid. Lower numbers were towards the north and continue to increase from left to right going south.

[8] Chris Scarre, "Monumentality," in *The Oxford Handbook of the Archaeology of Ritual and Religion*, ed. Timothy Insoll (Oxford: Oxford University Press, 2011), 9. According to Scarre, the association with larger, impressive structures comes after the seventeenth century.

[9] Ibid.

them in entirely novel and culturally specific ways. Hence monuments carry meanings far beyond the contexts of their original creation."[10]

Scarre's ideas of monumentality connect and apply well to Bell's insights of political rites. For example, if one examines Nehemiah's building of the wall in Jerusalem under Persian control through this lens, it seems that this mission had social, ritual, and religious complexities far beyond a construction project; that is, there is a human connection, as Scarre explains:

> Monuments connect not only to the landscapes in which they were built but also to the people who built and experience them.... Dramatic bursts of monument-building generate a sense of identity among those involved in the work and provide icons for the new political order.... Monumental construction is a particularly successful strategy in these circumstances since it disseminates ideology and allows leaders to promote their views, encourage social consensus, and consolidate economic resources.... The cooperative labour involved in these projects may be considered an act of social construction as much as it is one of monument-building.... The ceremonial context of construction is key to the creation and enlargement of these monuments.[11]

Even though this example deals with broader social structures beyond the site of Tell en-Naṣbeh, it nevertheless highlights the importance of monuments within a community and the need to search for this type of material culture within archeological sites. Governments or empires construct public buildings as testimony of their power and as a vehicle to develop this power.[12] Fogelin suggests two criteria to evaluate how and whether monuments serve this purpose: (1) "a religious structure should be located in a position associated with the people who are being legitimized—adjacent to a palace or in the capital city, for example," (2) "The second factor is visibility." People should be able to see it.[13]

An analysis of Stratum 2 architecture at Tell en-Naṣbeh reveals two buildings that may have served as monuments. Building 74.01 and 110.01 contain remains and building features associated with government buildings or palace-like structures, perhaps for officers with important administrative roles. In addition, their geographical position on high areas or places of high visibility

---

[10] Ibid.

[11] Ibid., 17.

[12] Lars Fogelin, "Deligitimizing Religion: The Archaeology of Religion as ... Archaeology," in *Belief in the Past: Theoretical Approaches to the Archaeology of Religion*, ed. David S. Whitley and Kelley Hays-Gilpin (Walnut Creek, CA: Left Coast, 2008), 134.

[13] Ibid.

suggests strategic importance. These structures contain a layout that is characteristic of a four-room building, but they also integrate additional rooms beyond the basic four-room house. Early scholars associated Building 110.01 with a sanctuary due to the floor plan's resemblance to early "cultic sites," but since then it has been suggested and accepted that this is not the case.[14] Keith Branigan in an article on the four-room buildings at Tell en-Naṣbeh argues that Building 194.01, 145.01, and 110.01 functioned as part of the military defense. He writes: "The close relation of these buildings to the city wall, and the fact that they were built on the inter-mural areas, suggests to the present writer that they must have fulfilled a military function."[15] Branigan also suggests these buildings functioned "as the houses of the officers in charge of the city's defences."[16] However, Branigan dates the structures to what he calls "the Middle Iron I-II," ca. 900 to 575 BCE, a range much earlier than Zorn's dating of Stratum 2.[17]

Even though I do not support Branigan's dating or his suggestion of a military function for these buildings, I agree with his assessment of the buildings' unique high quality construction, strategic position, and possible association with a government administrative building or palace for an important official. At the end of his article, Branigan mentions his hope of finding a fourth similar four-room structure at Tell en-Naṣbeh.[18] Zorn identifies this fourth structure and others in his 1993 study. Building 74.01, which I suggested above as a monument, fits this type. Zorn notes in his analysis the uniquely elaborate construction of these two buildings, and the possible function of Building 74.01 as a palace.[19]

What I consider significant in connection with these observations and our current knowledge of ritual typologies is the possible function that Buildings 74.01 and 110.01 might have served in terms of political rites. I refer to Bell's ritual notions discussed in Chapter 2, and how these connect with Scarre and Moore's insights of using architecture for political rites and government

---

[14] K. Branigan, "The Four-Room Buildings of Tell en-Naṣbeh," *IEJ* 16.3 (1966): 206–207.

[15] Ibid., 206. Branigan refers to these buildings as 1, 2, and 3 and references illustrations from McCown's original excavation report for the site in 1947. I cross-reference these and utilize Zorn's numbering since it assists in locating these on the site maps.

[16] Ibid., 208.

[17] Ibid. Branigan's dating comes from fn. 2 on ibid., 206.

[18] Ibid., 208.

[19] Zorn, "Tell en-Nasbeh: A Re-evaluation," 174.

ritualistic propaganda. Not until recently have scholars understood political rituals and the possible function that these government or official buildings might have played in promoting these ideals. I am not arguing that all large architecture or official buildings automatically falls within the possibility of a monument used in political or other type of ritual, but it merits attention to evaluate these structures with caution according to their attributes.

Even though Tell en-Naṣbeh's excavation methods and records have their limitations, and even though proving the presence of this type of rite is not definitive given the available data, I suggest that these two above-mentioned buildings' remains provide sufficient hints to propose this ritual function. I base this suggestion on two factors: first, the architectural features, and second, the close comparison of these buildings with Fogelin's two evaluation criteria discussed above.

Starting with the architectural features, Building 74.01 in figure 6 provides stronger evidence for resembling a palace.[20] It contains several key construction characteristics indicative of this type of architecture. The rooms associated with this building were: 149, 187–196, and 198.[21]

---

[20] I tabulate a summary of the construction features in table 23 of appendix D.

[21] Zorn, "Tell en-Nasbeh: A Re-evaluation," 165 and 424. Room 199 is missing from Zorn's table B.4.1, but present in his vol. 2 building description details. Conversely, Rooms 194, 195, and 198 are missing from his vol. 2, page 424, but present in that table. My review of the 1:100 maps led me to be inclusive of all these rooms for the building.

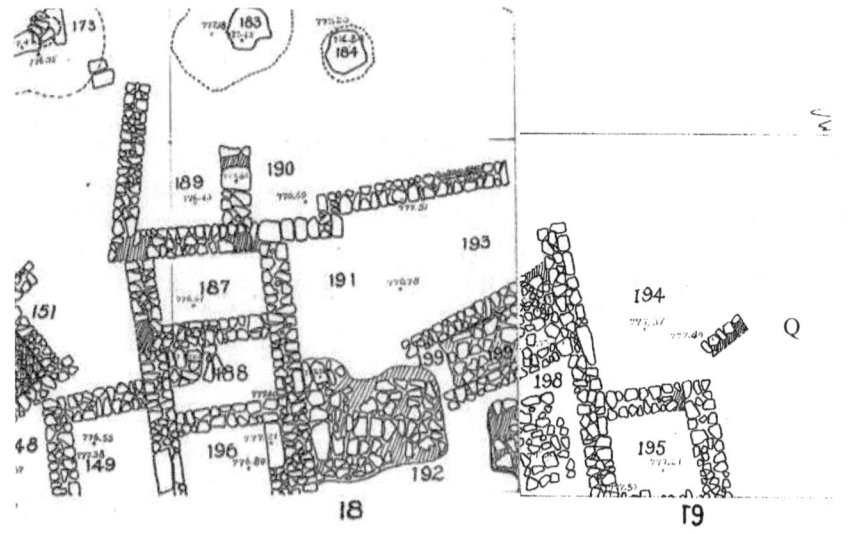

Figure 6. Tell en-Naṣbeh Building 74.01.

Source: Courtesy of Badè Museum, Berkeley, CA. Adapted by author from various 1:100 scale maps.

The building characteristics include the following: double-stone construction for most of the structure, rooms with stone paving, and a large stone-paved courtyard.[22] The floor in the courtyard had well-laid, large flat stones indicative of careful and elaborate construction.[23] The building had stone-paved floors in rooms 188, 192, and 198.[24]

Building 110.01 in figure 7 is also significant in terms of size. It encompassed rooms 266b, 267–269, 375, 376, 378, 379, 380a, 380b, and 400.[25] Walls in the building were well preserved, as were the pillars and floors. Most important, Room 376 contained in situ artifacts.[26] Zorn notes how the all of the

---

[22] Ibid., 424–25.
[23] Ibid., 425.
[24] Ibid., 169.
[25] Ibid., 165 and 538.
[26] Ibid., 538–39.

floor was preserved in cobblestones, a unique feature for most Persian period sites, and that it contained six monolithic stone pillars.[27] In addition to room 376, two other rooms, 379 and 380b, also had monolithic pillars.[28] All of these construction characteristics and the layout share similarities with those in Building 74.01 above. Zorn comments on the importance of Building 110.01: "Its size and complexity suggest that it was the home of an important individual, probably an official connected with the Babylonian appointed government."[29] I suggest that this function continued into the Persian period, given that the dating of this building extended at least to the middle of this period.[30] The reconstruction of this building may extend south to rooms from Building 127.01, making the complete complex of Building 110.01 even larger in size.[31]

---

[27] Ibid., 539.
[28] Ibid., 171.
[29] Ibid., 545.
[30] Ibid., 543–44.
[31] Ibid., 546.

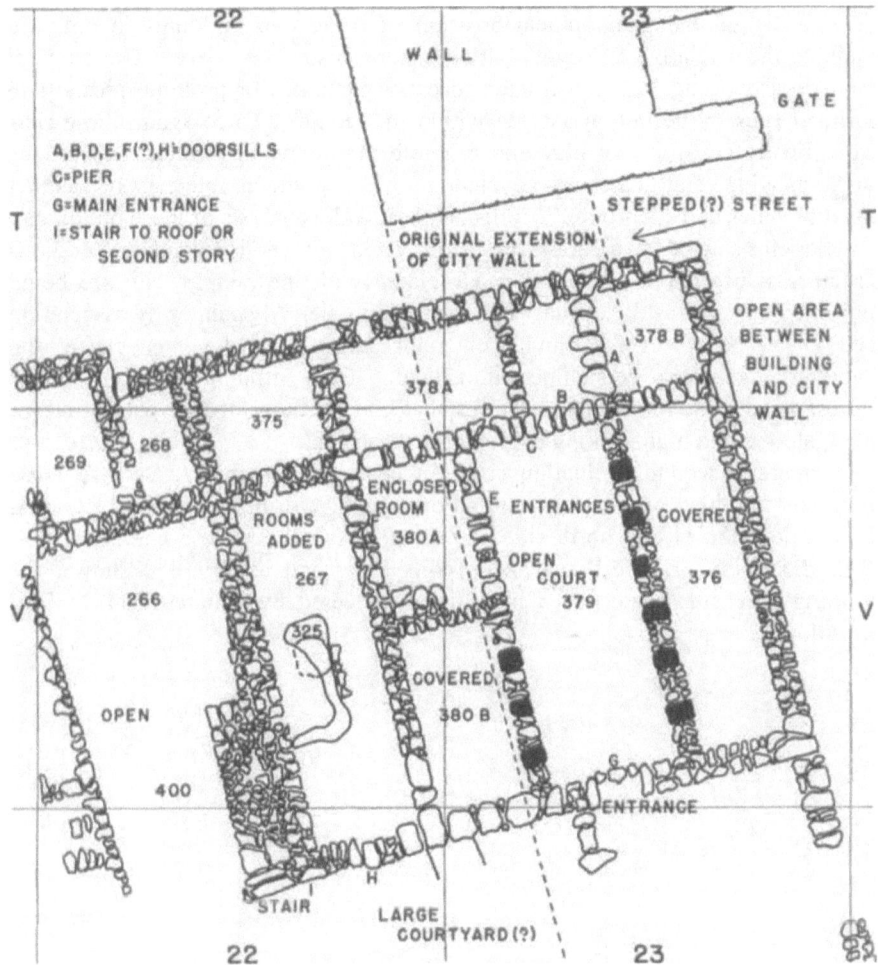

Figure 7. Tell en-Naṣbeh Building 110.01.

Source: McCown et al., *Archaeological and Historical Results*, fig. 51. Used by permission of the Badè Museum, Pacific School of Religion.

I analyzed the geographical position of these two buildings in order to evaluate them relative to Fogelin's two criteria discussed above.[32] Government sponsored buildings are constructed to carry meanings or promote ideals; and political rites by definition surface within this context. Once again, these rites "specifically construct, display and promote the power of political institutions (such as king, state, the village elders) or the political interests of distinct constituencies and subgroups."[33] I discuss below the analysis of these buildings.

Fogelin's first evaluation criterion cited above involved a religious structure's location in "a position associated with the people who are being legitimized," such as the capital city. As noted earlier, Mispah, or by association, Tell en-Naṣbeh, was the capital or main administrative center during the Babylonian and early Persian period in Judah.[34] Both Building 74.01 and 110.01 represent large architectural structures that can be described as palace-like or associated with a high-ranking administrative official.

Fogelin's second evaluation criterion dealt with visibility. Both of these buildings sat either on a high point and/or in a place of high visibility. Building 74.01's location on the north side of the tell fits both of these characteristics. Zorn did a topographical analysis of this area, and as figure 8 shows, the building was constructed at a high point reflected by squares Q17 to Q19 elevation.[35]

---

[32] I also examined the material culture present at these rooms. For details see appendix A. Zorn notes how buildings play an important part in how an empire shapes ideals, "human settlements are not established in isolation from their geographic and cultural environment. Buildings, installations and fortifications are constructed as a response to these two external forces and so the architecture of a site must be examined within this wider context." See ibid., 201.

[33] Bell, *Ritual: Perspectives and Dimensions*, 128.

[34] As noted earlier, there are proposals for viewing Ramat Raḥel as the main administrative center in the later Persian period.

[35] Please note that Building 74.01 extended over squares Q17 to 19.

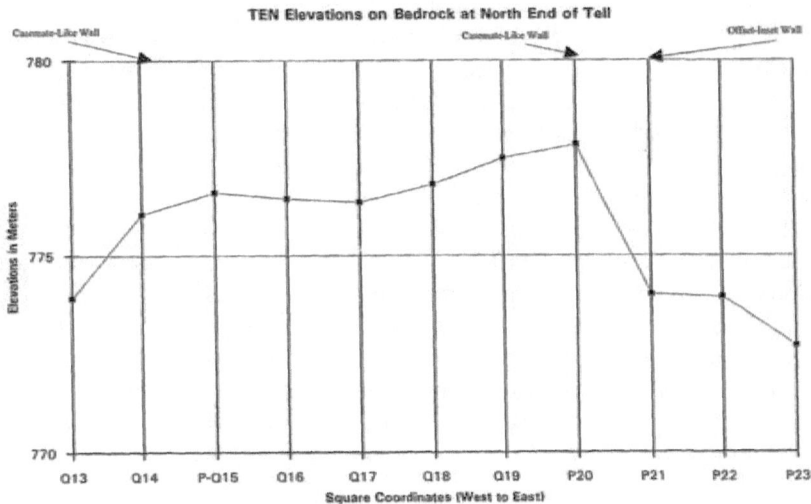

Figure 8. Tell en-Naṣbeh bedrock elevations in northern areas

Source: Zorn, "Tell en-Nasbeh: A Re-evaluation," p. 960. Used by permission.

Building 110.01's position next to the city gate commanded the attention of people coming in and out of the city. Both buildings were positioned at strategic locations at the settlement. Proximity to city gates infers possible connections with city administrative functions. It is my opinion that these large structures stood out from other architecture at the settlement and that these may have functioned for gathering people, official business, and other activities closely related to political rites. The large open courtyard architecture and expensive pillar construction with open access suggest a place in which public officials celebrated rituals. It was also likely that some of the rooms in both buildings contained a second floor, providing a potential platform for added visibility. Zorn identifies the potential for this second floor with some certainty in Building 110.01, Room 400.[36]

A second story in Building 110.01 contributes to issues of ritual and/or religious practices. A study of Israelite houses done by Philip J. King and

---

[36] Zorn, "Tell en-Nasbeh: A Re-evaluation," 171.

Lawrence E. Stager shows the importance of roof and second stories not only for daily living but also as a possible place for ritual: "The roof (*gāg*) and upper story (*'ăliyyâ*) of a house satisfied several purposes, including serving as the main living areas. During the warm months, the occupants had the option of sleeping out of doors on the rooftops.... The roof could also serve as a place for worship."[37] So even if only part of the building had a roof, it is still possible that these areas were utilized for rituals.

There are possible traces in addition to Zorn's analysis to support a roof or second story in Building 110.01. Various scholars have pointed to the relationship that exists between lamps and roofed areas or a second floor, although this correlation needs to be approached carefully.[38] An examination of the artifacts from the rooms in this building may shed light on this issue. There is the higher number of lamps in Rooms 378 and 379 when compared to other rooms at Tell en-Naṣbeh, as seen in table 9 below and compared to other rooms from tables in appendix A.[39] I suggest it is likely that Rooms 378 and 379 had at least covered areas, if not a second story.

---

[37] King and Stager, *Life in Biblical Israel*, 35.

[38] See for example, Brody, "Those Who Add House to House," 52. Also, Daviau, "Family Religion," 211.

[39] I consider that the rooms from Building 194.01 that have a higher number of artifacts might be associated with ritual. I discuss this further below.

TABLE 9 Building 110.01 Stratum 2 material culture

Artifact	Building 110.01										Total
	Rm. 266b	Rm. 267	Rm. 268	Rm. 269	Rm. 375	Rm. 376	Rm. 378	Rm. 379	Rm. 380a	Rm. 400	
Altars			1				1				2
Stands								3			3
Figurines, statuettes											0
Bowls	1	3	1	1	1	5	15	4		11	42
Cooking pot		2		2		1	7	5	1	6	24
Kraters											0
Baking-pan											0
Saucers and plates											0
Cups											0
Chalices							1				1
Jugs, juglets, flasks		1				2	6	2			11
Jars	2	8	4	1	2	8	12	7	8	2	54
Bottles											0
Lamps		1				1	2	2	1	1	8
Masks											0
Rattles										1	1
Zoomorphic vessels											0
Beads, amulets, pendants, other							2	5	1		8
Bones	1										1
Total per room	4	15	6	4	3	17	46	28	11	21	155

That these buildings served as a potential location for political ritual is more convincing when one considers how they were part of the building development process of Stratum 2. As Zorn notes and as discussed above, Stratum 3 structures at Tell en-Naṣbeh were leveled and Stratum 2 buildings erected on top of this earlier layer. This was part of a massive sponsored project, likely supported by the Babylonian and later Persian administration. What is important here is how this rebuilding may have supported religion. I draw on the work of Gösta Ahlström and his thesis that urbanization in the ancient Near East developed as a political process where state and religion worked together supported by royal administration.[40] These two buildings may have played a role in this state-sponsored development as it seems that they were utilized in political rites at Tell en-Naṣbeh.

4.1.1 City Gates

The importance of city gates for military, social, and administrative aspects of ancient living appears prominently in scholarly textual and archaeological literature. Yet archaeological sites with Persian period city gates remain few in numbers. Stern identifies the gates at Dor, Tel Megiddo, and Tel Lachish as the only remains from the Persian period, though he also considers the Valley Gate in Jerusalem as possibly dating to this period.[41] Jeffrey Zorn reevaluates the architecture of Tell en-Naṣbeh and concludes that the intragate walls and the outer gate continued to be used in the Persian period.[42] Until recently the potential for these architectural structures to be linked or used for ritual and religious practices has been classified as turbulent and obscure.[43] Tina Blomquist examines this issue and conclusively identifies cultic activities in Bethsaida and Tel Dan, and suggests possible evidence at eleven other sites, all of them dating to the Iron Age II. Although her study focuses on the Iron Age, it nonetheless contains information that is valuable for this study of the Persian period. I discuss below key aspects of city gates and how these relate to ritual or religious practices.

The origins of the synagogue trace back to city gates, making this area a potential location for ritual and religious activities.[44] As Blomquist argues, this area conveyed a sense of liminal space. "It is not," she writes, "a coincidence that the gates in the ancient Near East were places of judgement, execution,

---

[40] Gösta W. Ahlström, *Royal Administration and National Religion in Ancient Palestine*, SHANE, vol. 1 (Leiden: Brill, 1982).

[41] Stern, "The Assyrian, Babylonian, and Persian Periods (732–332 B.C.E.)," 466.

[42] Zorn, "Tell en-Nasbeh: A Re-evaluation," 1.175.

[43] Blomquist, *Gates and Gods*, 11–12.

[44] The city gates of the Persian period developed into independent areas that later became synagogues. For details, see Lee I. Levine, *The Ancient Synagogue: The First Thousand Years* (New Haven, CT: Yale University Press, 2005). Birger Olsson and Magnus Zetterholm, eds., *The Ancient Synagogue from Its Origins until 200 C.E.: Papers Presented at an International Conference at Lund University, October 14–17, 2001* (Stockholm: Almqvist & Wiksell, 2003). Joseph Gutmann, *Ancient Synagogues: The State of Research* (Chico, CA: Scholars Press, 1981).

asylum, display of booty and corpses, putting up of thrones and monuments and areas placed under the protection of deities."[45] She is careful when identifying borders and limits for city gates. I agree with her caution about defining what area constitutes the city gate, as these structures often included not just the three architectural elements mentioned above but also other nearby structures.[46]

City gates represent a good example of a location in which ritual and religious practices of various social strata could have taken place. This area was a public place in which officials or communal leaders could carry out ceremonies. This open and public characteristic of gates does not preclude the possibility for common people to either develop their own religious meaning of the official ritual or to use this area for their own rituals. Blomquist recognizes a plurality of cultic forms in city gates; she notes how they served "the occasional family cult" and she gives some support to Wolfgang Zwickel's view that they were the "cult place with small-scale rituals."[47] I agree with her view that the presence of domestic artifacts around city gates bears "witness to the diversity of cult practices, especially on the local or village community level," although I would also argue that this is not the only criteria for identifying ritual, as I discuss below.[48]

An analysis of Tell en-Naṣbeh' city gate provides an opportunity to explore ritual and religious practices during the Persian period. A review of what has been written about Tell en-Naṣbeh's city gate shows that at least one scholar feels strongly that it should not be included on the list of possible ritual sites.[49] Blomquist notes:

> It is time to remove Tell en-Naṣbeh from any further discussion on the archaeological evidence of cult practices at city gates for the following reasons: the pillar [referring to a large 'cigar-shaped' limestone pillar] has an uncertain provenance and its present shape could have been affected by standing exposed to the forces of weather for some period of time; the character of Building no.2 was not cultic, despite serious efforts in the past to prove the contrary; and no

---

[45] Blomquist identifies three architectural elements for ancient Near East city gates: (1) an opening, (2) a gatehouse, (3) a gate or passageway. See Blomquist, *Gates and Gods*, 16, 21.
[46] Ibid., 22.
[47] Ibid., 45.
[48] Ibid., 45–46.
[49] Perhaps Blomquist intends for the elimination of Tell en-Naṣbeh specific to the Iron Age. Her argument is not specific to a time period.

correspondence can be established between the use and find context of either the pillar figurines or scapula remains.[50]

It is my opinion that it is difficult to argue for or against the presence of rituals or religious practices at city gates based solely on the presence or absence of ritual artifacts. As seen and discussed previously, there are some types of rituals that may not leave behind material culture evidence. Therefore, as I discussed earlier, I propose a more open approach to the analysis that allows for two possibilities in seeing ritual or religious practices at the city gate: first, a comprehensive view of the possible architectural structures and areas that might have been part of the city gate complex, and second, an approach that recognizes the importance of the city gate as a possible site for political rites, even though specific ritual artifacts are not found in the remains. I pursue this strategy to make sure that structures and areas that were architecturally and socially closely connected to the city gate remain relevant. I discuss issues pertinent to these two possibilities below, first addressing the area for the city gate complex and then the city gate and its possible political rites.

Tell en-Naṣbeh archaeological excavations revealed two structures, an inner gate and an outer gate, as seen in figure 9, that together encompassed a city gate complex.[51]

---

[50] Blomquist, *Gates and Gods*, 109–110.

[51] The final excavation report describes how challenging it was for the original team first to identify and later to make sense of the two gate structures, as they postulated different theories of the relationship between the two gates. See McCown et al., "Archaeological and Historical Results," 195–201.

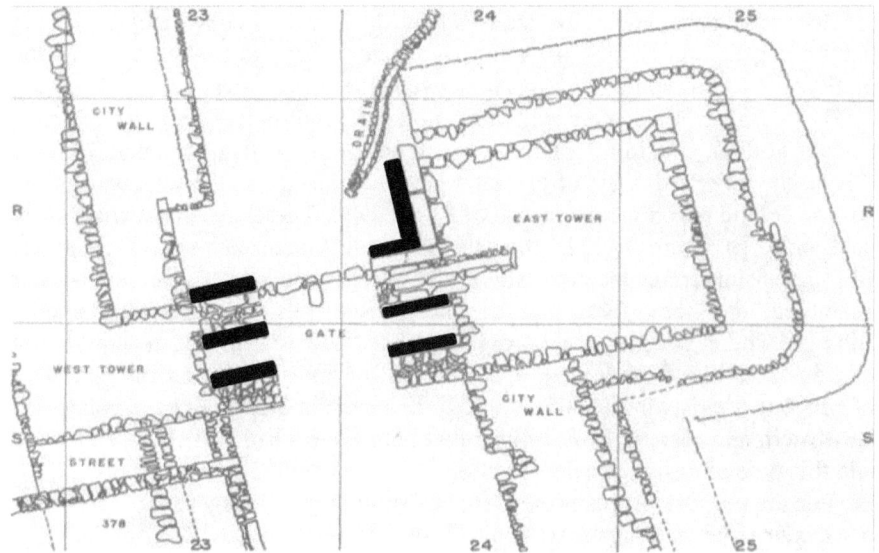

Figure 9. Tell en-Naṣbeh Outer Gate.
Note: Bench locations denoted by heavy black color.

Source: Adapted by author from McCown et al., *Archaeological and Historical Results*, fig. 47. Used by permission of the Badè Museum, Pacific School of Religion.

In Zorn's study he refers to the outer gate as Building 93.01 and the inner gate as Building 145.01 and provides a detailed analysis and critique of the original excavator's reconstructions.[52] He proposes that the final date for the use of the inner gate was the end of Stratum 3, probably starting with the Babylonian period, when the city was intentionally leveled for the building of Stratum 2.[53] The dating for the use of the outer gate extended to the latter part of the fifth century and possibly through the Persian period.[54] The construction of Building 93.02 over the outer gate indicates that it went out of use by Stratum

---

[52] Zorn, "Tell en-Nasbeh: A Re-evaluation," 332–38.
[53] Jeffrey R. Zorn, "An Inner and Outer Gate Complex at Tell en-Nasbeh," *BASOR* 307 (1997): 65.
[54] Zorn, "Tell en-Nasbeh: A Re-evaluation," 337. Also, Zorn, "An Inner and Outer Gate Complex at Tell en-Nasbeh," 65.

1.[55] Zorn also develops a later study solely dedicated to convincingly proving that both gates functioned as a massive gate complex, and articulating the relationship of Stratum 2 buildings in between these two gates.[56]

The original excavators and Zorn note the well-preserved state of stone benches at three locations: (1) on the north and south walls of Rooms 273a and 273c in the inner chambers of the outer gate; (2) outside on the west wall of the east tower; and (3) on the outer wall of Room 273c. These are shown with heavy black color in figure 9. These benches are an attribute commented on in the Bible as an important location where city elders, religious leaders, and others assembled, and they form part of ancient societies, in particular Israelite culture.[57] These benches may provide archaeological evidence to social and religious activities in this area, as supported by others sites and the extensive reference that exists in the Bible.[58] A stone or wood arch may have connected the western and eastern towers, given that both towers had sufficient strength to hold this type of design and construction.[59]

For the purpose of this present study the outer gate in figure 10 is the main focus, since the inner gate was not in use during Stratum 2. Zorn includes Building 93.01 with Rooms 273a, 273b, 273c, and 274–276 in the outer gate.[60] Depending on the physical layout of ancient city gates, this type of architecture often annexed other surrounding areas as part of the gate complex, forming a larger architectural and social space. Such areas included plazas, hallways, and other such spaces.

---

[55] Zorn, "Tell en-Nasbeh: A Re-evaluation," 497.

[56] Zorn, "An Inner and Outer Gate Complex at Tell en-Nasbeh."

[57] McCown et al., "Archaeological and Historical Results," 196. Zorn notes that the benches in Room 273a might have been a reconstruction by the excavators based on the presence of benches in 273c and agrees with this reconstruction based on the circumstances. See Zorn, "Tell en-Nasbeh: A Re-evaluation," 493.

[58] I recognize that the presence of these architectural features only indicate a structure for seating functions, as has been argued by Blomquist, *Gates and Gods*, 27. For a detailed study on ritual evidence at city gates, see ibid.

[59] McCown et al., "Archaeological and Historical Results," 196.

[60] See table 3 in this study.

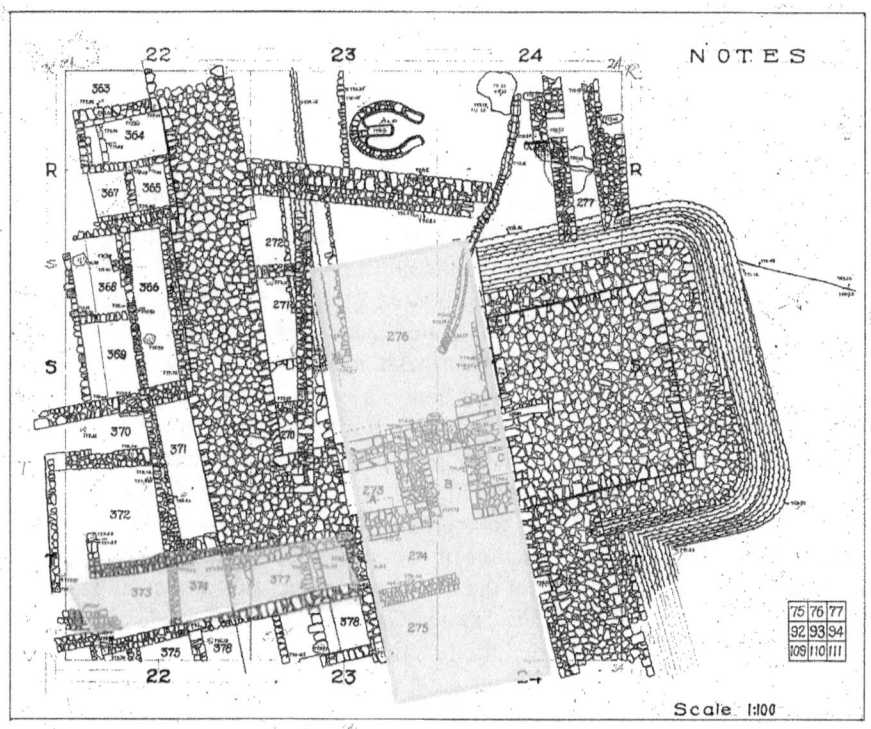

Figure 10. Tell en-Naṣbeh Outer Gate complex.

Note: author's proposed areas shaded.

Source: Badè Museum, Berkeley, CA. Author's adaptation of Map 1:100 Area 93. Used by permission.

Ze'ev Herzog notes how, beginning with the Iron Age, city gates evolved in their function:

> Iron Age gates had civilian functions above and beyond their purely military-defensive role. This conclusion is further supported by several installations in or next to the gates. Large plazas adjoining the gate inside the city that could

accommodate large audiences or serve as a market place were found at every site.[61]

The inner and outer city gates at Tell en-Naṣbeh represent a great example of this evolution, as it is evident that with the disuse of the inner gate and adoption of only the outer gate military function decreased after the Iron Age. The outer gate assumed a more civilian function during the Persian period. Tell en-Naṣbeh had Rooms 274 and 275 as part of a plaza that connected directly to the gate entry and its two inner chambers. On the north part of the outer gate Room 276 extended north for about 10 meters before reaching the edge of the east tower.

Zorn refers to what he calls the "Outer Gate Road," which included Rooms 373, 374, 377 on the east, and he describes this area as possibly an access road during the Persian period.[62] My own analysis of the literature and maps from Tell en-Naṣbeh's outer gate concurs with Zorn's assessment of how people entered the city during the Persian period.[63] It appears that the means of approach into Tell en-Naṣbeh was limited to the access road represented by Rooms 373, 374, and 377 due to topographical difficulties or buildings that would block access. The orientation of this gate access road towards the west gave direct access to the center of the city in a fairly straight and quick fashion. I suggest that what Zorn calls the "Outer Gate Road" might have served as a hallway or corridor that extended the function of the interior gate plaza, Rooms 274 and 275, in the area south of the gate. Even if this hallway did not function as the main entry point, it is likely that at the very least it functioned as an important access corridor for the reasons named above. Then, architecturally and socially, in addition to Building 93.01 and its accompanying rooms, Room 377 and possibly Rooms 373 and 374 formed part of the gate complex at Tell en-Naṣbeh. This proposed area is shaded in figure 10. I base this suggestion on the architectural features for this area which showed a stepped approach with a unique access to the center of the city, and the likelihood that people gathered in these areas for social and economic reasons, as trading and market activities might have taken place in such locations. King and Stager also recognize city gates and surrounding areas functioning in this manner: "The city gate (*ša'ar*) and the adjacent square were the place of public assembly, as well as the business center where commercial and legal transactions were conducted.... The account in 2 Chron. 32:6 says that Hezekiah gathered his commanders 'in the

---

[61] Zeev Herzog, "Fortifications (Levant)," *ABD* 2:852.
[62] See table 3 in this study.
[63] Zorn, "An Inner and Outer Gate Complex at Tell en-Nasbeh," 63.

plaza...' where he exhorted them to trust in Yahweh."[64] This case, although based on literary evidence, provides an excellent example of my initial argument for considering city gates as possible monuments, regardless of the presence or absence of ritual artifacts, when examining the potential for political rites or other types of rituals. I suggest this because the study next reviews the artifacts in this outer gate complex, and I think that it is important to be sensitive to small clues that may be present in the architecture or the context, independent of and supplementary to what is found in the ground.

The outer gate complex contained various kinds of artifacts and these provide material for making observations related to ritual and/or religious practices.[65] I analyzed the excavation records from the Badè Museum and in table 10 summarize the artifacts present in this area that in the past have been associated with ritual or religious practices.[66]

---

[64] King and Stager, *Life in Biblical Israel*, 234.

[65] From this point forward when I refer to the outer gate complex, I include the outer gate Building 93.01 with its rooms, and Rooms 373, 374, and 377.

[66] This analysis encompassed the review of my proposed areas by using the museum's millimeter cards for all the architecture that Zorn associated with certainty to Stratum 2. Artifacts that may be categorized as ritually related were summarized in a spreadsheet. These rooms and artifacts were cross-referenced and compared with Zorn's list of ritual artifacts to ensure that no artifacts were missed. The comprehensive list formed the data for the table.

TABLE 10 Outer gate complex Stratum 2 ritual material culture

Location	Material culture type[1]	Notes[2]
Building 93.01:		
Room 273a	1. Figurine head of Astarte, x1 2. Bowls 3. Two high base saucer lamps, x10, x11	1. Museum #B2012.1.82 (1698). Dull red-brown ware in mold with dark grey core, small white inclusions[3] 2. Miscellaneous rims 3. Fragments
Room 273b	No data	—
Room 273c	No data	—
Room 274	1. Bowls and juglets 2. Green-blue scarab, x29 3. Figurine head, x33 4. Saucer lamp, x35 5. Bronze flat piece with two holes, x36	1. Various types 2. Museum #1694 3. Fragment 4. Fragments 5. Fragment
Room 275	1. Figurine leg, x16 2. Three base saucer lamp, x18	1. Fragment 2. Fragments
Room 276	1. Figurine base, x2 2. High base saucer lamp, x4 3. Bowls and jars 4. Ring stand, x9 5. Bone; whistle (?), x10	1. Fragment 2. Fragment 3. Miscellaneous 4. Museum #1758 5. Museum #1706
Proposed Hallway:		
Room 373	No data	—
Room 374	No data	—
Room 377	1. Bronze fibula, x9 2. Saucers, x10 3. Figurine torso, x11	1. — 2. — 3. Fragment.

[1] The x number denotes the original excavators' method of numbering artifacts. When they found an item in an area, they started with number one and continued sequentially in the order of discovery. If three walls were discovered in that area, the x number became associated with the room number. If there were no rooms, the artifact remained with only an x number. For more details in the method of recording see Badè.

[2] The Museum numbers that start with a "B" represent the modern number that the museum utilizes today to catalog and manage artifacts. The numbers in parenthesis are the original museum numbers that the excavation and recording team assigned to artifacts. Some artifacts are in the process of being cataloged and may not yet have a modern museum number. Some of the descriptions in this column came from the observations and recording from the museum staff as recorded in the database.

³ Published on McCown, Muilenburg, Wampler, Bothmer and Harrison, *Archaeological and Historical Results*, 1947, 299, Plate 85.3. Also, Kletter, *The Judean Pillar-Figurines and the Archeaology of Asherah*, 1996, 190, Catalog #165.

I discuss some options for interpreting table 10 and draw some conclusions from these observations. First, there is evidence that this area contained artifacts related to ritual and/or religious practices. Even though this material culture was not found in situ, its presence may indicate some form of use near this location. The outer gate complex contained five figurines in total. In addition, the complex had two basalt bowl fragments, Room 274, x34 and Room 374, x8, suggestive of the type used in libation offerings. Finally, material culture other than figurines may indicate a context where rituals took place, and these should be considered as well. Second, another option is that some of these artifacts named above might have been part of the economic activity going on at the complex. If there were merchants selling these types of artifacts, then this complex area could certainly have functioned in such a capacity, although in my opinion the fact that these items were spread across several rooms rather than concentrated in one area diminishes this possibility.

As mentioned above, Blomquist argues for dismissing Tell en-Naṣbeh as a site with "cult practices."[67] She gives three reasons: (1) a limestone pillar and its unknown context near the inner gate, Building 145.02; (2) the observation that "Building 2"[68] in the inner gate area was not a temple or sanctuary but rather a four-room house; and (3) the lack of connection between use and context for the figurine or the scapula found in outer gate area.[69] Although she raises some good points pertaining to stratigraphic issues, her conclusions should be reevaluated and revised. Her first reason highlights a valid concern when considering the excavator's comments related to the limestone pillar.[70] The second reason, even though correct in terms of the building's identification as a four-room house, does not adequately account for the fact that rituals do occur outside of temples or sanctuaries. The fact that Building 145.02 was not a temple does not

---

[67] Blomquist, *Gates and Gods*, 110.

[68] This building corresponds with Zorn's Building 145.02. Blomquist's fn. 343 mentions that this building corresponded with Zorn's Building 145.01, however this represents an oversight, as seen by a closer examination of McCown et al., "Archaeological and Historical Results," 210, Fig. 52A.

[69] Blomquist refers to the figurine shown in the distribution map in ibid., Fig. 50C. She suggests a locus of 276 based on a cross-reference of map locations.

[70] These dealt with the possibility that local Arabs might have moved it there in modern times.

eliminate the city gate complex from other ritual or religious practice possibilities. Her third reason is difficult to argue for or against. As discussed above, the presence of these items does not definitively prove that rituals were taking place at these locations, but rather it provides strong support for the possibility. I suggest, however, that the outer gate area supports the possibilities for political rites and other types of religious activities as discussed above. The outer city gate is a potential context for ritual, as she has shown at other sites in her studies, in addition to the support that other scholars provide. As part of the reevaluation I point to other artifacts as shown in table 10 above. Some of these were not included in her discussion. In either case, as the table indicates, there were other artifacts in this outer gate complex. In addition, this process should consider newer investigations and conclusions of political rites at city gates complexes and the roles that they play, as discussed above. In light of my own analysis, I conclude that due to the importance of city gates and their role in the social and religious aspect of ancient societies, it would be prudent to remain open to the possibility of ritual taking place at Tell en-Naṣbeh's city gate complex, even with the current state of knowledge from past excavation results.

4.1.2 Temples

It appears that the three-type categorization for Persian period temple spaces that Stern suggests has not attracted alternative proposals from other scholars.[71] The first includes "Large, central, city temples," with the solar shrine at Tel Lachish as the only example available.[72] The second covers "Medium-sized sanctuaries," as seen only at three sites, all of which are outside of Yehud: Sarepta, Tel Michal, and Mizpe Yammim.[73] The third encompasses "Small (ca.1 sq.m.) chapels in which a sacred object stood: an idol or a *mazzebah*."[74] Such chapels so far have also been found outside of Yehud in Tel Dan and Tel Michal.[75] Even though Stern's three types cover temples and shrines well, it is my opinion that perhaps the organization of his 2001 book's Chapter 2 Temples and Cult Objects diminishes the possibility of investigating alternative locations and elements

---

[71] Stern, "The Assyrian, Babylonian, and Persian Periods (732–332 B.C.E.)," 478–79.

[72] Ibid. He comments that this is the only one of this type in Palestine. Others scholars see this temple as belonging to the Hellenistic period; see discussion in chapter 5 for more details.

[73] Ibid., 478–79.

[74] Ibid.

[75] Ibid., 478.

related to ritual. Some of these include nontraditional options such as monuments, city gates, household areas, burials, and natural open spaces, all or some of which may be part of family and household ritual and religion. He comments on the possibility of these non-temple based occurrences of ritual, but attributes these to non-Judean settlements, and, as quoted above, concludes that these were not connected with Jewish or Samaritan practices.[76]

There has been discussion as to the possibility of Tell en-Naṣbeh containing a temple during the Persian period. Scholars have investigated this area in connection to textual references that may shed light on the issue.[77] Zorn's reevaluation of the architecture does not reveal a structure that could be associated with any comparable temple or small sanctuary.[78] I also reviewed Stratum 2 architecture from the site and could not see any corresponding similarities to other well established temples in the region.[79] This lack of evidence from the early excavation records may suggest that Tell en-Naṣbeh did not have a temple, although a definite answer to this question is difficult to give since approximately one third of the site remains to be excavated and some architecture from Stratum 2 only survived to foundation levels. Zorn alludes to the possibility of a small shrine in Tell en-Naṣbeh, given that other settlements possessed these in ancient Israel.[80] To a certain extent the lack of a temple at Tell en-Naṣbeh results in most, if not all, of the material remains being related in some way or another to family and/or household rituals, except as noted above.

4.1.3 Houses and Other Household Areas

This study examined definitions and methodologies of family and household archaeology towards the end of chapter 1, and discussed the relationship that existed between family and household. I agree with Albertz and Schmitt's approach to definitions given there, as it fits well within the ancient Near East context. In essence, the term 'nuclear household' corresponds to "one conjugal family unit," described as a couple and its children. The term "extended household" encompasses the "nuclear household" plus any cohabitating single

---

[76] Ibid., 487–88.

[77] For a brief look at various positions see, Zorn, "Tell en-Nasbeh and the Problem of the Material Culture of the Sixth Century," 442–43.

[78] Ibid., 443.

[79] For example, see the Solar Shrine in Tel Lachish and its layout in chapter 5 of this study.

[80] Zorn, "Tell en-Nasbeh and the Problem of the Material Culture of the Sixth Century," 443.

relatives. It is also important to differentiate between the dynamic terms nuclear household and extended household versus houses and at times also household spaces. The former represents the human component and the latter the physical, space dimension. So to be clear in connection with this section's heading, this study explores "houses and other household areas" as a function of space in which nuclear and extended households lived or cohabitated.

The architecture remains provide an opportunity to explore what constitutes a house or a household area during the Persian period. There are various options to identify these spaces in Stratum 2 Tell en-Naṣbeh. First, this study discusses floor plans and building patterns from the Persian period, and then it focuses on identifying buildings that would fall within the parameters of houses and household areas. Stern's study identifies "most of the buildings in the Persian period were built on a surprisingly uniform plan, whether private or public."[81] He refers to this type of floor plan as the "open court house" composed of an open court, which was surrounded by rooms on some or all sides.[82] He concludes that this type of plan came into Palestine due to Assyrian influence and continued into the Persian period.[83] The only exception to this basic floor plan that he notes existed within the Residency at Tel Lachish, discussed in the next chapter. It is interesting to observe that this same basic type of floor plan with the open courtyard also existed during this period in Transjordan with the slight difference that these buildings often included tabuns or silos.[84]

The open courtyard functioned as an important area for families and households to gather and perform activities during the Persian period. Boyce notes how house layouts during the Persian period supported rituals:

> One of the features of a Median manor-house had been the hall, the centre of its life. Here presumably (as in the great houses of medieval Europe) the lord and his people sat, and meals were cooked at the wide hearth, which would have given out a comfortable warmth on winter days and nights. Even through the summer the fire would have burned there continually, blanketed when not needed under a layer of ash; and three times a day, in the pagan period, it would have received the ritual offerings. The intention of these offerings was to gratify Ātar, the god of fire; and they could be made accordingly by any adult

---

[81] Stern, *Material Culture of the Land of the Bible*, 54. Also Stern, "The Assyrian, Babylonian, and Persian Periods (732–332 B.C.E.)," 468–69.

[82] Stern, *Material Culture of the Land of the Bible*, 54.

[83] Ibid.

[84] Piotr Bienkowski, "The Persian Period," in *Jordan: An Archaeological Reader*, ed. Russell Adams (Oakville, CT: Equinox, 2008), 340.

member of the household who was in a state of ritual purity. The great innovation made in this ancient cult by Zoroaster had been to appoint fire as the symbol of righteousness, before which every member of his community should pray five times a day.[85]

Open courtyards appeared as one of the important recurring features in Persian period houses of the southern Levant. It would be critical to find an effective way to identify the above named fire rituals as a distinguishing element of family and household rituals for families that observed religious practices from Zoroastrianism.

At Tell en-Naṣbeh an analysis of Stratum 2 architecture reveals that of the thirteen buildings and three areas listed in table 3 that could be dated concretely to this stratum, seven were four-room buildings and one was a three-room building.[86] Unfortunately, the state of preservation on the other buildings makes it difficult to identify floor plans with certainty. Of these seven buildings Zorn notes the addition of more rooms in Buildings 110.01 and 125.01, and suggests that these may have functioned as possible storage or service areas.[87] As discussed earlier, these four-room and three-room Stratum 2 buildings were significantly larger in size with an average increase of 1.3 to 2.2 times the size of the largest Stratum 3 buildings.[88] Most of them had an approximate size of 10 meters by 12 meters by 13 meters.[89] The above mentioned thirteen buildings include Building 93.04 and Building 195.02. The remains of Building 93.04 were fragmentary. Building 195.02 had millimeter cards mostly for squares with a few cards for the rooms. Therefore, these two buildings are not discussed in the tables of appendix A. Of the eleven buildings listed in table 11 in appendix A it is likely that ten of these buildings functioned in whole, or some at least in part, as houses or household areas. Building 93.01, the outer gate complex, is the exception to this list.

How can one identify these spaces, or buildings, as houses or household areas in Stratum 2 Tell en-Naṣbeh? To answer this question, I review below the architecture of each building along with the notes that Zorn made for each room and building, and examine the type of artifacts found in each of these areas. I organize the discussion by sequential building number.[90]

---

[85] Boyce, "Under the Achaemenians," 51.
[86] See Zorn, "Tell en-Nasbeh: A Re-evaluation," 165–66, 172.
[87] Ibid., 172.
[88] Ibid., 173.
[89] Ibid., 59.
[90] I bold each building number for ease of reference.

Building 74.01 contained Rooms 149, 187–196, and 198.[91] As previously discussed this building contained elaborate construction features, and I suggested that it possibly functioned as a palace or residence for a high-ranking government official. The role that this building, along with Building 110.01, played as a whole in terms of monumental architecture did not diminish the likelihood that part of the building functioned as a house or household space. Zorn assigns to it a function of "a large public building. Perhaps it was an official residence, or a small palace."[92] Unfortunately, Rooms 149, 187, 188, 190, and 199 had no millimeter cards specific to the room number; the cards and excavation results exist only for the squares. However, the artifacts were recorded by squares. For this specific building the corresponding squares with associated rooms are Q17, Q18, and Q19. These areas had artifacts associated with ritual such as figurine fragments and chalices, but due to the lack of detail as to the exact location, these loci do not provide critical support.[93] Therefore, it is difficult to stipulate function without a complete and more accurate picture of these contexts. However, what can be gathered from these rooms suggests that there might have been a small amount of food preparation and/or food consumption taking place around the rooms for the central courtyard area, as Rooms 191, 192, 193, and 196 contained cooking pots, bowls, and the remains of animal bones.[94] What is interesting to note is the small number of recovered artifacts that are typically associated with domestic assemblages when compared to other buildings from Stratum 2. As table 11 shows, this building only had five bowls and five cooking pots. Most of the other buildings had well over ten of these artifacts. I interpret this as further support that this building served as a palace or government administrative structure, perhaps with occasional banquet or political ritual, as suggested above.

Building 93.03 encompassed Rooms 365–370.[95] All the rooms, except Room 367 had individual millimeter cards specific to each room. Zorn's analysis of the architecture reveals a four-room building and he identifies Rooms 368 and 369 as part of the central courtyard, Rooms 365 and 367 as the

---

[91] See figure 14 in appendix B for a reconstructed layout of the floor plan.

[92] Zorn, "Tell en-Nasbeh: A Re-evaluation," 427.

[93] Details of the millimeter cards, for square Q18: x5 a fragment of a figurine with possible torso of Astarte; x7–x9, limb bone fragments from large animals; x12, miniature couch; x18 figurine fragment of saddle; x71–x73, figurine fragments. For square Q19: x2 zoomorphic spout of head of dog; x3, base fragment of chalice.

[94] There was an artifact in Room 196 that had a resemblance to an altar and I have listed it that way, although it is difficult to ascertain due to the fragmentary nature of it.

[95] See figure 15 appendix B.

back rooms of the building, and he suggests that Room 370 probably functioned as an alley.[96] He concludes with the following: "There is nothing to indicate more than a domestic role for this structure."[97] A review of the recovered artifacts by rooms in table 14 appendix A shows that most of the rooms in this building had a representation of artifacts that have been associated with the domestic setting. There were fragments for bowls, cooking pots, jug and juglets, jars, lamps, and bivalve shells. The highest recurrence of these artifacts was located in Rooms 366 and 368. I suggest that part of Room 366 could have been a space for food preparation or food storage given the number and type of artifacts present. Of particular interest for this study and for the archaeology of ritual and religion was the presence of two figurines in Room 366 and one figurine in Room 369. In addition, Room 370 contained an artifact that I suggest resembles an incense altar. The details of these artifacts are described in table 6 and table 7 above. It is interesting to note that Rooms 366 and 368 also had two lamps each, a rather higher number than most of the other rooms in Stratum 2. As discussed earlier, this may suggest a roof and/or a second story. This is more likely for Room 366 as its east wall backed up to the large city wall. It is also possible that these lamps had a ritual function.

Building 110.01 contained Rooms 266b, 267–269, 375, 376, 378, 379, 380a, 380b, and 400.[98] All the rooms in this building had individual millimeter cards specific to them. Zorn identifies this building as a "4-Room house complex" based on extensive photographic evidence and the well-preserved state of the walls.[99] Rooms 376, 378, 379, 380a, and 380b constituted the main floor plan for the core portion of the four-room house.[100] Room 376 contained an entire cobble floor with in situ vessels. Room 379 functioned as the main courtyard with the other rooms in the core functioning as side rooms. To the west of the core rooms and the main four-room house, the building had an annex structure. Zorn suggests that some of the rooms in the core areas functioned as living quarters, with the likelihood of other activities in the second story. He interprets the function of the building relative to the gate as follows:

> That this structure was built adjacent to the gate, over part of the original town wall, and belongs to Stratum 2 may indicate that whoever lived there may have had some connection with activities customary to gate areas. Its size and

---

[96] Zorn, "Tell en-Nasbeh: A Re-evaluation," 501–02.
[97] Ibid., 503.
[98] See figure 16 in appendix B for a reconstructed layout of the floor plan.
[99] Zorn, "Tell en-Nasbeh: A Re-evaluation," 538.
[100] Ibid.

complexity suggest that it was the home of an important individual, probably an official connected with the Babylonian appointed government.[101]

I agree with Zorn's interpretations in terms of the building's connection with the outer gate as discussed in the section for Monuments. A review of the contents in each of the rooms brings about some interesting observations. First, the large number of artifacts in Room 378 and Room 379 including: bowls, cooking pots, jugs, juglets, jars, and white shells. Room 378 might have functioned as a food preparation area or storage space. Room 379 also had a significant number of domestic artifacts including bronze fibulas, bracelets, and a needle. In terms of ritual artifacts, Room 378 contained two altars, and Room 379 had three stands, as described in table 6. In addition, Room 378 also had a chalice, vessel x37, with only a small portion missing. Both rooms also contained two lamps with the possible interpretations, as suggested earlier. Collectively, Building 110.01 had the highest number of stands, bowls, cooking pots, jugs, juglets, flasks, and jars from all the buildings in Stratum 2, as seen in table 11 in appendix A.

I also suggest that Building 110.01's function as a potential palace or house for an administrative official does not negate its potential for there to exist family or household rituals and/or religious practices. As John Holladay points out, rituals and religious expression existed at different levels of society, and it was quite possible that Buildings 110.01 and 74.01, even though potentially palaces or large houses, may have rooms where important administrative officials or family members could have performed religious activities.[102] Patricia A. McAnany further explores this idea in her study and concludes with some insights that are worth mentioning in this discussion:

> Notwithstanding this re-orientation, it is wise to keep in mind that the so-called popular religion of domestic ritual often co-exists, either in cooperation or conflict, with institutionalized religions that serve the interests of the state, resulting in multiple ideologies. Quite often, ritual is seated at the crux of power negotiations between the household and the state; thus, as we enhance

---

[101] Ibid., 545.

[102] Holladay, "Religion in Israel and Judah under the Monarchy," 267–68. I find that even though this study examines Iron Age archaeology, some of its ideas and conclusions should hold true to Stratum 2 archaeology at Tell en-Naṣbeh.

our understanding of domestic ritual, we also learn something of the reach of the power of the state.[103]

In addition, Darby's study suggests that "figurine rituals were performed by a large percentage of the populace regardless of socioeconomic status."[104]

Building 125.01 was composed of Rooms 472, 473, 477, 638, 641, 643, 647, 659.[105] All the rooms had individual millimeter cards specific to them. Zorn interprets this structure as a four-room building and notices the open courtyard to which the excavators did not assign a number.[106] This area resided in the central location of the building with Room 477 on the north side and Room 641 on the south. Room 643 contributes to the stratigraphy of the building, as its floor contained in situ artifacts.[107] Like Building 110.01, this building also contained an annex with Rooms 473, 638, and possibly 472 on the east side of the structure, and it may be the house of a well-to-do individual or government official at Tell en-Naṣbeh.[108] Of special interest to ritual and religious practice possibilities are the altar in the shape of a tubular votive stand in Room 477 x20 and the zoomorphic vessel in Room 473, x13 in table 6 and table 8, respectively. It is also worth noting that as a whole Building 125.01 contained the highest number of finds in the beads, amulets, pendants and other small artifacts category when compared to the rest of the buildings in Stratum 2. These items included bronze fibulas, perforated shells, bronze rings, Kohl sticks, and iron fibula.

Building 127.01 represented a structure with a smaller number of spaces: Rooms 97, 106, and 108.[109] The excavators associated specific millimeter cards with each of these rooms. However, Room 97's records might be either incomplete or lacking details due to the state of the notes on the millimeter card. This issue might have contributed to the small number of recovered artifacts for this room and possibly others in this building, as seen in appendix A. Zorn interprets this structure as a possible four-room building, and notes its close

---

[103] Patricia A. McAnany, "Rethinking the Great and Little Tradition Paradigm from the Perspective of Domestic Ritual," in *Domestic Ritual in Ancient Mesoamerica*, ed. Patricia Plunket (Los Angeles, CA: Cotsen Institute of Archaeology, University of California Los Angeles, 2002), 119.

[104] Darby, *Interpreting Judean Pillar Figurines*, 401.

[105] See figure 17 in appendix B for a reconstructed layout of the floor plan.

[106] Zorn, "Tell en-Nasbeh: A Re-evaluation," 568.

[107] Ibid., 569.

[108] Ibid., 570.

[109] See figure 18 in appendix B for a reconstructed layout of the floor plan.

resemblance in layout and construction with Building 110.01.[110] The building also contained a *tannur* or oven on the NW corner of Room 108, although the minimal amount of recovered material makes it challenging to formulate an opinion as to the likelihood that this house belonged to a potter. Of special interest for ritual discussions is the figurine head fragment from Room 108, x3 as described in table 7.

Building 127.03 contained Rooms 333, 334, 335, 336.[111] All of these rooms had specific millimeter cards. Zorn classifies this structure as a four-room building, and stipulates that it served a domestic function.[112] This structure connected with Building 144.01 on its east side. A review of the recovered artifacts from this building in conjunction with the floor plan may suggest that Room 333 functioned as a food preparation area due to the presence of bowls, a juglet, jars, and a cooking pot. It also might have been a covered room given that a lamp was found there. My review and analysis of the information available for this building did not reveal ritual practices.

Building 144.01 had Rooms 318, 324–327, 331, and 332.[113] This building is positioned east of Building 127.03 as shown in figure 19 of appendix B. All of these rooms possessed millimeter cards. Zorn identifies this structure as a three-room building, although the architecture provided some challenges in its full reconstruction.[114] Room 331 contained five stairways coming down from the plaza area just east of the room.[115] The artifacts in these rooms provide a wide range of assemblages from the domestic setting including: bowls, cooking pots, jugs, jars, and small items. The total number of artifacts for this building represents the second largest assemblage for the whole Stratum 2 architecture, only surpassed by Building 110.01. This building also contained important artifacts associated with ritual and/or religious practices. For example, Room 324 had a flat-topped altar, x27 as described in table 6; Room 326 contained a fragment x4 that I suggest resembles an altar; Room 327, x13 included a basalt stand; and Room 331 had a zoomorphic vessel, x8 as described in table 8.

Building 145.02 represented another structure with a smaller number of spaces, which included Rooms 224 to 227. All of the rooms had specific

---

[110] Zorn, "Tell en-Nasbeh: A Re-evaluation," 594–95.
[111] See figure 19 in appendix B for a reconstructed layout of the floor plan.
[112] Zorn, "Tell en-Nasbeh: A Re-evaluation," 605.
[113] See figure 19 in appendix B for a reconstructed layout of the floor plan. Room 318 may share walls with Building 128.01. See ibid., 690.
[114] Ibid., 690–92.
[115] Ibid., 171.

millimeter cards.[116] Zorn identifies this structure as a four-room building and notes the likelihood of Room 226 functioning as the central courtyard for what seemed to be a house for an official due to its well-constructed nature.[117] In addition to domestic assemblages for food preparation, the contents of the rooms had some interesting artifacts including: bone remains in Rooms 224 and 226 and bronze artifacts in 226 and 227. Based on the data available this building did not reveal ritual activities.

Building 160.10 had Rooms 463, 468, 565, 567, 569, and 574.[118] Each of the room's millimeter cards had associations with their respective rooms. The architectural remains of this building to a height barely above foundation level made it challenging to identify and propose potential functions, although Zorn suggests that some of the rooms might have functioned as storerooms.[119] The material culture from the rooms contained a wide distribution of domestic artifacts as seen in table 21 of appendix A. Overall, Building 160.10 placed fifth out of the eleven buildings from Stratum 2 in terms of total number of recovered artifacts. Room 463 had a large inventory of bowls, cooking pots, kraters, jugs, juglets, jars, and loom weights. Material culture of special interest for ritual included: Room 463, x19, a fragment of a possible altar categorized by excavators in the millimeter card as pedestal fragment of a chalice. I suspect that this may be a fragment of an altar since it has a depression in the center, and was the shape of similar incense altars. Further research in this area may bring additional insights. The same room also contained two animal figurines x20 and x51 as described in table 7. Even though I did not include it with the numbers for altars, Room 463 also had a limestone mortar, x53. Here, too, I suspect what was identified as a mortar was actually another altar.

Lastly, **Building 194.01** encompassed Rooms 20 to 26. However, Rooms 20, 21, 25, and 26 lacked specific millimeter cards. Only Rooms 22, 23, and 24 had these. Zorn identifies this structure as a four-room building with a central courtyard in Rooms 23–25, based on the architecture.[120] Kiln 106, located southwest of this building, dates to Stratum 3 and therefore has no relationship to Building 194.01.[121] This building had a wide distribution of recovered

---

[116] Room 225 had only a fossil x1 and three fragments x2–x4 of decorated wall vessels which did not contain enough material to identify their type.

[117] Zorn, "Tell en-Nasbeh: A Re-evaluation," 714.

[118] See figure 21 in appendix B for a reconstructed layout of the floor plan.

[119] Zorn, "Tell en-Nasbeh: A Re-evaluation," 787–88.

[120] Ibid., 900.

[121] Ibid., 901–02. If not so, it would make for an easy explanation of the large number of assemblages that the excavators recovered from this area.

artifacts, and, in fact, it was surprising to see the large number of items, given that these were mostly distributed over Rooms 23 and 24. For example, Room 24 had the second highest number of bowls for all the rooms, and Room 23 had the fourth highest number. These two rooms also contained the highest and second highest number of cooking pots. In terms of jars, each of the rooms had twenty, the highest number of any other room from Stratum 2. The same can be said for lamps, as Room 23 had six and Room 24 had four. I discuss this further below. Building 194.01 placed third in terms of number of recovered artifacts, an amazing fact given that this represented finds recorded in only two of its rooms.

The excavators also recovered material culture related to ritual and religious practices in Rooms 23 and 24. In fact, Room 23 contained two figurine fragments and one zoomorphic vessel as described in table 7 and table 8 respectively. The number of lamps appears to be well above any other room for Stratum 2, suggesting the possibility of a roof or a second story. It is interesting to note that Badè identified this building as a potential sanctuary based on the tripartite architecture of the three front rooms, even though in later excavations this arrangement met the layout of four-room buildings, and his theory was discredited based on the form of the architecture.[122] However, as Zorn notes, the question of whether this building was used for cultic purposes remains viable.[123]

4.1.4 Natural Landscape

Ritual loci in natural landscape include at least two identifiable locations: ritualized open spaces and caves. Studies in anthropology and archaeology demonstrate how humans, past and present, use naturally formed areas as special places to relate to deities or carry out activities with religious significance.[124] This type of space must have seemed like an attractive option to the inhabitants of the ancient Near East, given the landscape with special features like open and high places as well as caves. In addition, there is textual evidence for such locations being used for these purposes within the southern Levant.[125]

---

[122] Ibid., 900.

[123] Ibid.

[124] Insoll, *Archaeology, Ritual, Religion*, xiii–xv. Also, Juan Manuel Tebes, "The Archaeology of the Desert Cults and the Origins of Israel's God," *NEAF* 58 (2015): 13.

[125] See Gen 8:20, 12:7, 13:18, 15:7–12, 22:1–3. For a closer time to the Persian period, see 2 Chr 33:3.

What is more interesting, and more important in my view, is how significant natural landscapes are to early Judaism and overall to Israelite religion, and how little this source of data is discussed in biblical scholarship that focuses on these topics.[126] It is likewise surprising to see how few research agendas take such areas into account when developing site surveys and excavation plans. I recognize that it is more tangible for the archaeology of ritual and religion to emphasize artifacts and material culture that can be physically examined and interpreted. As I discussed in chapter 1, Joyce identifies this problem and traces its roots to structuralism, as scholars have tended to define ritual in connection with spaces, repetitive activities, and material culture that is tangible and easier to identify.[127] It is understandable why this issue represents a challenge for biblical scholars and archaeologists of ritual and religion. Capturing aspects of this theoretical issue in their study of landscapes, Randi Haaland and Gunnar Haaland write, "what we are dealing with here are the ritual perspectives of the viewer and the components in the environment that are perceived as loaded with ritual significance."[128] However, I believe that by expanding our perspectives and engaging more with anthropological and cross-disciplinary areas, evidence of rituals and religious practices may start to emerge in some of these natural landscapes.

Literary evidence from the Bible informs us of how Israelites and practitioners of early Judaism were prohibited from making or worshiping idols, or any image that would represent the God of Israel. For example, this is seen in several of the early mandates in the Ten Words or Commandments of the Bible, such as Exod 20:3–5. At the same time, the Bible also mentions how people worshipped or related to God in open spaces with naturally made altars, rocks, trees, et cetera. In fact, the biblical text in Exod 20:24 is specific about altars, and more specifically in Exod 20:25–26 it describes how not to build one. I would suggest that central to the Israelite religion is the understanding that God manifested himself on earth and that people interfaced with him via the elements seen in natural landscapes.

---

[126] I use the term early Judaism to specifically address the practices during the Persian period.

[127] Joyce, "Archaeology of Ritual and Symbolism," 721.

[128] Randi Haaland and Gunnar Haaland, "Landscape," in *The Oxford Handbook of the Archaeology of Ritual and Religion*, ed. Timothy Insoll (Oxford: Oxford University Press, 2011), 25.

Juan Manuel Tebes argues that the origin of Yahweh's worship can be traced to the southern areas such as the Negev and the Sinai Peninsula.[129] He describes his findings in the following manner: "Open air sanctuaries are the most common type of cultic places in the southern desert regions.... The most significant components of the material culture that can be related to cultic practices are standing stones(mazzeboth), open courtyard shrines, cairns, high places."[130] Even though some of these sites may date to an earlier period, he argues convincingly using data from a later period that these ritual customs are slow to evolve. He writes: "even when locals formally converted ... they frequently modified in one way or the other their new faiths' cultural elements, adapting them to their millennia-old heritage."[131]

The present study discussed previously how people utilized areas outside of the city walls for performing rituals or religious practices, although their practices fell outside of the orthodox parameter of the controlling majority. The walls for the city of Tell en-Naṣbeh expanded out after Stratum 3, and the exterior walls of Stratum 2 are well defined in the site map. We now turn to ritualized open spaces and caves.

Of special interest for ritual and/or religious practices in open spaces are areas with running water, pools, ponds, high places, special rock formations, trees, et cetera.[132] It is challenging to reconstruct the potential for any ancient rituals that took place in the open space without conducting a survey of the site's surrounding areas. However, a look at a topographical map of Tell en-Naṣbeh's surroundings identifies certain features and contours in the landscape that can be mentioned as possible loci. I have utilized the ancient maps prepared by C. R. Conder and H. H. Kitchener for the Palestine Exploration Fund during the years of 1872 to 1877 in past research.[133] These maps can be valuable in identifying details and features that were present in the ancient landscape, but are no longer

---

[129] Tebes, "The Archaeology of the Desert Cults and the Origins of Israel's God," 13–14.

[130] Ibid., 13.

[131] Ibid.

[132] These locations are more critical given that rituals in Zoroastrianism are practiced in these areas.

[133] C. R. Conder and H. H. Kitchener, "Map of Western Palestine in 26 Sheets," (London: Committee of the Palestine Exploration Fund, 1880), Electronic edition titled "Survey of Western Palestine: The Maps." CD-ROM copyrighted by Todd Bolen, 2004. These maps were digitized by Todd Bolen, Ph.D. and are available at www.bibleplaces.com. I utilize the electronic versions of these maps.

visible now or present in modern maps due to urban development. The final excavation report for Tell en-Naṣbeh discussed topography briefly.[134]

Water has been utilized for ritual since the early days as evidenced in many archaeological and artistic renditions. Terje Oestigaard summarized the function of water in ritual in the following way:

> Water is always in a flux. The fluid matter changes qualities and capacities wherever it is, and it always takes new forms. This transformative character of water is forcefully used in ritual practices and religious constructions. Water represents the one and the many at the same time, and the plurality of ritual institutionalizations and religious perceptions puts emphasis on water's structuring principles and processes in culture and the cosmos.... Purification rituals may take place in almost every ritual from daily to annual ceremonies, but especially in life-cycle rites with a particular emphasis on death rituals.[135]

These observations on the characteristics of water and its use in rituals fit well with the typology of ritual discussed in chapter 1. Water may be an important component of calendrical rites, rites of exchange and communion, rites of affliction, feasting, fasting, and festival rites, and perhaps even political rites. In addition to water's use in purification functions, the link that existed in relating the presence or lack of water in connection with the human need for it gave it a special place in ritual contexts. Droughts placed severe stress on ancient Near East cultures, and, as evidenced in various literary works, rituals were targeted to deities to mitigate or help in securing adequate supply.[136]

What sort of water sources were in the proximity of Tell en-Naṣbeh?[137] As depicted in the Palestine Exploration Fund map below in figure 11, Tell en-Naṣbeh was surrounded by seasonal sources of water from Wady Jiliân on the

---

[134] McCown et al., "Archaeological and Historical Results," 50–52.

[135] Terje Oestigaard, "Water," in *The Oxford Handbook of the Archaeology of Ritual and Religion*, ed. Timothy Insoll (Oxford: Oxford University Press, 2011), 38, 39.

[136] See for example how Egyptians perceived the powers associated with Osiris and the water levels in the Nile. Refer to ibid., 42–43.

[137] I realize that the use of the PEF map, although depicting landscape features and topography from the late 1800s, may not represent an accurate rendition of the conditions present during the Persian period. However, this map provides for us a view into the past not available in modern maps. Many of the ancient landscape features have been preserved in these maps. See, for example, the Roman road next to Tell en-Naṣbeh, various tombs, locations of khirbet or ancient ruins, et cetera. For more information on the benefits of using these maps, refer to Hopkins, "Nineteenth-Century Maps of Palestine."

east and Wady Duweit on the west.[138] The latter is a tributary of the former.[139] In addition the map shows a small spring, Åin Jâd, to the south that was likely a seasonal source. Zorn conducted a brief study of the hydrology in Tell en-Naṣbeh and noted that there are only seasonal streams around the site.[140] As one moves further out, there are two springs within 1 km and six within a 5 km radius of the site.

Figure 11. Ancient map of Tell en-Naṣbeh and its surroundings.

Source: Conder and Kitchener, *Map of Western Palestine in 26 Sheets*, 1880. Illustration taken from CD-ROM edition titled "Survey of Western Palestine: The Maps. Copyrighted by Todd Bolen, 2004. Courtesy of Todd Bolen, Ph.D. Used by permission.

It is interesting to note where some of the burial sites, labeled as "Tombs" on the map, sit relative to the water sources. The tombs' placements lie just

---

[138] I utilize the Arabic names for ease of reference with the PEF map since names are in Arabic there. The English names are Wadi Jilyan and Wadi Duweit, respectively.
[139] McCown et al., "Archaeological and Historical Results," 53.
[140] Zorn, "Tell en-Nasbeh: A Re-evaluation," 208–09.

north at the intersection of the two streams and some east of them, making these water sources reachable with a short walk. Therefore, I would suggest that water played an important role in burial rituals. The other elements of open spaces, such as special rock formations or trees, I cannot discuss at this time due to a lack of data.

Caves formed special places beneath the earth where humans performed rituals and/or religious practices. Some of these formations were part of burial sites while others existed as secluded areas dedicated to these functions. Haaland and Haaland note how "caves lend themselves to metaphoric associations with the female body. They are, in a way, 'natural' settings for ritual activities like initiations and shamanistic performances."[141] Holladay identifies caves as possible cult areas, and specifically referred to the extramural Cave 193 of Tell en-Naṣbeh.[142] The final Tell en-Naṣbeh excavation report dedicated a chapter to caves at the site and discussed how these types of loci had not been a high priority for the excavation team due to the concerted effort to dig within the city walls.[143]

In summary, this chapter provides suggestions for the types of locations and material culture that may be associated with ritual and religious practices during the Persian period in the southern Levant. This data informs the review and analysis of Tell en-Naṣbeh available at the Badè Museum. The investigation presents and discusses various loci and material culture that may be associated with ritual and/or religious practices, and highlights with special interest those locations that have been associated with domestic settings, as possible sources of family and household ritual. In the next chapter I evaluate briefly other sites in the Shephelah that have Persian period material culture to see how they compare with the evidence found in TEN.

---

[141] Haaland and Haaland, "Landscape," 27.

[142] Holladay, "Religion in Israel and Judah under the Monarchy," 274–75.

[143] McCown et al., "Archaeological and Historical Results," 67. See chapter 8 of vol. 1. Many of the caves were associated with tombs and fall outside of the scope of this study, although a review of these types of caves would be a good future research project.

5. PERSIAN PERIOD RITUAL MATERIAL CULTURE FROM OTHER YEHUD SITES

What type of archaeological evidence related to ritual and religion exists at other Yehud sites? How are these related to family and household rituals and religious practices? This chapter briefly responds to these questions with published data. Due to the large number of sites in Yehud, the study selects the region of the Shephelah as a test case and examines only the most important findings from sites where Persian period ritual and/or religious material culture has been identified.

5.1 Shephelah Sites

In chapter 2, this study discussed the geographical boundaries of the Shephelah and some of the issues associated with defining its borders. In general, most scholars agree that the following sites fall within the region of the Shephelah: Tel ʿAzekah, Tel Batash (Timnah), Gezer, Tel Lachish (Tell ed-Duweir), Maresha, Tell eṣ-Ṣafi (Gath), and Tel Zayit. As indicated earlier, Tel Lachish and Maresha are at times associated with the province of Idumea rather than Judah. I suggest that these settlements may be part of a border zone reflecting a mix of cultures and religions. These associations may bear more weight in terms of political affiliations than social or religious reality.

This region raises several challenges for my project. First, some of the settlements in the Shephelah were excavated early in the 1900s and their site reports do not contain much data pertaining to the archaeology of ritual and religion; or in some cases this type of information was not recorded in association with stratigraphy. For example, Stern mentions twelve "Palestinian altars" in connection with R. A. S. Macalister's early 1900s excavation at Gezer, but Stern gives only the locus, or context, for one of them, and that one came from a tomb.[1] Second, excavation from some sites reveals only minimal evidence from the Persian period and, more specifically, lacks information on

---

[1] Stern, *Material Culture of the Land of the Bible*, 184, 186.

houses or household areas from this phase. Excavation objectives tended to target earlier strata and/or focused on larger structures. Third, recent excavations at Tel ʻAzekah, Gezer, Maresha, and Tel Zayit, to my knowledge, have not yet produced final excavation reports, so the data is not yet available for research. Tel ʻAzekah is unearthing exciting discoveries and the publications from the years of excavations will contribute greatly to the understanding of the Shephelah and the province of Judah, but these reports are not yet available. Expedition teams at Gezer have posted some of their field reports online, but more complete data is not yet available. The Tel Zayit team is working on the publication of their report, according to their web site.[2]

5.2 Archaeology Related to Ritual and Religion

Since the previous chapter already introduced discussions of the different ritual material culture, the format for presenting the data for the Shephelah sites follows a structure and order based on the categories for ritual loci. The following sections therefore present ritual artifacts as part of the respective context or loci where excavators found them.

5.2.1 Ritual Loci: Architecture and Natural Landscape

5.2.1.1 Monuments

The excavations at Tel Lachish provide archaeologists with a unique architectural structure from the Persian period that I categorize within the realm of monuments.[3] This building, known as The Residency, serves as a well-preserved example of this type of architecture. Stern discusses this structure under the heading "Domestic Architecture," and he concludes that it was a palace. But part of this structure may have served domestic functions. Its location and impressive layout leads me to conclude, as I did with TEN Building 74.01, that this building also meets the two previously discussed criteria to qualify as a monument. The first is the location of the structure in association with the people who are legitimized. Palaces function in this manner and The Residency is a structure located at a strategic location. Tel Lachish served an important role during this time. Tel Lachish, like Tell en-Naṣbeh, also was an

---

[2] See http://www.zeitah.net
[3] Stern, *Material Culture of the Land of the Bible*, 57.

administrative center during the Persian period.⁴ The second criterion is visibility. This building is in a central location in the tel where it is visible by the people. The function of The Residency has been interpreted by other scholars in different ways. For example, Ruth Amiran and Immanuel Dunayevsky conclude that this building shows Achaemenid influence, while Aharoni argues that it more closely resembles an Assyrian courthouse.⁵ *The New Encyclopedia of Archaeological Excavations in the Holy Land* includes a floor plan of this structure.⁶ Stern notes that one figurine from pit 47:15L was found near the palace.⁷ I suggest that The Residency merits consideration for political rites and for other Persian government sponsored events which may include ritual practices.

5.2.1.1.1 City Gates

Excavations at Tel Lachish discovered a possible statue next to the outer city gate, although the fragmentary nature of the structure and the lack of content make its ritual function questionable.⁸ Blomquist describes it as follows: "Its central part consisted of dressed stone blocks of varying length, laid without mortar and enclosed by two further squares of undressed stones."⁹

The excavation report from Tel Batash, or the biblical city of Timnah, did not produce significant results for Stratum I, the Persian period stratum. The only evidence of occupation during this time came from the city gate Area C, and these remains were fragmentary, with the exception of the discovery of a complete jar.¹⁰ A pit in this area also contained dog bones, although they appeared to be randomly thrown there with little data available to make possible connections with a ritual related to Zoroastrianism.¹¹

---

⁴ David Ussishkin, "Lachish," *NEAEHL* 3:910.
⁵ Stern, *Material Culture of the Land of the Bible*, 54.
⁶ Ussishkin, "Lachish," *NEAEHL* 3:911.
⁷ Stern, *Material Culture of the Land of the Bible*, 158–59.
⁸ Blomquist, *Gates and Gods*, 81–82.
⁹ Ibid., 82.
¹⁰ George L. Kelm and Amihai Mazar, "Three Seasons of Excavations at Tel Batash: Biblical Timnah," *BASOR* 248 (1982): 32.
¹¹ George L. Kelm and Amihai Mazar, "Tel Batash (Timnah) Excavations: Third Preliminary Report, 1984–1989," *BASORSup* 27 (1991): 65.

5.2.1.2 Temples

Tel Lachish provides other contributions to the archaeology of ritual and religion of the Persian period specific to temples with Building 106 ("solar shrine") and Building 10 as seen in figure 12. The archaeological evidence, based on the alignment of the buildings on an east-west axis, and the presence of altars and other cultic objects, provides strong support for their interpretation as ritual sites. The excavators discovered ritual artifacts of various types: (1) figurines in assemblage 522; (2) one figurine and thirty limestone altars in assemblage 515; (3) several figurines in rooms of Building 106; (4) an open bronze lamp; (5) a marble plaque with decorations used for libations.[12] The two assemblages have been interpreted as having come from favissae of Building 106.[13]

---

[12] Stern, *Material Culture of the Land of the Bible*, 63, 158–59.
[13] Ibid., 159.

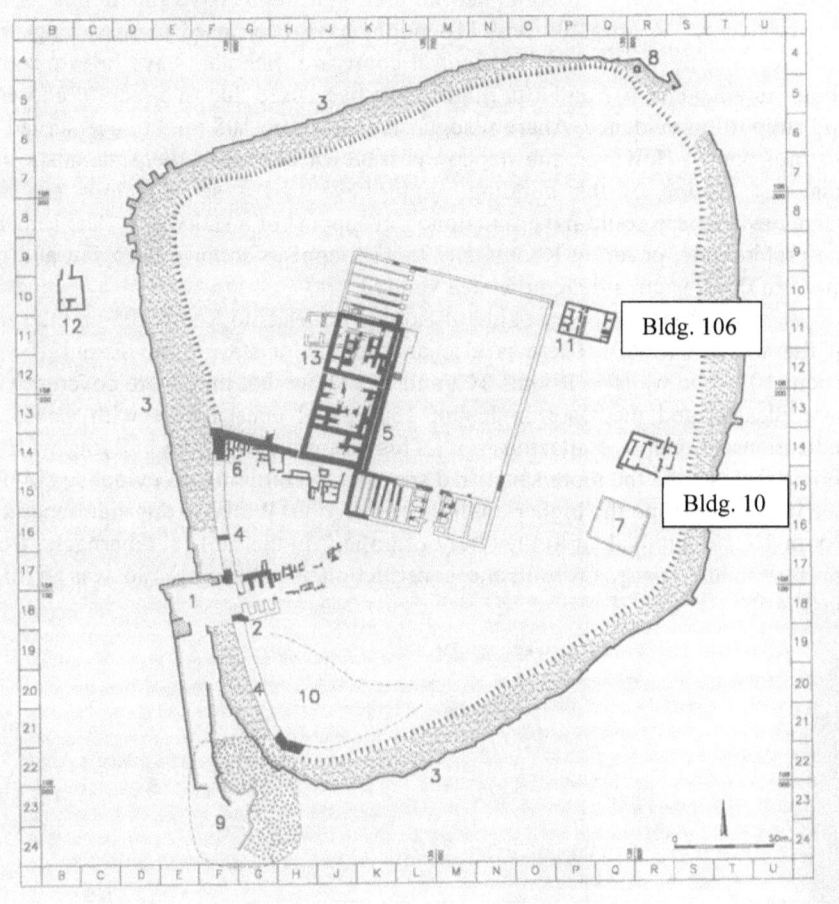

Figure 12. Map of Tel Lachish with Buildings 106 and 10.

Source: Author's modification of Ussishkin, *The Renewed Archaeological Excavations at Lachish (1973–1994)*, 1:34. Courtesy of The Institute of Archaeology of Tel Aviv University. Used by permission.

I studied both buildings when I visited the site in June 2012 and discuss below some possible interpretations and functions for the various buildings and rooms. Building 106 represents an excellent example of a temple, given its architectural floor plan and building characteristics as seen in figure 13. The eastern wall of room 110 contained an area that might have functioned as the external door.[14] Rooms 109 and 110 might have been used as a waiting area prior to entering Room 106, the central courtyard. Scholars have been puzzled about how Rooms 107 and 108 might have been used due to a lack of contents and supporting evidence. Aharoni suggests that Room 108 might have served as a store-room.[15] However, the narrow passageway between them suggests that this east section of the building might have had a second floor and the passageway space could have functioned in support of a stairway.[16] The roof for the eastern side, covering Rooms 107 to 110, appears to have been flat and the space of the western side/temple area vaulted.[17]

A set of stairs on the east side of Room 106 leads to Room 105 and the rest of the western rooms. There is also another set of stairs from Room 105 to Room 102. The walls in Rooms 102 and 105 show that they were covered with hard plaster, and the floor in Room 105 reveal construction with slabs, all indications of quality craftsmanship.[18] This western side of the building with its rooms represented the more sanctified space of the building, as evidenced by the rise in elevation and the higher quality construction. Walls on this side separated Room 102, an equivalent to the "holy of holies" in the biblical tabernacle, from the rest of the space. Overall, the construction for Building 106 was of high quality.[19]

---

[14] Yohanan Aharoni and Universiṭat Tel-Aviv. Makhon le-arkhe'ologyah, *Investigations at Lachish: The Sanctuary and The Residency (Lachish V)*, Publications of the Institute of Archaeology, Tel Aviv University (Tel Aviv: Gateway, 1975), 3.
[15] Ibid.
[16] Ibid.
[17] Ibid.
[18] Ibid.
[19] Ibid.

PERSIAN PERIOD RITUAL MATERIAL CULTURE FROM OTHER YEHUD SITES   127

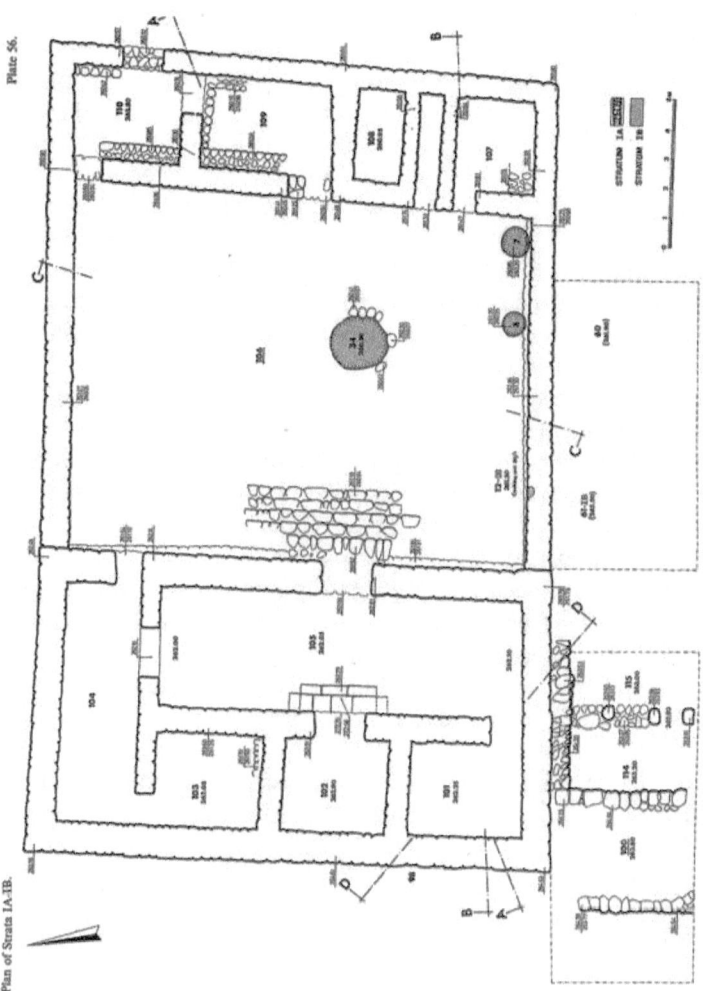

Figure 13. Details of Buildings 106 at Tel Lachish.

Source: Aharoni, *Investigations at Lachish: The Sanctuary and the Residency (Lachish V)*, Pl. 56. Courtesy of The Institute of Archaeology of Tel Aviv University. Used by permission.

Building 10 bears a close resemblance to Building 106 and the excavators concluded that they both shared architectural features.[20] Building 10 had minimal content although what it did have dated in form to the fourth and third centuries BCE.[21] It is my opinion that these two structures stand as testimony of ritual space and practices in the Persian period. I believe that ritual artifacts found in Building 106 and Building 10 support this suggestion. Archaeologists unearthed eleven libation and incense altars from Building 106: one from Room 106, one small trachyte incense altar from Room 105, and nine limestone altars on a bench in Room 104.[22] The dating for the pottery related to these nine altars corresponds to the Persian period. In addition to the nine altars from Room 104, archaeologists found another limestone incense stand/altar with carved door panels flanked with pillars imitating a house or shrine in Building 10, Room 11.[23] Excavators also discovered fragments of two figurines; the first is definitely from the Persian period, while the identification of the second is unclear. The first, No.71, is a clay figurine of a standing human found on the surface of Area GW.[24] Unfortunately, only the square base of the statuette remains. The second, No. 9, may be the forepart of a horse and rider and was also found on the surface.[25]

Since there have been several proposals as to the dating of Building 106 and Building 10, I offer a brief discussion and then share my position on this issue. Starkey, the first archaeologist to excavate the site, dates Building 106 to the Persian period.[26] He was murdered during the excavation and the responsibility for publishing the findings passed to Olga Tufnell, who dated the construction of Building 106 with hesitation.[27] David Ussishkin, the lead excavator from a more recent expedition, agrees with Starkey and Stern's analysis in dating Building 106 to the Persian period.[28] Aharoni conducted new excavations in Building 106

---

[20] Ibid., 9.

[21] Ibid., 11.

[22] Ibid., 5.

[23] Ibid., 11.

[24] Raz Kletter, "Clay Figurines," in *The Renewed Archaeological Excavations at Lachish (1973–1994)*, ed. David Ussishkin, SMNIA 22 (Tel Aviv: Emery and Claire Yass Publications in Archaeology, 2004), 2060.

[25] Ibid., 2066.

[26] David Ussishkin, ed., *The Renewed Archaeological Excavations at Lachish (1973–1994)*, SMNIA 22 (Tel Aviv: Emery and Claire Yass Publications in Archaeology, 2004), 96.

[27] Ibid.

[28] Ibid.

and the Residency as part of a comparative study with the Arad temple, and he dates Building 106 to the Hellenistic period, specifically to ca. 200 BCE.[29] He also interprets Building 10 as a Persian period structure that served as the precursor of Building 106.[30] Fantalkin and Tal support Aharoni's position, as they date the construction of Building 106 to what they term the "third phase," during the Late Persian and/or Early Hellenistic occupation.[31]

It is my opinion that the analysis pertaining to the dating of these buildings would benefit from a more explicit presentation and consideration of a key piece of information that is at times neglected in the discussions. According to the excavation reports, the Wellcome-Marston British Expedition of the 1930s cleared the plastered floors of the main hall, Room 105 and the adyton, and Room 102; their excavations in the courtyard 106 and the eastern Rooms 107 to 110 went below floor level.[32] Findings from later excavations found artifacts in debris, pits, and fills and excavators used these to argue for a later date. All these loci constitute non-stratigraphic remains that are inaccurate for dating. For example, three of the coins from post-Persian periods were found "in the debris," as well as a "fragment of a heavy ware, fusiform unguentarium" found "in the fill" of Room 105.[33] I support a Persian period date for the dating of this building based on the unconvincing arguments for a Hellenistic period phase coupled with the discovery of Persian period altars within this building, which in all likelihood were contemporaneous with the building.

The dating of Building 106 is not the only unsettled issue. The identification of who was worshipped there and the kind of ritual activity that occurred also elicit various proposals. Tufnell and Stern base the religious affiliation on the ritual contents and the orientation of the altar; as they note, the "libation altar on the open axis line suggest[s] a solar cult."[34] However, Aharoni, and then later Fantalkin and Tal, suggest that the shrine was an Israelite, Yahwistic shrine from the Hellenistic period.[35] The support for this interpretation comes from the altar

---

[29] Aharoni and Universiṭat Tel-Aviv. Makhon le-arkhe'ologyah, *Investigations at Lachish*, 3–4, 9.

[30] Ibid., 9.

[31] Fantalkin and Tal, "Redating Lachish Level I," 171.

[32] Aharoni and Universiṭat Tel-Aviv. Makhon le-arkhe'ologyah, *Investigations at Lachish*, 3.

[33] Ibid., 3–4.

[34] Ussishkin, *The Renewed Archaeological Excavations at Lachish (1973–1994)*, 96.

[35] Alexander Fantalkin and Oren Tal, "The Persian and Hellenistic Pottery of Level I," in *The Renewed Archaeological Excavations at Lachish (1973–1994)*, ed. David

found southwest of the city gate in cave 534, which contained the inscription of a possible Yahwistic name.[36]

5.2.1.3 Houses and Other Household Areas

The 2008 excavations at Gezer have identified parts of two buildings/complexes in Field B and the western end of Field A that the staff initially dated to the Persian-Hellenistic period, although the report placed a stronger emphasis on them being associated with a Hellenistic dating.[37] Of special interest for possible connections with Zoroastrianism rituals was the discovery of three dog burial sites in the north side of Field B. The report did not cover many details of these burials so it is difficult to suggest an interpretation.

Excavations at Maresha identify potential Persian period houses in the upper and lower cities, although to my knowledge there is no ritual material culture associated with these houses.[38] There seems to be a close connection with houses and underground caves, and it appears that the material culture from some of these houses was dumped below in the caves.

5.2.1.4 Natural Landscape

At Tel Lachish three caves, including the cave mentioned above, southwest of the gate in Areas 506, 512, and 534, contained 200 limestone altars, some of them with decorations and one of them with an Aramaic inscription.[39] In Maresha excavators recovered a mix of figurines that they date to the Persian period. Unfortunately, their non-stratigraphic loci do not help to approach domestic questions as Adi Erlich notes:

> the Maresha assemblage comes from fills of caves, and therefore the original contexts of its items are unknown. It is most likely that the Maresha figurines were originally used in houses, as they have been found together with other

---

Ussishkin, Monograph Series / Tel Aviv University 22 (Tel Aviv: Emery and Claire Yass Publications in Archaeology, 2004), 2, 191.

[36] Fantalkin and Tal, "Redating Lachish Level I," 176.

[37] Steven M. Ortiz and Samuel R. Wolff, "The Renewed Excavations of Tel Gezer, 2006–2008: 2008 Field Report," (2008). www.telgezer.com.

[38] Amos Kloner, "Mareshah (Marisa)," *NEAEHL* 5:1918–19.

[39] Aharoni and Universiṭat Tel-Aviv. Makhon le-arkheʾologyah, *Investigations at Lachish*, 5. The one with the Aramaic inscription came from Cave 534.

domestic finds, and their wide dispersal points to an origin scattered rather than centralized.[40]

Maresha may be able to provide important information to the archaeology of ritual and religion if excavators are able to find Persian period houses with this type of material culture or caves that contain artifacts in stratigraphic contexts.

This chapter discusses the Persian period ritual material culture from key Shephelah sites containing Persian period archaeology. These include: Tel 'Azekah, Tel Batash (Timnah), Gezer, Tel Lachish (Tell ed-Duweir), Maresha, Tell eş-Şafi(Gath), and Tel Zayit. I suggest that while Tel Lachish provides a valuable representation of a Persian period temple, the rest of the sites do not contain as much Persian period architecture or ritual material culture as Tell en-Naşbeh.

---

[40] Adi Erlich, "Recherches Pluridisciplinaires Sur Une Province de L'Empire Achéménide," *Transeu* 32 (2006): 55.

6. SUMMARY AND CONCLUSIONS

This study demonstrates that there has not been much research done on the topic of family and household ritual and religion for the Persian period. It suggests that while textual information proved useful in better understanding religious practices during this time period, these data were neither fully representative nor normative. Given this state of affairs, the study identifies ritual loci and artifacts from Persian period Tell en-Naṣbeh, as a case study of the rituals and religious practices of families and households in Persian period Judah.

In light of the available literature, chapter 1 shows that a multi-disciplinary approach was methodologically most advantageous. I explore how biblical scholarship utilizes theories and methods from these disciplines in the study of ritual and religion. Definitions of ritual and religion, family and household, and the identification of the six ritual typologies were important aspects to focus. I conclude that while these disciplines do not agree on all fronts on issues of definitions and approaches, the theories and methods from the archaeology of ritual and religion serve well in other studies and provide a solid base for the present study.

Chapter 2 provides information on Judah and the southern Levant as a contextual structure to examine Ezra as a representative case of a Persian period biblical text. I utilize Bell's typology categories of ritual to test and to investigate the type of data that was available pertaining to family and household rituals and religious practices. The chapter also introduces a brief discussion of geographical issues with Yehud, possible Persian influence on religion, language, and other contextual issues. I include this information due to its importance in contributing to the understanding of how these factors shaped ritual and religious practices in Persian period Yehud. My conclusions from the analysis of Ezra validate earlier suggestions that references to family and household practices in the text deal with official ceremonies in the reestablishment of the Jerusalem Temple. The text does not provide information about how families performed rituals and/or religious practices in houses or household areas, and there is no indication of rituals in relationship to domestic settings. I further validate this conclusion by referring to Albertz's views and conclusions on the topic.

In chapter 3 I introduce the importance of Tell en-Naṣbeh as a Persian period settlement in the province of Judah and include a discussion of the challenges associated with this early excavation. Among these, I highlight that this study utilizes Stratum 2 as a representative layer for Persian period material culture, even though it is difficult to isolate a pure Persian period range, as Zorn's reevaluation of Stratum 2 also include the years 586–537 BCE. At the same time, as I investigated Tell en-Naṣbeh and other sites in Judah, I gained a renewed appreciation for its importance and significance in contributing to research in the archaeology of ritual and religion due to its architectural exposure and the wide range of material culture that it offers when using original documentation in comparison to other sites. Part of the chapter also reviews the literature that had been written related to the archaeology of ritual and religion for the Persian period with a focus on two of Stern's books. My analysis of this literature concludes that there was still a gap in research in ritual and religion at the family and household level for the Persian period, and more investigations are needed to further understand these areas. This review and the analysis of the architecture and material culture at Tell en-Naṣbeh led me to develop and to propose a typology for components related to ritual and religion based on loci and artifacts. I discuss each of the categories for ritual artifacts, and as I present the Tell en-Naṣbeh collection I indicate where these items were excavated on the site, thus contextualizing the ritual objects. This analysis demonstrates how vast and comprehensive was the Tell en-Naṣbeh collection of domestic and ritual material culture.

Chapter 4 investigates architecture and natural landscape as potential loci for ritual and/or religious practices. I discuss how there was a need to examine locations with care and to maintain an open perspective on where family and household ritual could have taken place. With this in mind, I examine monuments, city gates, temples, and houses and household areas. My investigation led me to conclude and argue for the importance of Tell en-Naṣbeh's city gate complex as a key area for ritual during the Persian period. The chapter develops a detailed investigation of the buildings in Stratum 2 with a focus on houses and household areas. I argue in this chapter for the importance of natural landscape as key loci for ritual and examine how open spaces and caves served this function.

Chapter 5 discusses the Persian period ritual material culture from the Shephelah as a representative section of Yehud sites. These include: Tel 'Azekah, Tel Batash (Timnah), Gezer, Tel Lachish (Tell ed-Duweir), Maresha, Tell eṣ-Ṣafi(Gath), and Tel Zayit. I conclude that while Building 106 in Tel Lachish provides an excellent example of a Persian period temple, the rest of the sites do not contain as much Persian period architecture or ritual material culture as Tell en-Naṣbeh does. This observation elevates the importance of Tell en-Naṣbeh as a strategic site for the study of family and household ritual.

I introduce below the set of questions that developed from my investigation before discussing my observations on possible rituals and religious practices at Tell en-Naṣbeh. Some have wider applications, while others tend to focus more on family and household ritual and religion, and are as follows: (1) how did ritual or religious practices take place in the house or household areas?;[1] (2) how can these rituals be identified in terms of the six ritual types outlined by Bell?; (3) what rooms or functional areas were involved?; (4) can the evidence support gendered rituals? If so, what are the connections with other material culture that tends to have a gender affiliation?; (5) how can one distinguish economic status based on architecture and artifacts?; (6) what type of variations were there in rituals, if any, between economic classes?; (7) did Tell en-Naṣbeh materials support Stern's argument that "cultic" material culture came from people foreign to Judah? If not, what other options might exist?; and (8) does the material culture indicate Persian influence manifested with Zoroastrianism practices? If so, how? Since I have discussed already the specifics of the loci and the artifacts, this section focuses more on addressing the above questions and relating these to the data presented in chapters 3, 4, and 5. I address questions six to eight towards the end of this section after having examined all the data.

My review and analysis of the data for the site leads me to conclude that Tell en-Naṣbeh was a settlement where rituals and religious practices took place at various levels of social strata. This seems to be true also of other settlements, as evidenced by Blomquist and Albertz' observations referred to earlier in this study. Since the monument and city gate areas deal mostly with political rites and less with family and household ritual connections, here I will review them only briefly. I suggest that Building 74.01, a likely palace, and Building 110.01 might have served as monuments for the performance of political rites at the level of official or government sponsored religion based on their architectural features that met Fogelin's two evaluation criteria.[2] Building 74.01 records provide an incomplete picture for specific inquiries, although the layout and some of the findings may support a proposal that the courtyard area in Room 193 served as an open space for political rites and possibly other types of rituals.

---

[1] In these questions I use the terms house and household areas, but intend also to cover other areas where family and household rituals or religious practices might have taken place. This takes into account rituals at multiple social strata, and the practice of these rituals at places such as the city gates, et cetera.

[2] I follow Albertz definition of the term "official religion." See Albertz and Schmitt, *Family and Household Religion in Ancient Israel and Levant*, 54.

Building 110.01 shares some similarities in terms of ritual artifact distribution in Room 379, the courtyard, and Room 400, another open or possibly secondary courtyard.

In addition to these buildings, I also suggest that the city gate complex functioned as a monument and that its architectural layout would have been functional and beneficial for political rites, independent of whether or not there were "cultic" artifacts at the outer gate complex. I suggest that the presence of these types of artifacts in the Tell en-Naṣbeh city gate complex add support to this argument. In connection with these objects, I highlight the possibility that these may have been part of family and household ritual that took place in a monumental space.

I propose that family and household rituals and religious practices occurred at Tell en-Naṣbeh and I present data to corroborate this thesis. After having developed the framework to investigate potential ritual loci and artifacts discussed earlier, the identification of areas where family and household ritual took place was among the main objectives, along with the relationship that these loci have with ritual artifacts. A review of Zorn's architectural study and my own analysis of the buildings lead me to conclude that of the eleven buildings from Stratum 2 shown on table 11 in appendix A ten were strong candidates for houses or household areas in whole or at least in part. Out of these ten houses or household areas, six show evidence for family and household ritual or religious practices.

In my review and analysis, I identify those buildings that contained material culture associated with ritual or religious practice.[3] **Building 93.03**, a four-room house showed strong evidence for ritual based on the existence of three figurines, and one possible incense altar. If one follows my proposed interpretation of Room 366 as a food preparation or food storage space, then these data support the idea that rituals were taking place in close proximity to food related functions. This room also was situated next to the courtyard and this may suggest that rituals were done in a more open or public style. The courtyard in ancient Judean households served in many instances as the food preparation space as noted by King and Stager.[4]

Room 369 contained a whole female JPF figurine with cupped breasts and a pinched face, as seen in figure 26 of appendix C. The context of this figurine adds support to the suggestion that these figurines functioned in the domestic

---

[3] I discard analyzing Building 74.01 since most rooms do not have specific millimeter cards.

[4] King and Stager, *Life in Biblical Israel*, 64.

setting for protection and healing.⁵ It is interesting to note the close proximity to food preparation or food storage and the possible connection that this may reveal. Could this figurine be part of the domestic kitchen domain, such as a guardian or symbol for petitions for the family's provisions? If one explores this further in terms of gender and family functional areas, food preparation areas were more frequently associated with women. Would this mean that women were more involved in relating petitions and prayers as part of their rituals? Carol Meyers indicates a close connection as she interprets Judean Pillar Figurines. She writes: "They are the physical expression of a woman's prayers for fertility and successful lactation; as tangible and visible objects, they represent what women seek.... They surely were part of women's religious culture."⁶

This type of interpretation relates to Bell's typology of ritual. It is my opinion that this context may have been used in rites of passage, such as childbirth, special initiations for boy and girls, et cetera. Calendrical rites would also fit within this scenario with connections to agricultural activities like the harvest and changes in seasons. Rites of exchange and communion might be part of the family ritual for such things as petitions for a good harvest, plentiful crops, health of the household, et cetera.

What economic or ethnic observations may be derived from this context? The building's architecture contained a mix of below average and more expensive features. For example, the floors did not have stones or paving, and it was likely a one story structure; however, the building did include monolithic pillars.⁷ In terms of size, Building 93.03 ranked the lowest in terms of total square meters out of all the four-room building plans, as seen in table 23 of appendix D. The house contained dimensions of 12.5m in length by 8.5+ m in width for a total of 106.25 square meters.⁸ The building contained no evidence for a second story.⁹ I suggest that given the above information the residents of this structure lived in a house that would be considered average in comparison to other four-room houses at Tell en-Naṣbeh.¹⁰ In terms of ethnic factors, the presence of a Judean type of figurine and a building construction following a

---

⁵ See Darby, *Interpreting Judean Pillar Figurines*, 404.

⁶ Meyers, *Households and Holiness*, 29.

⁷ Zorn, "Tell en-Nasbeh: A Re-evaluation," 169–71.

⁸ See table 23 in appendix D. The average for all Stratum 2 buildings is 133.35 meters. See ibid., 173.

⁹ Zorn does not include this building in his list of buildings with this feature. See ibid., 171.

¹⁰ There is a relationship between quality, expensive building features and economic status.

localized Judean plan suggests that families from this group who self-identified as Judean lived in this building.

Building 110.01 is also a four-room structure with architectural features resembling a palace or an important house for a government official. In addition to possible political rites, this building also contained ritual artifacts and other domestic vessels. It is probable that there was ritual at the family and household level in varied contexts in this building. As discussed earlier, Room 378 likely served as food storage or food preparation space, and the presence of the altar and chalice in this room suggests that house rituals took place in close connection with the storage and processing of food. Room 379, the courtyard for Building 110.01, also was in close proximity. This, too, may indicate the close relationship between kitchen functions and rituals. Some of the previous comments regarding these spaces, ritual, and gender may apply to this building as well.

This building provides clues to suggest economic status. First, the architectural features show that this structure was built with quality materials and expensive features.[11] For example, Room 376 had an entire cobble floor, Room 380a had a stone-paved floor, Rooms 379 and 380b had monolithic pillars, and Room 400 showed various staircases leading to a second story for the building. Second, the size of the structure and the number of rooms suggest a significant investment of time and resources in its construction. This building had eleven rooms, the second highest number out of all the other Stratum 2 buildings. The dimensions, as seen in appendix D, were 13m in length by 10m in width for a total square meter area of 130. In terms of size, this building ranked third out of all the other buildings. Third, it is interesting to note that this building contained the highest number of artifacts with a total of 155, as seen in table 11 of appendix A. This large inventory of objects came with a price to its original inhabitants. Room 379 also contained bronze artifacts, items typically indicative of wealth. I suggest that with these three observations, it is likely that the residents of this palace/house lived in a structure that reveals a wealthy status.

Regarding the types of rituals that might have taken place in this building, I previously discussed political rites functioning within monumental architecture. In addition, the context and the ritual artifacts suggest possible domestic rituals, although the specific types are more difficult to discern. The presence of the rattle in Room 400 is of special interest, but more research is needed on these types of artifacts to try and understand their role in ritual.

---

[11] See appendix D for a summary of these.

Building 125.01, another four-room building, showed evidence for ritual in the presence of one zoomorphic vessel and one altar. I discussed previously how interpretations of zoomorphic vessels placed them in both ritual and domestic settings. Tell en-Naṣbeh's collection includes 30 of these artifacts. If one accepts ritual function, then these vessels served in libation offerings. Rooms 641 or 643 might have served as food preparation or food storage areas due to the large number of artifacts there associated with these functions. The altar came from Room 477, the courtyard for the building, and the zoomorphic vessel from Room 473, a space just east of the courtyard. It is likely that the entrance to this building was on its east side given that this would provide the more logical flow pattern coming from the city gate and the rest of the city. If this is the case then Room 473 likely functioned as a living quarter in connection with the entrance. This may highlight a connection between a more public and visible use of the zoomorphic vessel in rituals and an individual of high social and economic status.

This house displayed characteristics indicative of a high economic status. Rooms 477, 641, and 638 had stone-paved floors.[12] In addition, Room 477 contained monolithic pillars.[13] The size of this house also places it as the second largest of all the houses in Stratum 2 Tell en-Naṣbeh. The dimensions were 13m in length by 11m in width for a total area of 143 square meters, as seen in table 23 in appendix D. Zoomorphic vessels are linked with wealthy status due to their complexity in manufacture and their rarity.[14] Given these observations, I suggest that this house belonged to a family of high economic status.

In terms of ritual typologies, the zoomorphic vessel suggests that libation rituals were conducted in this house. If this is the house of a wealthy or government official, then one may infer that feasting rites formed part of the social activities. This observation is supported by the fact that the vessel was excavated from a room next to the courtyard, and that in the courtyard itself an altar was found. The zoomorphic vessel also fits well with rites of exchange and communion for offerings or libations with the expectation to receive favorable results.

I identify **Building 144.01**, a three-room house, as a potential structure for family and household ritual based on the following artifacts: two altars, one stand, and one zoomorphic vessel. The previous comments with regards to zoomorphic vessels apply here as well. Room 324 and Room 325 may have

---

[12] Zorn, "Tell en-Nasbeh: A Re-evaluation," 170.

[13] Ibid., 171.

[14] Albertz and Schmitt, *Family and Household Religion in Ancient Israel and Levant*, 67.

been food preparation or food storage spaces, and Room 327 the adjoining courtyard. Room 331 appeared to have a possible entrance into the building.[15] It is in this room that the excavators found the zoomorphic vessel. I find it interesting to note the recurrence of a zoomorphic vessel, just like in Building 125.01, in an entryway or a space closely associated with an entrance, once again denoting possible rituals in a more open and public fashion. Could this also be a household of a government official or wealthy individual(s)? This building shared walls with other structures on the east and west, and it may be that these other structures functioned in relationship with Building 144.01.

In terms of ritual typology, the artifacts present suggest rites of exchange and communion as these altars functioned for burning incense and other aromatics. Some of these rituals may be affiliated with petitions. The zoomorphic vessel was likely used for this type of ritual in addition to feasting rites as discussed above. Rites of affliction may also be a possibility given that they were used for healing, exorcising, et cetera.

Several observations can be made in regards to economic issues. Building 144.01 displayed costly construction characteristics with Room 326 and Room 331 having stone-paved floors.[16] In addition, this building also had seven monolithic pillars.[17] As indicated previously, the building contained the second highest amount of artifacts out of all the Stratum 2 buildings. This ranking also occurred based on the incidence of bowls and cooking pots. All of these things suggest that the family that lived in this house was likely of a high economic status.[18]

As a side note, and in support of the previous suggestion of the city's entry being by the outer gate complex and leading west through the proposed corridor or hallway, this building's entrance was located on the west side facing towards the center of town. The entry's location adds weight to that proposal since traffic would need to come from the west side of the building. Building 125.01's entry would be in alignment with this suggestion.

As discussed previously **Building 160.10**'s reduced architecture limits what can be investigated. Two possible interpretations of its function surface: (1) a storehouse; or (2) a three-room or four-room house.[19] If the latter is assumed

---

[15] Zorn, "Tell en-Nasbeh: A Re-evaluation," 688.
[16] Ibid., 170.
[17] Ibid., 171.
[18] Room 324 contained two Greek coins, x16 and x17, dated from 400 to 250 BCE.
[19] Zorn notes the challenges with this building and suggests a possible storehouse. I find that this structure has some similarities with Building 93.03.

then, the ritual artifacts in Room 463 become relevant in a domestic setting. With this assumption, then Room 565 might be identified with a courtyard and Rooms 463 and 569 with food preparation or food storage areas. I find that there are some architectural similarities of the floor plans of this building and Building 93.03, although a conclusive opinion is difficult due to the minimal wall remains. I cannot help but wonder if Rooms 463 and 569 in this building functioned the same as Room 366 in Building 93.03.

If this is the case, then the animal figurines found in Room 463 may have served a similar function as the JPFs of Building 93.03 discussed above, given that the former have been associated with fertility and plentitude.[20] Given these interpretations, rituals described for JPF's may also apply here to animal figurines. Darby's study suggests a similar interpretation, in which she notes the "strong correlation between anthropomorphic and zoomorphic figurines in the same loci."[21]

In terms of economic investigations, the architecture left minimum evidence. Although, if one assumes a domestic setting of a three or four-room house, then at least a minimal resemblance to Building 93.03 exists. Zorn does not identify building dimensions, but a cursory look at the site maps shows a floor plan layout of about the same size as Building 93.03, around 100 square meters. This represents an average size house.

Building 194.01, a four-room house, showed strong evidence for family and household ritual based on the presence of three figurines, a high number of lamps, and one zoomorphic vessel. The high number of bowls and jars in Rooms 23 and 24, designated as the courtyard, indicates the possibility that the residents of this house had their food preparation and serving functions in this area, rather than in separate rooms as has been seen in earlier examples. This should be considered preliminary, since as has been pointed out above, specific millimeter cards do not exist for four rooms in this building. The zoomorphic vessel came from Room 23, a space associated with the main entrance for the building, a location paralleled by the two other buildings with zoomorphic vessel fragments mentioned above. As Zorn states: "The entrance to Building 194.01 was almost certainly by way of a door in this court's NW wall."[22] With this scenario, rituals at this house may have been conducted in a more public fashion, as discussed above for previous examples.

---

[20] Albertz and Schmitt, *Family and Household Religion in Ancient Israel and Levant*, 66.

[21] Darby, *Interpreting Judean Pillar Figurines*, 182, 210.

[22] Zorn, "Tell en-Nasbeh: A Re-evaluation," 899.

Given the kinds of artifacts recovered, I suggest that rituals of various types were practiced in this house. Similar rites as discussed above with regard to figurines and zoomorphic vessels apply here. The high number of lamps suggests the possibility that these were involved in something more than simple illumination of rooms. How could these artifacts have served in rituals? All of the fragments were of the high base saucer type. My survey of the literature did not reveal any specifics with regard to Persian period ritual, so this could be an area for further investigation.[23]

In terms of details that relate to possible economic status, this house had building characteristics of lower quality than some of the other ones previously examined. For example, floors contained no stones or paving, there were no monolithic or other type of pillars, and the building lacked a second story. The building dimensions were 12m in length by 10m in width for a total of 120 square meters divided in seven rooms. This building ranked fifth in terms of total space out of all the Stratum 2 buildings. What is somewhat unusual is the high number of food preparation and food storage artifacts in relation to the house size and construction quality and the fact that the artifacts were distributed only over two rooms. I suggest that this house was average in terms of economic status when compared to other Stratum 2 houses.

I will now address questions six to eight presented above. In terms of variants in rituals and their possible relationship to economic status, I do not see consistent patterning in all the buildings. However, I think that in some cases buildings considered to be of high quality construction, and possibly affiliated with wealthy residents, contained zoomorphic vessels. This was the case with Building 125.01 and Building 144.01. These houses, in turn, showed no presence of figurines, as these surfaced mostly in average quality houses. It has been discussed that figurines were cheap artifacts and more common in comparison to the more expensive zoomorphic vessels.[24]

Persian influence of ritual or religious practices may be present in political rites that took place in, or around, monuments. Scholars associate the presence and influence of Zoroastrianism in relationship to natural landscapes and dog burials. The Tell en-Naṣbeh records on natural landscapes are limited, and this study finds no details of dog burials. Both of these areas need further

---

[23] Eric Lapp conducts a study of lamps in Roman times. See Eric Christian Lapp, "The Archaeology of Light: The Cultural Significance of the Oil Lamp from Roman Palestine" (Ph.D. Dissertation, Duke University, 1997).

[24] However, as articulated by Darby there is no correlation between figurines and the lower economic classes. See Darby, *Interpreting Judean Pillar Figurines*, 401.

investigation and possibly additional surveys and/or excavations in order to further elucidate the question.

Several closing remarks are in order with regards to these observations, and to address the remaining question that deals with Stern's thesis. First, it is my opinion that the Tell en-Naṣbeh remains strongly demonstrate the presence of figurines and other ritually related artifacts in Judah during the Persian period. This observation counters Stern's thesis about a "religious revolution" in Judah during the Persian period. It is quite possible that his position reflects the past tendency to view JPFs in a negative way and as items of "black magic" or "cultic" practices not complementary to traditional Israelite religion. I suggest that these figurines need to be seen through the lens of family and household ritual and religious practices.[25] With this perspective, and as the above contexts show, these figurines emerge as artifacts of household rituals that were likely used as part of Yahwistic rituals conducted by Judean families.

Second, the analysis of the architecture and the artifacts for Stratum 2 showed recurring instances of zoomorphic vessels recovered from entrances and more public areas. At least in two instances, these vessels were present in houses with expensive construction and likely wealthy inhabitants. Could these residents be associated with Persian government officials or Judeans holding important roles in the Persian government? This area may be promising for further study in order to better understand the relationship of economic status, ethnicity, and ritual practices. The collection from Tell en-Naṣbeh, with its broad range of household architecture and object records from the original excavation of the site, is uniquely positioned to fill that investigative avenue.

The importance and contributions of Tell en-Naṣbeh extend beyond filling this last suggested research gap. It is clear in my presentation of contemporary materials from the Shephelah that other Yehud Persian period sites do not offer the information that allow researchers to move towards a more complete picture of family and household rituals. Here again, Tell en-Naṣbeh can contribute to the research taking place at other Judean sites. As this study demonstrates, Tell en-Naṣbeh's Stratum 2 architecture and domestic material culture are one-of-a-kind in the southern Levant, and these provide an ideal context for the study of family and household rituals and/or religious practices.

This study provides an interdisciplinary investigation that fills a gap in biblical and archaeological scholarship by demonstrating how the architecture and material culture from Persian period Tell en-Naṣbeh can be utilized to study

---

[25] Darby argues for a similar position in her study: "scholars should not assume that ancient Near Eastern figurine rituals fell outside the realm of official religion or that they were frowned upon by those in official positions." See ibid., 400.

ritual and religious practices at the family and household level. The observations and conclusions from this study contribute to a better understanding of these rituals and practices in the province of Yehud, thus increasing our comprehension of the variety of religious beliefs and practices present in early Judaism.

APPENDIX A: TELL EN-NAṢBEH MATERIAL CULTURE DISTRIBUTION FOR STRATUM 2

TABLE 11 Building totals for Stratum 2

Artifact	Building number											Total
	74.01	93.01	93.03	110.01	125.01	127.01	127.03	144.01	145.02	160.10	194.01	
Altars	1	0	0	2	1	0	0	2	0	1	0	9
Stands	0	1	1	3	0	0	0	1	0	0	0	5
Figurines, statuettes	0	5	3	0	0	1	0	0	0	2	3	14
Bowls	5	22	20	42	16	2	7	30	0	15	23	189
Cooking pots	5	17	16	24	15	1	2	18	4	13	15	137
Kraters	0	2	0	0	3	0	0	0	0	7	2	14
Baking-pans	0	1	0	0	0	0	0	0	0	0	0	1
Saucers and plates	0	0	1	0	0	0	0	0	0	0	0	1
Cups	0	0	0	0	0	0	0	0	0	0	0	0
Chalices	0	0	0	1	0	0	0	0	0	0	0	1
Jugs, juglets, flasks	0	3	9	11	1	1	2	8	2	6	6	49
Jars	0	35	19	54	41	0	8	32	1	41	40	277
Bottles	0	1	2	0	0	0	0	1	0	0	0	4
Lamps	2	6	7	8	5	0	1	6	1	3	10	50
Masks	0	0	0	0	0	0	0	0	0	0	0	0
Rattles	0	0	0	1	0	0	0	0	0	0	0	1
Zoomorphic vessels	0	0	0	0	1	0	0	1	0	1	0	3
Beads, amulets, pendants, other	0	5	5	8	10	1	2	8	7	5	2	53
Bones	3	0	0	1	0	0	0	0	5	0	0	12
Total per building	16	98	83	155	93	6	22	108	20	93	102	
Ranking per total artifacts	10	4	7	1	5*	11	8	2	9	5*	3	

Note: Building 93.04 does not have a table because it was fragmentary and challenging to identify. See Zorn 1993, p. 503–504. There is also no table for Building 195.02 because there were no millimeter cards for some of the rooms, only for the square. * Buildings that had equal ranking.

APPENDIX A

TABLE 12 Building 74.01 Stratum 2 material culture

Artifact:	Building 74.01[1]					Totals
	Rm. 189	Rm. 191	Rm. 192	Rm. 193	Rm. 196	
Altars					1	1
Stands						0
Figurines, statuettes						0
Bowls	3	1		1		5
Cooking pots		1	1	1	2	5
Kraters						0
Baking-pans						0
Saucers and plates						0
Cups						0
Chalices						0
Jugs, juglets, flasks						0
Jars						0
Bottles						0
Lamps		2				2
Masks						0
Rattles						0
Zoomorphic vessels						0
Beads, amulets, pendants, other						0
Bones		1	2			3
Total per room	3	5	3	2	3	16

[1] Rooms 149, 187, 188, 190, and 199 had no millimeter cards for the room number, only for the squares.

TABLE 13 Building 93.01 Stratum 2 material culture

Artifact:	Outer Gate Complex							Total
	Building 93.01 (Outer Gate, Plaza)				?	Outer Gate Hallway		
	Rm. 273a	Rm. 274	Rm. 275	Rm. 276	Rm. 373	Rm. 374	Rm. 377	
Altars								0
Stands				1				1
Figurines, statuettes	1	1	1	1			1	5
Bowls	3	7	4	1	5	1	1	22
Cooking pots	2	3	4	2	3	2	1	17
Kraters		1	1					2
Baking-pans		1						1
Saucers and plates								0
Cups								0
Chalices								0
Jugs, juglets, flasks		2					1	3
Jars	3	12	6	1	5	3	5	35
Bottles						1		1
Lamps	1	1	1	1	1		1	6
Masks								0
Rattles								0
Zoomorphic vessels								0
Beads, amulets, pendants, other		3		1			1	5
Bones								0
Total per room	10	31	17	8	14	7	11	98

?: Unknown as to possible architecture.

APPENDIX A   149

TABLE 14 Building 93.03 Stratum 2 material culture

Artifact:	Building 93.03					Total
	Rm. 365	Rm. 366	Rm. 368	Rm. 369	Rm. 370	
Altars					1	1
Stands						0
Figurines, statuettes		2		1		3
Bowls	2	6	7	1	4	20
Cooking pots	1	7	2	3	3	16
Kraters						0
Baking-pans						0
Saucers and plates					1	1
Cups						0
Chalices						0
Jugs, juglets, flasks		4	1	3	1	9
Jars	5	7	3	2	2	19
Bottles		2				2
Lamps	1	2	1	2	1	7
Masks						0
Rattles						0
Zoomorphic vessels						0
Beads, amulets, pendants, other		2	2	1		5
Bones						0
Total per room	9	32	16	13	13	83

TABLE 15 Building 110.01 Stratum 2 material culture

Artifact:	Building 110.01										Total
	Rm. 266b	Rm. 267	Rm. 268	Rm. 269	Rm. 375	Rm. 376	Rm. 378	Rm. 379	Rm. 380a	Rm. 400	
Altars			1				1				2
Stands								3			3
Figurines, statuettes											0
Bowls	1	3	1	1	1	5	15	4		11	42
Cooking pot		2		2		1	7	5	1	6	24
Kraters											0
Baking-pan											0
Saucers and plates											0
Cups											0
Chalices							1				1
Jugs, juglets, flasks		1				2	6	2			11
Jars	2	8	4	1	2	8	12	7	8	2	54
Bottles											0
Lamps		1				1	2	2	1	1	8
Masks											0
Rattles										1	1
Zoomorphic vessels											0
Beads, amulets, pendants, other							2	5	1		8
Bones	1										1
Total per room	4	15	6	4	3	17	46	28	11	21	155

APPENDIX A 151

TABLE 16 Building 125.01 Stratum 2 material culture

Artifact:	Building 125.01								Total
	Rm. 472	Rm. 473	Rm. 477	Rm. 638	Rm. 641	Rm. 643	Rm. 647	Rm. 659	
Altars			1						1
Stands									0
Figurines, statuettes									0
Bowls	1	2	3	3	2	1	1	3	16
Cooking pots		1	1		5	5	3		15
Kraters			1	2					3
Baking-pans									0
Saucers and plates									0
Cups									0
Chalices									0
Jugs, juglets, flasks			1						1
Jars	4	5	7	3	9	8	4	1	41
Bottles									0
Lamps			2	1	1	1			5
Masks									0
Rattles									0
Zoomorphic vessels		1							1
Beads, amulets, pendants, other	1	4	1	1	2	1			10
Bones									0
Total per room	6	13	17	10	19	16	8	4	93

TABLE 17 Building 127.01 Stratum 2 material culture

Artifact:	Building 127.01			Total
	Rm. 97	Rm. 106	Rm. 108	
Altars				0
Stands				0
Figurines, statuettes			1	1
Bowls	1		1	2
Cooking pots		1		1
Kraters				0
Baking-pans				0
Saucers and plates				0
Cups				0
Chalices				0
Jugs, juglets, flasks	1			1
Jars				0
Bottles				0
Lamps				0
Masks				0
Rattles				0
Zoomorphic vessels				0
Beads, amulets, pendants, other			1	1
Bones				0
Total per room	2	1	3	6

TABLE 18 Building 127.03 Stratum 2 material culture

Artifact:	Building 127.03				Total
	Rm. 333	Rm. 334	Rm. 335	Rm. 336	
Altars					0
Stands					0
Figurines, statuettes					0
Bowls	5		1	1	7
Cooking pots	1		1		2
Kraters					0
Baking-pans					0
Saucers and plates					0
Cups					0
Chalices					0
Jugs, juglets, flasks	1			1	2
Jars	2	2	2	2	8
Bottles					0
Lamps	1				1
Masks					0
Rattles					0
Zoomorphic vessels					0
Beads, amulets, pendants, other		1	1		2
Bones					0
Total per room	10	3	5	4	22

TABLE 19 Building 144.01 Stratum 2 material culture

Artifact:	Building 144.01							Total
	Rm. 318	Rm. 324	Rm. 325	Rm. 326	Rm. 327	Rm. 331	Rm. 332	
Altars		1		1				2
Stands					1			1
Figurines, statuettes								0
Bowls	3	5	7	1	6	4	4	30
Cooking pots	6	3	4	1	1	2	1	18
Kraters								0
Baking-pans								0
Saucers and plates								0
Cups								0
Chalices								0
Jugs, juglets, flasks		2	5			1		8
Jars	9	6	5	3	5	2	2	32
Bottles						1		1
Lamps	1	1	1		1	1	1	6
Masks								0
Rattles								0
Zoomorphic vessels						1		1
Beads, amulets, pendants, other	3	4			1			8
Bones						1		1
Total per room	22	22	22	6	15	13	8	108

TABLE 20 Building 145.02 Stratum 2 material culture

Artifact:	Building 145.02			Total
	Rm. 224	Rm. 226	Rm. 227	
Altars				0
Stands				0
Figurines, statuettes				0
Bowls				0
Cooking pots		3	1	4
Kraters				0
Baking-pans				0
Saucers and plates				0
Cups				0
Chalices				0
Jugs, juglets, flasks	1		1	2
Jars		1		1
Bottles				0
Lamps	1			1
Masks				0
Rattles				0
Zoomorphic vessels				0
Beads, amulets, pendants, other	3	2	2	7
Bones	2	3		5
Total per room	7	9	4	20

TABLE 21 Building 160.10 Stratum 2 material culture

Artifact:	Building 160.10						Total
	Rm. 463	Rm. 468	Rm. 565	Rm. 567	Rm. 569	Rm. 574	
Altars	1						1
Stands							0
Figurines, statuettes	2						2
Bowls	6	1	2	2	3	1	15
Cooking pots	6			1	4	2	13
Kraters	6		1				7
Baking-pans							0
Saucers and plates							0
Cups							0
Chalices							0
Jugs, juglets, flasks	5	1					6
Jars	15	6	2	2	12	4	41
Bottles							0
Lamps				2	1		3
Masks							0
Rattles							0
Zoomorphic vessels							0
Beads, amulets, pendants, other	4				1		5
Bones							0
Total per room	45	8	5	7	21	7	93

TABLE 22 Building 194.01 Stratum 2 material culture

Artifact:	Building 194.01			Total
	Rm. 22	Rm. 23	Rm. 24	
Altars				0
Stands				0
Figurines, statuettes		2	1	3
Bowls	1	10	12	23
Cooking pots		7	8	15
Kraters			2	2
Baking-pans				0
Saucers and plates				0
Cups				0
Chalices				0
Jugs, juglets, flasks	1	3	2	6
Jars		20	20	40
Bottles				0
Lamps		6	4	10
Masks				0
Rattles				0
Zoomorphic vessels		1		1
Beads, amulets, pendants, other	1	1		2
Bones				0
Total per room	3	50	49	102

APPENDIX B: TELL EN-NAṢBEH STRATUM 2 BUILDING RECONSTRUCTIONS

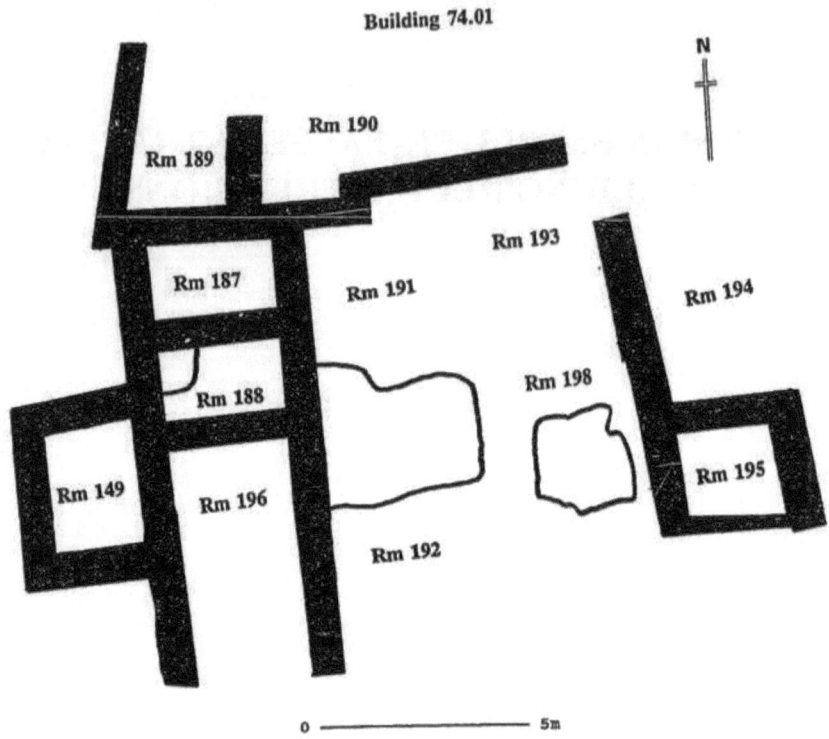

Figure 14. TEN Building 74.01.

Source: Zorn, "Tell en-Nasbeh: A Re-evaluation," 1029. Used by permission.

APPENDIX B 161

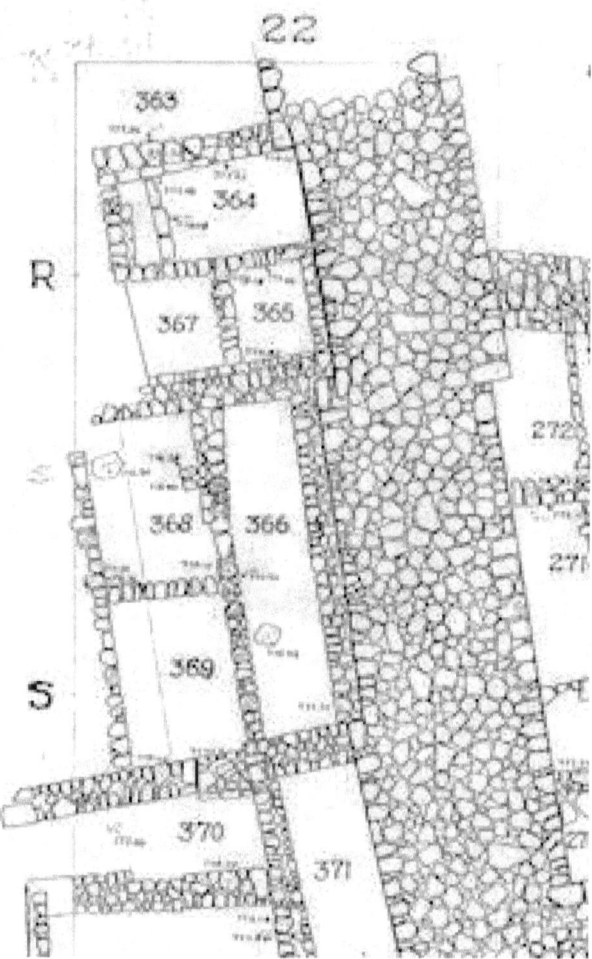

Figure 15. TEN Building 93.03.

Source: Badè Museum, Berkeley, CA. Author's adaptation of Map 1:100 Area 93. Used by permission.

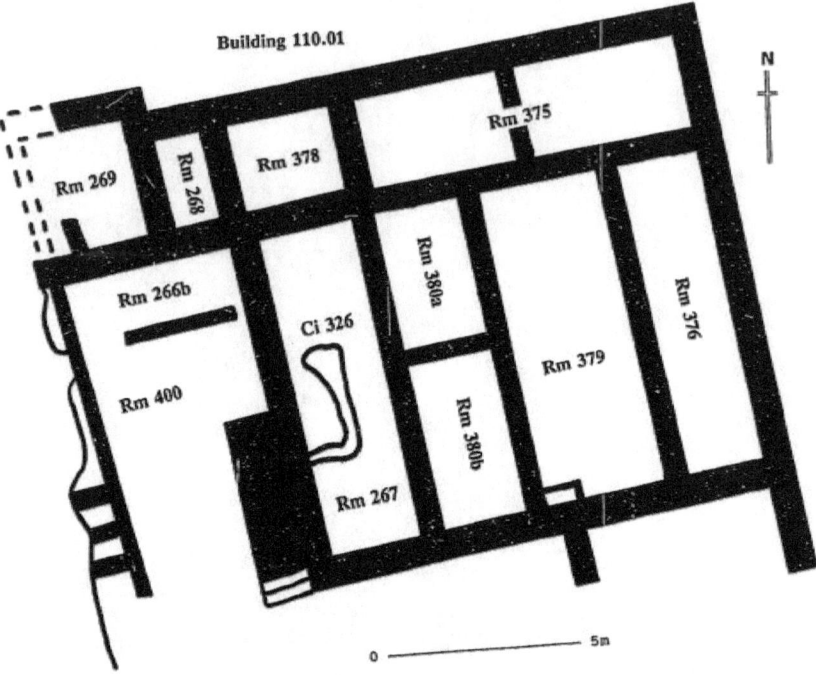

Figure 16. TEN Building 110.01.

Source: Zorn, "Tell en-Nasbeh: A Re-evaluation," 1032. Used by permission.

APPENDIX B   163

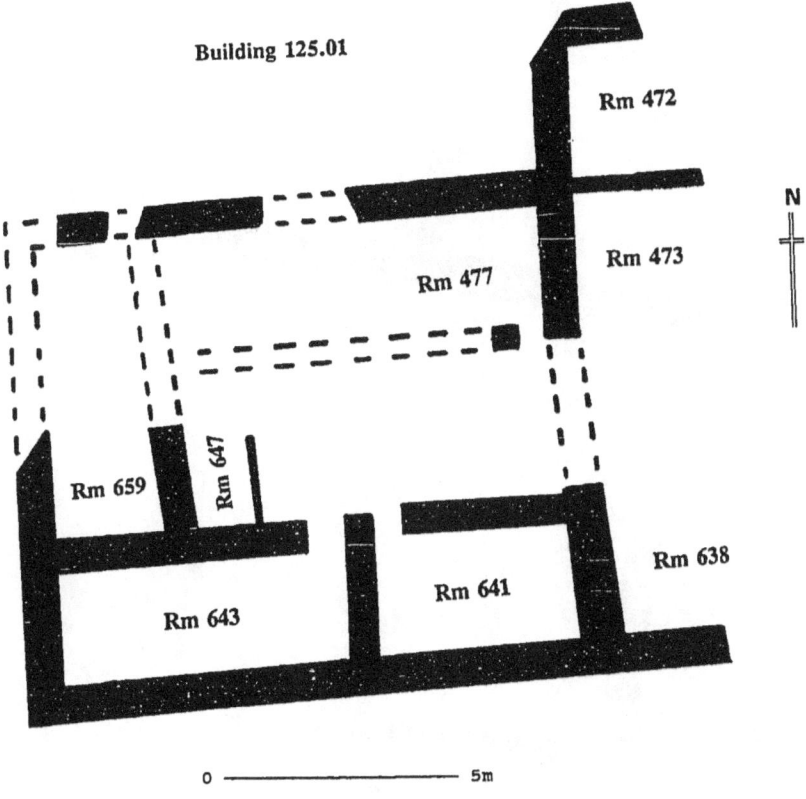

Figure 17. TEN Building 125.01.

Source: Zorn, "Tell en-Nasbeh: A Re-evaluation," 1034. Used by permission.

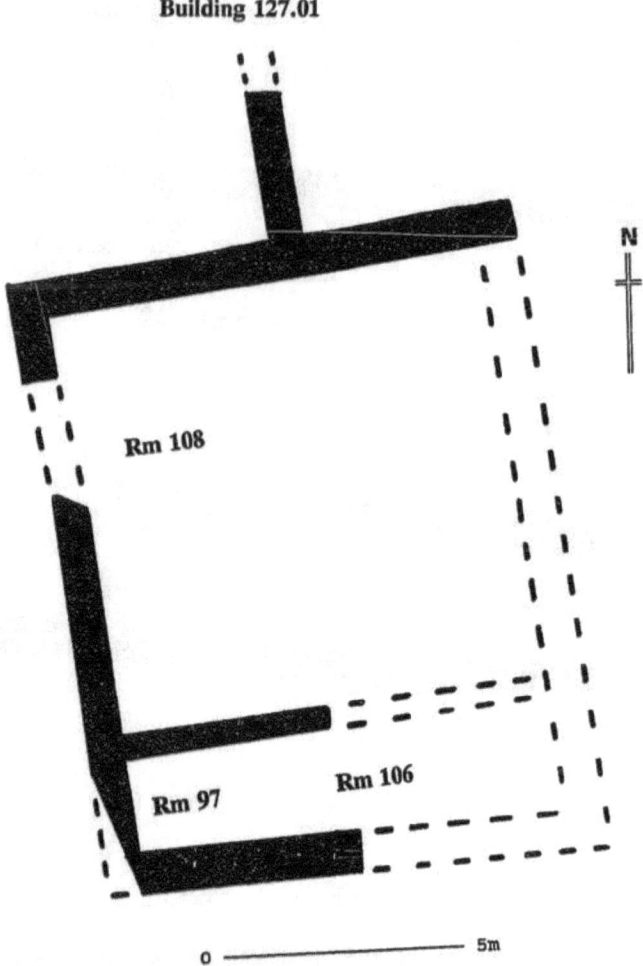

Figure 18. TEN Building 127.01.

Source: Zorn, "Tell en-Nasbeh: A Re-evaluation," 1039. Used by permission.

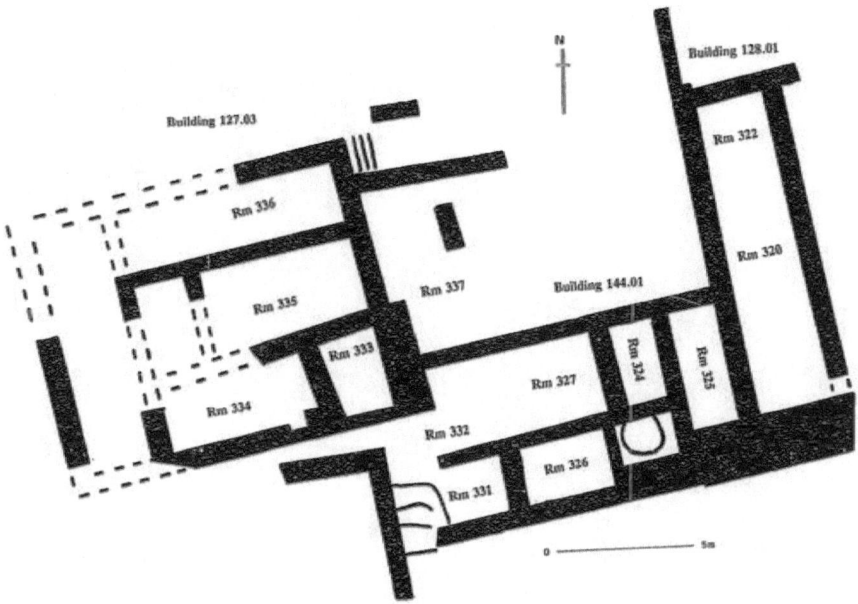

Figure 19. TEN Buildings 127.03 (left), 144.01 (center).

Source: Zorn, "Tell en-Nasbeh: A Re-evaluation," 1039, 1040. Used by permission.

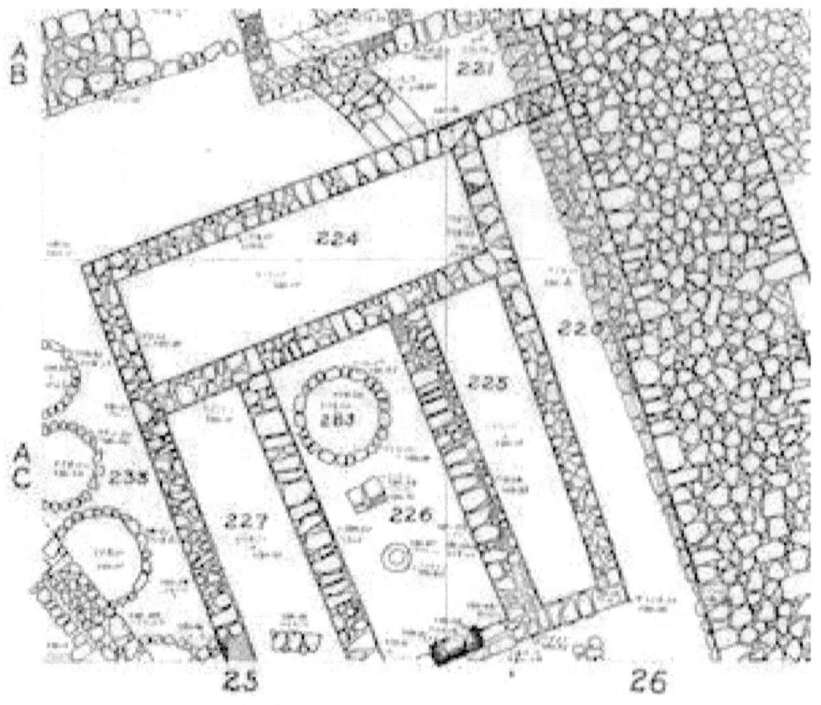

Figure 20. TEN Building 145.02.

Source: Badè Museum, Berkeley, CA. Author's adaptation of Map 1:100 Area 145. Used by permission.

APPENDIX B   167

Building 160.10

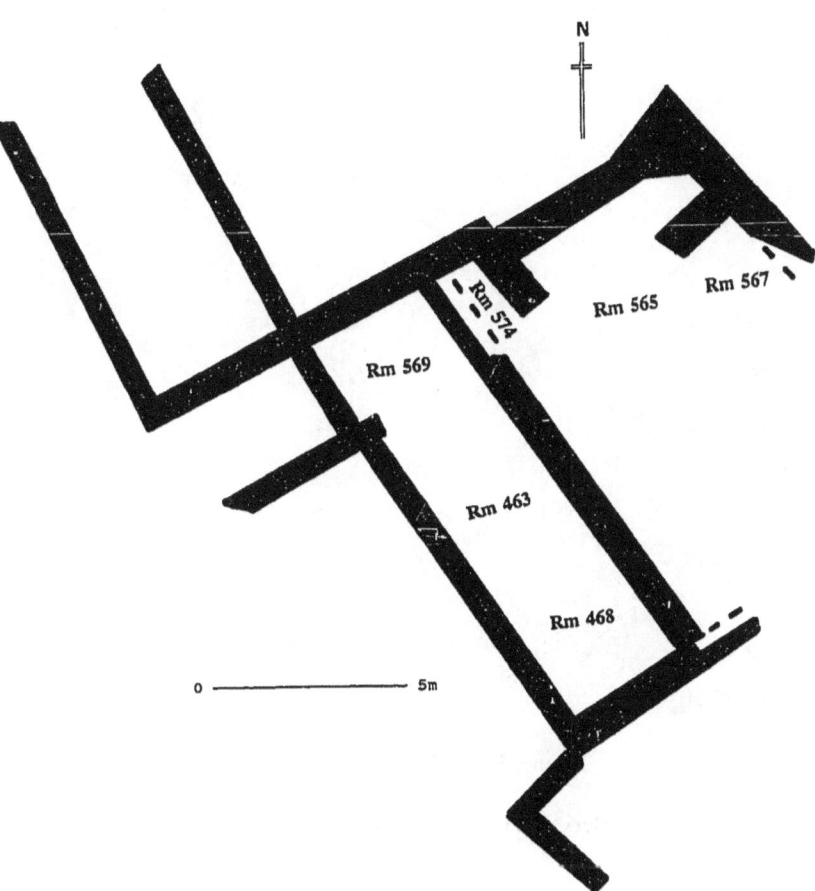

Figure 21. TEN Building 160.10.

Source: Zorn, "Tell en-Nasbeh: A Re-evaluation," 1055. Used by permission.

168 HOUSEHOLD AND FAMILY RELIGION IN PERSIAN PERIOD JUDAH

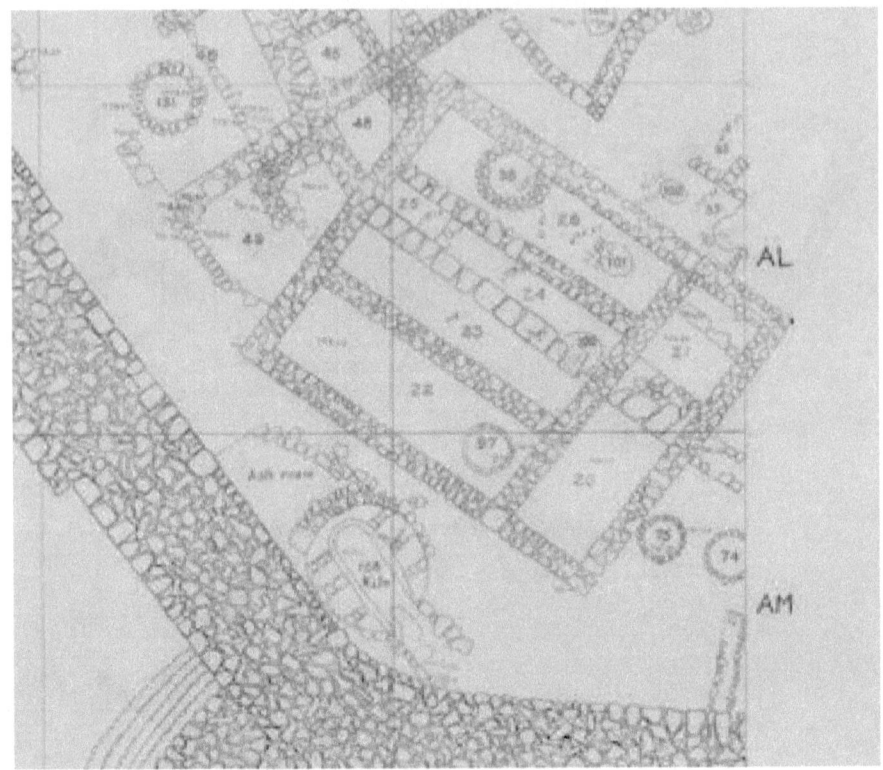

Figure 22. TEN Building 194.01.

Source: Badè Museum, Berkeley, CA. Author's adaptation of Map 1:100 Area 194. Used by permission.

APPENDIX C: PHOTOGRAPHS OF TELL EN-NAṢBEH RITUAL ARTIFACTS STRATUM 2

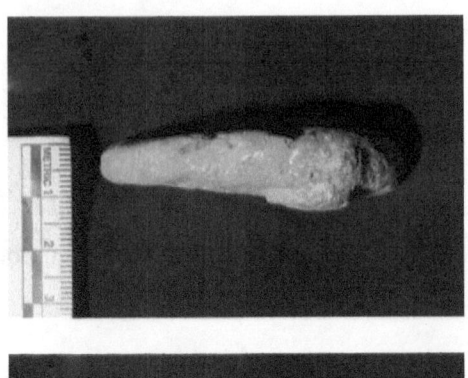

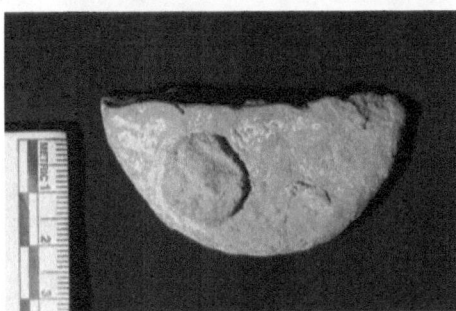

Figure 23. Altar fragment; Bldg. 144.01, Rm. 324, x27.

Note: Side, top, and bottom view. Badè Museum number B2013.1.89.

Source: Artifacts courtesy of Badè Museum, Pacific School of Religion, Berkeley, CA. Photographed by author.

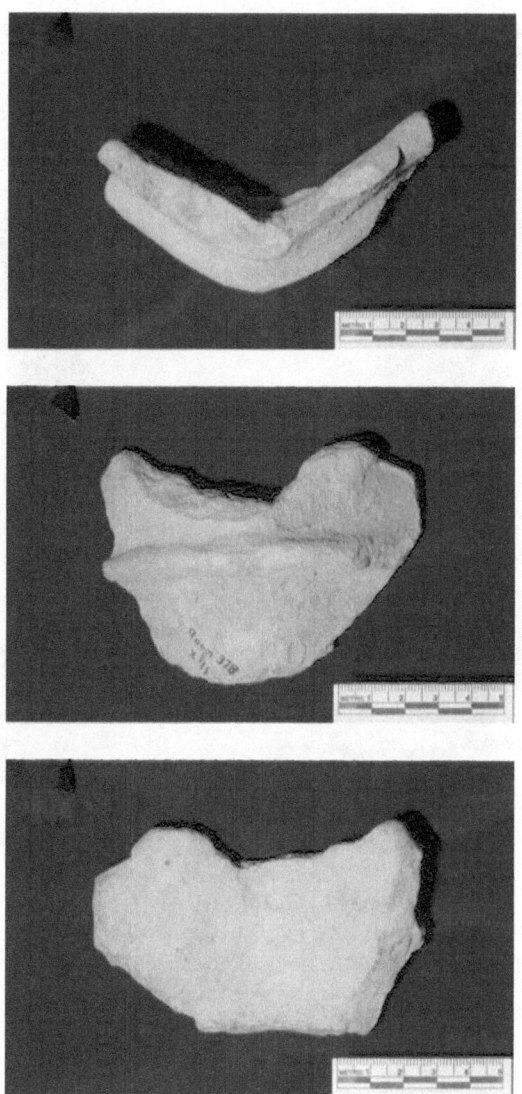

Figure 24. Incense altar fragment; Bldg. 110.01, Rm. 378, x41.

Note: Top, front, and back view. Badè Museum number B2014.1.105.

Source: Artifacts courtesy of Badè Museum, Pacific School of Religion, Berkeley, CA. Photographed by author.

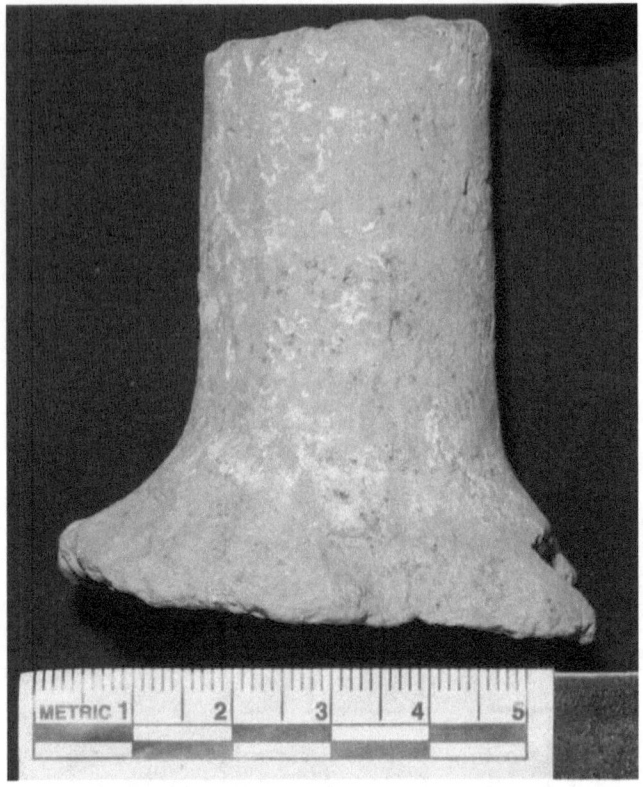

Figure 25. Pillar base figurine fragment; Bldg. 93.03, Rm. 366, x29.

Note: Badè Museum number B2012.1.61.

Source: Artifacts courtesy of Badè Museum, Pacific School of Religion, Berkeley, CA. Photographed by author.

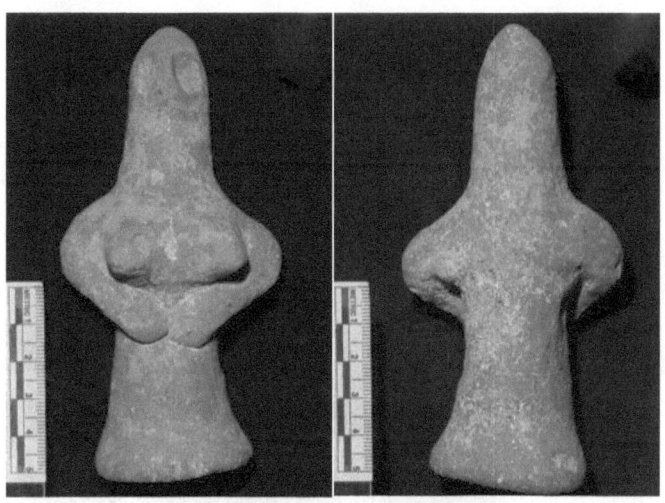

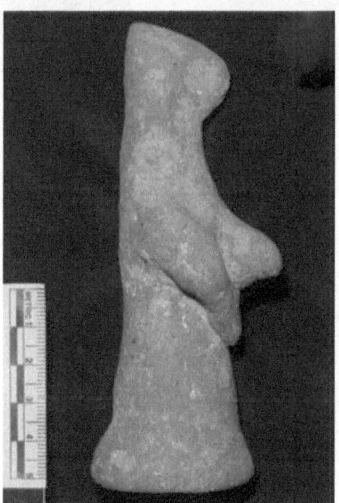

Figure 26. JPF; Bldg. 93.03, Rm. 369.

Note: Front, back, and side view. Badè Museum number B2012.1.140.

Source: Artifacts courtesy of Badè Museum, Pacific School of Religion, Berkeley, CA. Photographed by author.

Figure 27. Animal figurine fragment; Bldg. 160.10, Rm. 463, x20.

Note: Back and front view. Badè Museum number B2012.1.19

Source: Artifacts courtesy of Badè Museum, Pacific School of Religion, Berkeley, CA. Photographed by author.

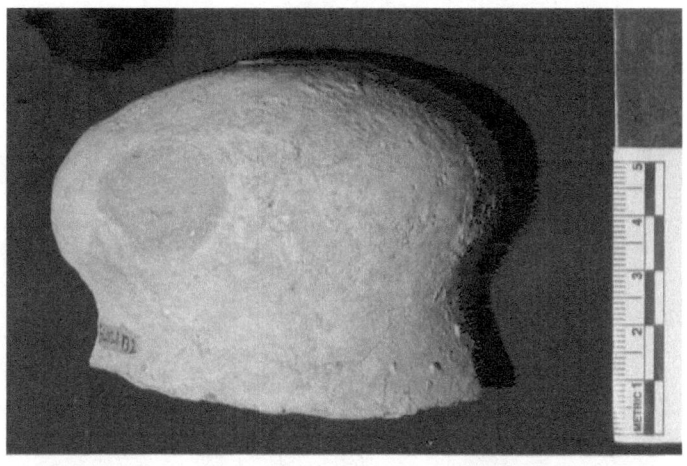

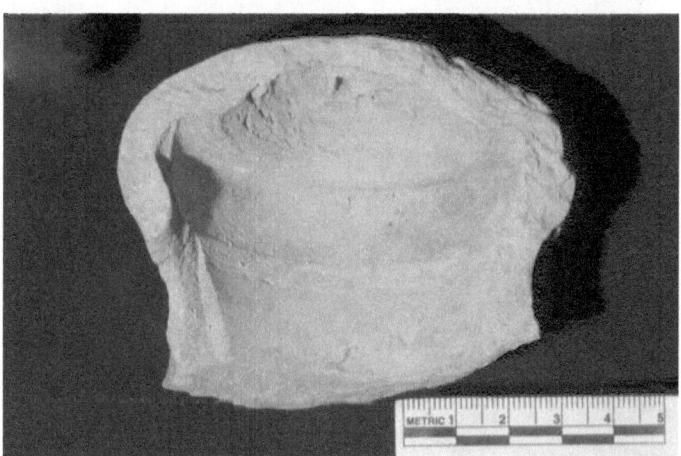

Figure 28. Rattle fragment from Bldg. 110.01, Rm. 400, x19.

Note: Badè Museum number B2012.1.132.

Source: Artifacts courtesy of Badè Museum, Pacific School of Religion, Berkeley, CA. Photographed by author.

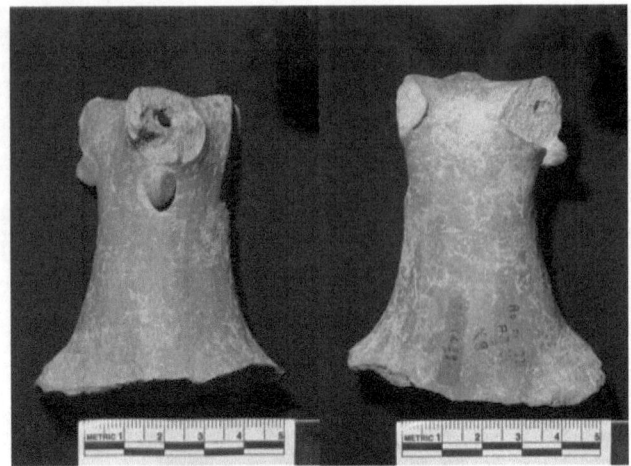

Figure 29. Zoomorphic vessel; Bldg. 144.01, Rm. 331, x8.

Note: Front, back and side view. Badè Museum number B2014.1.39

Source: Artifacts courtesy of Badè Museum, Pacific School of Religion, Berkeley, CA. Photographed by author.

APPENDIX D: TELL EN-NAṢBEH STRATUM 2 BUILDING SPECIFICATION

TABLE 23 TEN Stratum 2 building characteristics

	Bldg. 74.01	Bldg. 93.03	Bldg. 110.01	Bldg. 125.01	Bldg. 127.01	Bldg. 127.03	Bldg. 144.01	Bldg. 145.02	Bldg. 160.10	Bldg. 194.01
Type	Palace	4-room	4-room	4-room	4-room	4-room	3-room	4-room	Store-house	4-room
Size										
Length		12.5	13	13		13		12.5		12
Width		8.5	10	11		11.5		10		10
Total Square Meters	NA	106.3	130	143	NA	149.5	NA	125	NA	120
Ranking[1]		6	3	2		1		4		5
Total Rooms	12	6	11	8	3	4	7	4	6	7
Construction Features:[2]										
Paved Floors	Rms. 188, 192, 198	None	Rms. 376, 380a	Rms. 477, 638, 641	None	Rm. 334	Rms. 326, 331	None	None	None
Pillars	None	9	9	1	None	None	7	None	None	None
Stairs	None	None	3+	None	None	None	5; plaza down to Rm. 331	1; step down to Rm. 226	None	None
Roof		Rms. 366, 369 (P)								
Second Story				Yes, Rm. 400						

[1] Based on total square meters calculations. [2] Unless otherwise stated, these are based on Zorn, "Tell en-Nasbeh: A Re-evaluation of the Architecture and Stratigraphy of the Early Bronze Age, Iron Age and Later Periods." (P) represents my proposal.

BIBLIOGRAPHY

Aharoni, Yohanan. *The Land of the Bible: A Historical Geography*. 2nd rev. ed. London: Burns & Oates, 1979.

Aharoni, Yohanan, and Universiṭat Tel-Aviv. Makhon le-arkhe'ologyah. *Investigations at Lachish: The Sanctuary and The Residency (Lachish V)*. Publications of the Institute of Archaeology, Tel Aviv University. Tel Aviv: Gateway, 1975.

Ahlström, Gösta W. *Royal Administration and National Religion in Ancient Palestine*. Vol. 1. SHANE. Leiden: Brill, 1982.

Albertz, Rainer. *From the Exile to the Maccabees*. Vol. 2 of *A History of Israelite Religion in the Old Testament Period*. Louisville, KY: Westminster John Knox, 1994.

———. "Personal Piety." Pages 135–46 in *Religious Diversity in Ancient Israel and Judah*. Edited by Francesca Stavrakopoulou, and John Barton. London: T&T Clark, 2010.

Albertz, Rainer, and Rudiger Schmitt. *Family and Household Religion in Ancient Israel and Levant*. Winona Lake, IN: Eisenbrauns, 2012.

Amiran, Ruth. *Ancient Pottery of the Holy Land: From Its Beginnings in the Neolithic Period to the End of the Iron Age*. New Brunswick, NJ: Rutgers University Press, 1970.

Badè, William Frederic. *A Manual of Excavation in the Near East: Methods of Digging and Recording of the Tell en-Nasbeh Expedition in Palestine*. Berkeley, CA: University of California Press, 1934.

Bell, Catherine M. "Response: Defining the Need for a Definition." Pages 277–288 in *The Archaeology of Ritual*. Edited by Evangelos Kyriakidis. Los Angeles, CA: Cotsen Institute of Archaeology, University of California, Los Angeles, 2007.

———. *Ritual: Perspectives and Dimensions*. New York: Oxford University Press, 2009.

Berlin, Adele, Marc Zvi Brettler, Michael A. Fishbane, and Jewish Publication Society. *The Jewish Study Bible*. Oxford: Oxford University Press, 2004.

Berlinerblau, Jacques. "The 'Popular Religion' Paradigm in Old Testament Research: A Sociological Critique." Pages 53–76 in *Social-Scientific*

Old Testament Criticism: A Sheffield Reader. Edited by David J. Chalcraft. Sheffield: Sheffield Academic, 1997.
Bienkowski, Piotr. "The Persian Period." Pages 335–52 in *Jordan: An Archaeological Reader*. Edited by Russell Adams. Oakville, CT: Equinox, 2008.
Blenkinsopp, Joseph. *Ezra-Nehemiah: A Commentary*. Philadelphia, PA: Westminster, 1988.
Bloch-Smith, Elizabeth. *Judahite Burial Practices and Beliefs about the Dead*. JSOTSup 123. Sheffield: JSOT Press, 1992.
Blomquist, Tina Haettner. *Gates and Gods: Cults in the City Gates of Iron Age Palestine; An Investigation of the Archaeological and Biblical Sources*. ConBot 46. Stockholm: Almqvist & Wiksell, 1999.
Bodel, John P., and Saul M. Olyan, eds. *Household and Family Religion in Antiquity*, Ancient World: Comparative Histories. Malden, MA: Blackwell, 2008.
Boyce, Mary. *Under the Achaemenians*. Vol. 2 of *A History of Zoroastrianism*. Leiden: Brill, 1982.
Branigan, K. "The Four-Room Buildings of Tell en-Naṣbeh." *IEJ* 16.3 (1966): 206–08.
Briant, Pierre. *From Cyrus to Alexander: A History of the Persian Empire*. Winona Lake, IN: Eisenbrauns, 2002.
Brody, Aaron J. "Mizpah, Mizpeh." *NIDB* 4:116–17.
———. "'Those Who Add House to House': Household Archaeology and the Use of Domestic Space in an Iron II Residential Compound at Tell en-Naṣbeh." Pages 45–56 in *Exploring the Longue Durée: Essays in Honor of Lawrence E. Stager*. Edited by J. David Schloen. Winona Lake, IN: Eisenbrauns, 2009.
———. "The Archaeology of the Extended Family: A Household Compound from Iron II Tell en-Nasbeh." Pages 237–54 in *Household Archaeology in Ancient Israel and Beyond*. Edited by Assaf Yasur-Landau, Jennie R. Ebeling, Laura B. Mazow, and American Schools of Oriental Research. Leiden: Brill, 2011.
Carter, Charles E. *The Emergence of Yehud in the Persian Period: A Social and Demographic Study*. JSOTSup 294. Sheffield: Sheffield Academic, 1999.
Chicago Manual of Style. 16th ed. Chicago: University of Chicago Press, 2010.
Conder, C. R., and H. H. Kitchener. "Map of Western Palestine in 26 Sheets." London: Committee of the Palestine Exploration Fund, 1880. Electronic edition titled "Survey of Western Palestine: The Maps." CD-ROM copyrighted by Todd Bolen, 2004.

Cook, J. M. *The Persian Empire*. New York: Schocken Books, 1983.
Cornelius, Izak. "'East Meets West': Trends in Terracotta Figurines." Pages 67–93 in *A "Religious Revolution" in Yehud?: The Material Culture of the Persian Period as a Test Case*. Edited by Christian Frevel, Katharina Pyschny, and Izak Cornelius. Fribourg, Switzerland; Göttingen: Academic Press Fribourg; Vandenhoeck & Ruprecht, 2014.
Darby, Erin. *Interpreting Judean Pillar Figurines: Gender and Empire in Judean Apotropaic Ritual*. FAT 2/69. Tübingen: Mohr Siebeck, 2014.
Daviau, P. M. Michèle. "Family Religion: Evidence for the Paraphernalia of the Domestic Cult." Pages 199–229 in *The World of the Aramaeans*. Edited by John William Wevers, Michael Weigl, and Paul-Eugène Dion. Sheffield: Sheffield Academic, 2001.
Davies, Gordon F. *Ezra and Nehemiah*. Berit Olam. Collegeville, MN: Liturgical Press, 1999.
Davila, James R. "Ritual in the Jewish Pseudepigrapha." Pages 158–83 in *Anthropology and Biblical Studies: Avenues of Approach*. Edited by Louise Joy Lawrence, and Mario I. Aguilar. Leiden: Deo, 2004.
De Tarragon, Jean-Michel. "Ammon (Person)." *ABD* 1:194–96.
Erlich, Adi. "Recherches Pluridisciplinaires Sur Une Province de L'Empire Achéménide." *Transeu* 32 (2006): 45–62.
Fantalkin, Alexander, and Oren Tal. "The Persian and Hellenistic Pottery of Level I." in *The Renewed Archaeological Excavations at Lachish (1973–1994)*. Edited by David Ussishkin. Tel Aviv: Emery and Claire Yass Publications in Archaeology, 2004.
———. "Redating Lachish Level I: Identifying Achaemenid Imperial Policy at the Southern Frontier of the Fifth Satrapy." Pages 167–99 in *Judah and the Judeans in the Persian Period*. Edited by Oded Lipschits, and Manfred Oeming. Winona Lake, IN: Eisenbrauns, 2006.
Fensham, F. Charles. *The Books of Ezra and Nehemiah*. NICOT. Grand Rapids, MI: Eerdmans, 1982.
Fernández S.J., Andrés. *Comentario a los Libros de Esdras y Nehemías*. Madrid: Consejo Superior de Investigaciones Científicas, 1950.
Fogelin, Lars. "Deligitimizing Religion: The Archaeology of Religion as ... Archaeology." Pages 129–41 in *Belief in the Past: Theoretical Approaches to the Archaeology of Religion*. Edited by David S. Whitley, and Kelley Hays-Gilpin. Walnut Creek, CA: Left Coast, 2008.
Foster, Catherine P., and Bradley J. Parker. "Introduction: Household Archaeology in the Near East and Beyond." Pages 1–12 in *New Perspectives on Household Archaeology*. Edited by Bradley J. Parker, and Catherine P. Foster. Winona Lake, IN: Eisenbrauns, 2012.

Frevel, Christian, Katharina Pyschny, and Izak Cornelius, eds. *A "Religious Revolution" in Yehud?: The Material Culture of the Persian Period as a Test Case*, OBO 267. Fribourg, Switzerland: Academic Press Fribourg; Göttingen: Vandenhoeck & Ruprecht, 2014.

Geertz, Clifford. *The Interpretation of Cultures: Selected Essays*. New York: Basic Books, 1973.

Grabbe, Lester L. *Ezra-Nehemiah*. New York: Routledge, 1998.

———. *A History of the Jews and Judaism in the Second Temple Period*. LSTS. London: T&T Clark, 2004.

Guinan, Michael. "Aramaic, Aramaism." *NIDB* 1:228–31.

Gutmann, Joseph. *Ancient Synagogues: The State of Research*. Chico, CA: Scholars Press, 1981.

Haaland, Randi, and Gunnar Haaland. "Landscape." Pages 24–37 in *The Oxford Handbook of the Archaeology of Ritual and Religion*. Edited by Timothy Insoll. Oxford: Oxford University Press, 2011.

Hershman, Debby. *Face to Face: The Oldest Masks in the World*. Jerusalem: Israel Museum, 2014.

Herzog, Zeev. "Fortifications (Levant)." *ABD* 2:844–852.

Holladay, John S. Jr. "Religion in Israel and Judah under the Monarchy: An Explicitly Archaeological Approach." Pages 249–99 in *Ancient Israelite Religion: Essays in Honor of Frank Moore Cross*. Edited by Patrick D. Miller, Paul D. Hanson, and S. Dean McBride. Philadelphia, PA: Fortress, 1987.

Hopkins, I. W. J. "Nineteenth-Century Maps of Palestine: Dual-Purpose Historical Evidence." *Imago Mundi* 22 (1968): 30–36.

Insoll, Timothy. *Archaeology, Ritual, Religion*. London: Routledge, 2004.

———. "Introduction: Ritual and Religion in Archaeological Perspective." Pages 1–5 in *The Oxford Handbook of the Archaeology of Ritual and Religion*. Edited by Timothy Insoll. Oxford: Oxford University Press, 2011.

Japhet, Sara. *From the Rivers of Babylon to the Highlands of Judah: Collected Studies on the Restoration Period*. Winona Lake, IN: Eisenbrauns, 2006.

Joyce, Rosemary A. "What Should an Archaeology of Religion Look Like to a Blind Archaeologist?" *Archaeological Papers of the American Anthropological Association* 21 (2012): 180–88.

———. "Archaeology of Ritual and Symbolism." Pages 721–26 in *International Encyclopedia of the Social and Behavioral Sciences*. Edited by James D. Wright. Oxford: Elsevier, 2015.

Kaliff, Anders. "Fire." Pages 51–62 in *The Oxford Handbook of the Archaeology of Ritual and Religion*. Edited by Timothy Insoll. Oxford: Oxford University Press, 2011.
Kelm, George L., and Amihai Mazar. "Three Seasons of Excavations at Tel Batash: Biblical Timnah." *BASOR* 248 (1982): 1–36.
———. "Tel Batash (Timnah) Excavations: Third Preliminary Report, 1984– 1989." *BASORSup* 27 (1991): 47–67.
King, Philip J., and Lawrence E. Stager. *Life in Biblical Israel*. Lousville, KY: Westminster John Knox, 2001.
Kletter, Raz. *The Judean Pillar-Figurines and the Archeaology of Asherah*. British Archaeological Reports (BAR) International Series 636. Oxford: John and Erica Hedges Ltd. and Archaeopress, 1996.
———. "Clay Figurines." in *The Renewed Archaeological Excavations at Lachish (1973–1994)*. Edited by David Ussishkin. Tel Aviv: Emery and Claire Yass Publications in Archaeology, 2004.
Kloner, Amos. "Mareshah (Marisa)." *NEAEHL* 5:1918–25.
———. "The Identity of the Idumeans Based on the Archaeological Evidence from Maresha." Pages 563–73 in *Judah and the Judeans in the Achaemenid Period: Negotiating Identity in an International Context*. Edited by Oded Lipschits, Gary N. Knoppers, and Manfred Oeming. Winona Lake, IN: Eisenbrauns, 2011.
Koehler, Ludwig, Walter Baumgartner, M. E. J. Richardson, and Johann Jakob Stamm. *HALOT* Electronic edition.
Kottsieper, Ingo. "And They Did Not Care to Speak Yehudit." Pages 95–124 in *Judah and the Judeans in the Fourth Century B.C.E.* Edited by Oded Lipschits, Gary N Knoppers, and Rainer Albertz. Winona Lake, IN: Eisenbrauns, 2007.
Kuhrt, Amélie. "The Persian Empire, c. 550–330 BC." Pages 51–60 in *Art et civilisation de l'Orient hellénisé: Rencontres et échanges culturels d'Alexandre aux Sassanides. Hommage à Daniel Schlumberger*. Edited by Pierre Leriche. Paris: Picard, 2014.
Kyriakidis, Evangelos. "Archaeologies of Ritual." Pages 289–308 in *The Archaeology of Ritual*. Edited by Evangelos Kyriakidis. Los Angeles: Cotsen Institute of Archaeology, University of California, Los Angeles, 2007.
Lapp, Eric Christian. "The Archaeology of Light: The Cultural Significance of the Oil Lamp from Roman Palestine." Ph.D. Dissertation, Duke University, 1997.
Lapp, Paul W. "The Pottery of Palestine in the Persian Period." Pages 179–97 in *Archäologie und Altes Testament: Festschrift für Kurt Galling*. Edited by Arnulf Kuschke, and Ernst Kutsch. Tübingen: Mohr Siebeck, 1970.

Lawrence, Louise J. "A Taste for 'The Other': Interpreting Biblical Texts Anthropologically." Pages 9–25 in *Anthropology and Biblical Studies: Avenues of Approach*. Edited by Louise Joy Lawrence, and Mario I. Aguilar. Leiden: Deo, 2004.

Lemos, T. M. "Cultural Anthopology." Pages 157–65 in *The Oxford Encyclopedia of Biblical Interpretation*. Edited by Steven L. McKenzie, 1. Oxford: Oxford University Press, 2013.

Levine, Lee I. *The Ancient Synagogue: The First Thousand Years*. New Haven, CT: Yale University Press, 2005.

Lipschits, Oded. *The Fall and Rise of Jerusalem: Judah under Babylonian Rule*. Winona Lake, IN: Eisenbrauns, 2005.

———. "Achaemenid Imperial Policy and the Status of Jerusalem." Pages 19–52 in *Judah and the Judeans in the Persian Period*. Edited by Oded and Manfred Oeming Lipschits. Winona Lake, IN: Eisenbrauns, 2006.

———. "Persian Period Finds From Jerusalem: Facts and Interpretations." *JHebS* 9 (2010): 1–29.

Lipschits, Oded, Yuval Gadot, and D. Langgut. "The Riddle of Ramat Raḥel: The Archaeology of a Royal Persian Period Edifice." *Transeu* 41 (2012): 57–79.

Llinares García, Mar. *Los Lenguajes del Silencio: Arqueologías de la Religión*. Akal Universitaria. Madrid: Akal Ediciones, 2012.

Magen, Yitzhak. "Bells, Pendants, Snakes, and Stones: A Samaritan Temple to the Lord on Mt. Gerizim." *BAR* 36.6 (2010): 26–35, 70.

Marcus, Joyce. "Rethinking Ritual." Pages xii, 319 p. in *The Archaeology of Ritual*. Edited by Evangelos Kyriakidis. Los Angeles: Cotsen Institute of Archaeology, University of California, Los Angeles, 2007.

McAnany, Patricia A. "Rethinking the Great and Little Tradition Paradigm from the Perspective of Domestic Ritual." Pages 115–19 in *Domestic Ritual in Ancient Mesoamerica*. Edited by Patricia Plunket. Los Angeles, CA: Cotsen Institute of Archaeology, University of California Los Angeles, 2002.

McCown, Chester Charlton, James Muilenburg, Joseph Carson Wampler, Dietrich Von Bothmer, and Margaret Harrison. *Archaeological and Historical Results*. Vol. 1 of *Tell en-Nasbeh Excavated under the Direction of the Late William Frederic Badè*. Berkeley, CA: Palestine Institute of Pacific School of Religion and American Schools of Oriental Research, 1947.

Meyers, Carol. "Terracottas without Texts: Judean Pillar Figurines in Anthropological Perspective." Pages 115–30 in *To Break Every Yoke: Essays in Honor of Marvin L. Chaney*. Edited by Robert B. Coote,

Norman K. Gottwald, and Marvin L. Chaney. Sheffield: Sheffield Phoenix, 2007.
Meyers, Carol L. *Households and Holiness: The Religious Culture of Israelite Women*. Facets. Minneapolis, MN: Fortress, 2005.
———. "Household Religion." Pages 118–34 in *Religious Diversity in Ancient Israel and Judah*. London: T&T Clark, 2010.
Myers, Jacob M. *Ezra Nehemiah: Introduction, Translation, and Notes*. Vol. 14. The Anchor Bible. Edited by William Foxwell Albright and David Noel Freedman. Garden City, NY: Doubleday, 1965.
Nakhai, Beth Alpert. "Varieties of Religious Expression in the Domestic Setting." Pages 347–60 in *Household Archaeology in Ancient Israel and Beyond*. Edited by Assaf Yasur-Landau, Jennie R. Ebeling, Laura B. Mazow, and American Schools of Oriental Research. Leiden: Brill, 2011.
Negbi, Ora. *A Deposit of Terracottas and Statuettes from Tel Ṣippor*. 'Atiqot 6. Jerusalem: The Department of Antiquities and Museums, The Israel Exploration Society, 1966.
Oestigaard, Terje. "Water." Pages 38–50 in *The Oxford Handbook of the Archaeology of Ritual and Religion*. Edited by Timothy Insoll. Oxford: Oxford University Press, 2011.
Olsson, Birger, and Magnus Zetterholm, eds. *The Ancient Synagogue from Its Origins until 200 C.E.: Papers Presented at an International Conference at Lund University, October 14–17, 2001*. Stockholm: Almqvist & Wiksell, 2003.
Ortiz, Steven M., and Samuel R. Wolff. "The Renewed Excavations of Tel Gezer, 2006–2008: 2008 Field Report." (2008). www.telgezer.com.
Overholt, Thomas W. *Cultural Anthropology and the Old Testament*. Guides to Biblical Scholarship Old Testament Series. Minneapolis, MN: Fortress, 1996.
Pagán, Samuel. *Esdras, Nehemías y Ester*. Comentario Bíblico Hispanoamericano. Miami, FL: Editorial Caribe, 1992.
Pfoh, Emanuel. "Introduction: Anthropology and the Bible Revisited." Pages 3–12 in *Anthropology and the Bible: Critical Perspectives*. Edited by Emanuel Pfoh. Piscataway, NJ: Gorgias, 2010.
Polak, Frank H. "Sociolinguistics and the Judean Speech Community in the Achaemenid Empire." Pages 589–628 in *Judah and the Judeans in the Persian Period*. Edited by Oded Lipschits, and Manfred Oeming. Winona Lake, IN: Eisenbrauns, 2006.
Poorthuis, Marcel, Joshua Schwartz, and Joseph Turner. *Interaction between Judaism and Christianity in History, Religion, Art and Literature*. Jewish and Christian Perspectives Series. Leiden: Brill, 2009.

Rainey, Anson F., and R. Steven Notley. *The Sacred Bridge: Carta's Atlas of the Biblical World*. Second Emended and Enhanced ed. Jerusalem: Carta, 2014.

Rainville, Lynn. "Techniques for Understanding Assyrian Houses." Pages 139–64 in *New Perspectives on Household Archaeology*. Edited by Bradley J. Parker, and Catherine P. Foster. Winona Lake, IN: Eisenbrauns, 2012.

Renfrew, Colin. "The Archaeology of Religion." Pages 47–54 in *The Ancient Mind: Elements of Cognitive Archaeology*. Edited by Colin Renfrew, and Ezra B.W. Zubrow. Cambridge: Cambridge University Press, 1994.

———. "The Archaeology of Ritual, Cult, and of Religion." Pages 109–22 in *The Archaeology of Ritual*. Edited by Evangelos Kyriakidis. Los Angeles: Cotsen Institute of Archaeology, University of California, Los Angeles, 2007.

Ritmeyer, Leen and Kathleen. *Jerusalem in the Time of Nehemiah*. Jerusalem: Carta, 2005.

Roaf, Michael. *Cultural Atlas of Mesopotamia and the Ancient Near East*. New York: Facts on File, 1990.

Sáenz-Badillos, Ángel. *História de la Lengua Hebrea*. Sabadell: AUSA, 1988.

Scarre, Chris. "Monumentality." Pages 9–23 in *The Oxford Handbook of the Archaeology of Ritual and Religion*. Edited by Timothy Insoll. Oxford: Oxford University Press, 2011.

Schniedewind, William. "Aramaic, the Death of Written Hebrew, and Language Shift in the Persian Period." Pages 135–52 in *Margins of Writing, Origins of Cultures*. Edited by Seth L. Sanders. Chicago: University of Chicago Press, 2006.

Schoville, Keith. *Ezra-Nehemiah*. Joplin, MI: College Press, 2001.

Shepherd, William R. 1923. "Reference Map of Ancient Palestine," *Historical Atlas*, Henry Holt and Company, https://www.lib.utexas.edu/maps/historical/history_shepherd_1923.html.

Silverman, Jason M. "Persian Influence on Jewish Apocalyptic." *PIBA* 32 (2009): 49–60.

———. "Iranian-Judean Interaction in the Achaemenid Period." Pages 133–68 in *Text, Theology, and Trowel: New Investigations in the Biblical World*. Edited by Lidia Matassa, and Jason M. Silverman. Eugene, OR: Pickwick, 2011.

Society of Biblical Literature. *The SBL Handbook of Style*. 2nd ed. Atlanta: SBL Press, 2014.

Stager, Lawrence. "Biblical Philistines: A Hellenistic Literary Creation?" Pages 375–84 in *"I Will Speak the Riddles of Ancient Times": Archaeological and Historical Studies in Honor of Amihai Mazar on the Occasion of*

His Sixtieth Birthday. Edited by Aren M. Maeir, Pierre de Miroschedji, and Amihay Mazar. Winona Lake, IN: Eisenbrauns, 2006.

Stavrakopoulou, Francesca, and John Barton. *Religious Diversity in Ancient Israel and Judah*. London: T&T Clark, 2010.

Steinmann, Andrew E. *Ezra and Nehemiah*. Saint Louis, MI: Concordia, 2010.

Stern, Ephraim. *Material Culture of the Land of the Bible in the Persian Period 538–332 B.C.* Warminster, England: Aris & Phillips, 1982.

———. "The Phoenician Architectural Elements in Palestine during the Late Iron Age and the Persian Period." Pages 302–09 in *The Architecture of Ancient Israel: from the Prehistoric to the Persian Periods*. Edited by Aharon Kempinski, and Ronny Reich. Jerusalem: Israel Publication Society, 1992.

———. *The Assyrian, Babylonian, and Persian Periods (732–332 B.C.E.)*. Vol. 2 of *Archaeology of the Land of the Bible*. New York: Doubleday, 2001.

———. "Chronological Tables: The Historical Archaeological Periods." *NEAEHL* 5:2126.

Tebes, Juan Manuel. "The Archaeology of the Desert Cults and the Origins of Israel's God." *NEAF* 58 (2015): 13–15.

Ussishkin, David. "Lachish." *NEAEHL* 3:897–911.

———, ed. *The Renewed Archaeological Excavations at Lachish (1973–1994)*, SMNIA 22. Tel Aviv: Emery and Claire Yass Publications in Archaeology, 2004.

Van der Toorn, Karel. *Family Religion in Babylonia, Syria, and Israel: Continuity and Changes in the Forms of Religious Life*. SHANE. Leiden: Brill, 1996.

Van der Toorn, Karel, Rainer Albertz, Hripsime Haroutunian, and Jamsheed K. Choksy. "Religious Practices of the Individual and Family." Pages 423–437 in *Religions of the Ancient World: a Guide*. Edited by Sarah Iles Johnston. Cambridge, MA: Belknap Press of Harvard University Press, 2004.

VanderKam, James C. "Calendars: Ancient Israelite and Early Jewish." *ABD* 1:816–820.

Williamson, Hugh G. M. *Ezra and Nehemiah*. Edited by R. N. Whybray. Sheffield: Sheffield Academic, 1987.

Wilson, Robert R. *Sociological Approaches to the Old Testament*. Guides to Biblical Scholarship. Edited by Gene M. Tucker. Philadelphia, PA: Fortress, 1984.

Winn Leith, Mary Joan. "Israel among the Nations: The Persian Period." Pages 366–419 in *The Oxford History of the Biblical World*. Edited by Michael D. Coogan. New York: Oxford University Press, 1998.

Wolff, Samuel R. "Mortuary Practices in the Persian Period of the Levant." *NEA* 65.2 (2002): 131–37.

Wortham, Robert. *Social-Scientific Approaches in Biblical Literature*. Texts and Studies in Religion. Lewiston, NY: Mellen, 1999.

Wright, John W. "Remapping Yehud: The Borders of Yehud and the Geneologies of Chronicles." Pages 67–89 in *Judah and the Judeans in the Persian Period*. Edited by Oded Lipschits, and Manfred Oeming. Winona Lake, IN: Eisenbrauns, 2006.

Zorn, Jeffrey R. "Nasbeh, Tell en-." *NEAEHL* 3:1098–1102.

———. "Tell en-Nasbeh: A Re-evaluation of the Architecture and Stratigraphy of the Early Bronze Age, Iron Age and Later Periods." Ph.D. Dissertation, University of California, Berkeley, 1993.

———. "This Old Site: Issues in the Reappraisal of Early Excavations." Pages 59–70 in vol. 2 in *Archaeology's Publication Problem*. Edited by J. Aviram, and Hershel Shanks. Washington, DC: Biblical Archaeology Society, 1996.

———. "An Inner and Outer Gate Complex at Tell en-Nasbeh." *BASOR* 307 (1997): 53–66.

———. "Tell en-Nasbeh and the Problem of the Material Culture of the Sixth Century." Pages 413–47 in *Judah and the Judeans in the Neo-Babylonian Period*. Edited by Oded Lipschits, and Joseph Blenkinsopp. Winona Lake, IN: Eisenbrauns, 2003.

ANCIENT SOURCES INDEX

1. Hebrew Bible/Old Testament

Genesis
8:20	114
12:7	114
13:18	114
15:7–12	114
22:1–3	114

Exodus
20:3–5	115
20:24	115
20:25–26	115

Leviticus
4:22–26	42
9:3	42
23:34	41
23:39	41

Numbers
7	42
29:12–38	41

1 Chronicles	22, 23

2 Chronicles
	22, 23
32:6	100
33:3	114

Ezra
	5, 21, 22, 23, 35, 36, 37, 39, 40, 45, 46, 47, 48, 133
1–6	22, 37
1:1	40, 45, 46
1:2–4	40
1:4	41, 45, 46
1:6	41, 45, 46
2:64	37
2:68–70	41, 45, 46
2:70–3:1	39
3	42
3:2	41
3:3	39, 45, 46
3:4	41, 45
3:5	41, 45
3:6	41
3:10–11	42, 45
4:1	39
4:1–2	42
4:1–5	39
4:4	39
4:23	42, 45
5:8	24
6:16–17	42, 45
6:19	42
6:19–22	42, 45
6:20	43
6:21	39
6:22	43
7–10	37
7:3–5	40
7:11	43, 45
7:12–26	43, 45
7:14	43
8:21–23	43, 45
8:35	43, 45
9:3–10:1	43, 45
10:5–6	44
10:7–11	44, 45
10:19	44

Nehemiah
	3, 21, 22, 23, 35, 36, 37, 39, 47, 48

1–12	37
1:3	24
2:19	39
3:33–35	39
4:1–2	39
5:1	39
7:6	24
7:66–68	37
9:2	39
10:29	39
11:3	24
13:24–25	35
1 Maccabees	49
Job	47
Psalms	
9–10	47
12	47
14	47
35	47
69	47
70	47
75	47
82	47
109	47
140	47
Proverbs	
1–9	47
Ezekiel	
43:18–27	42

MODERN AUTHORS INDEX

Aharoni, Yohanan	24, 27, 126, 127, 128, 129, 130	Carter, Charles E.	24
		Choksy, Jamsheed K.	2
		Conder, C. R.	116, 118
Ahlström, Gösta W.	93, 94	Cook, J. M.	30
Albertz, Rainer	1, 2, 8, 18, 19, 47, 48, 58, 61, 63, 66, 69, 70, 71, 73, 74, 76, 77, 78, 82, 133, 135, 139, 141	Cornelius, Izak	60, 61, 69, 70, 71
		Darby, Erin	69, 71, 111, 137, 141, 142, 143
		Daviau, P. M. M.	58, 61, 66, 68, 70, 73, 74, 77, 92
Amiran, Ruth	73		
Badè, William F.	4, 50, 51, 66, 82, 102, 114,	Davies, Gordon F	23, 40
Barton, John	2	Davila, James R.	16
Baumgartner, Walter	41	De Tarragon, J.-M.	39
Bell, Catherine M.	5, 13, 14, 15, 16, 17, 18, 22, 46, 84, 85, 90, 133, 135, 137,	Erlich, Adi	130, 131
		Fantalkin, Alexander	24, 26, 129, 130
		Fensham, F. Charles	22
		Fernández, Andrés	40
Berlin, Adele,	40	Fogelin, Lars	84, 86, 90, 135
Berlinerblau, Jacques	21	Foster, Catherine P.	18
Bienkowski, Piotr	106	Frevel, Christian	61
Blenkinsopp, Joseph	23, 40, 41, 42, 43, 44	Gadot, Yuval	50
		Geertz, Clifford	11
Bloch-Smith, E.	63	Grabbe, Lester L.	23, 24
Blomquist, Tina H.	73, 94, 95, 96, 98, 103, 104, 123, 135	Guinan, Michael	36
		Gutmann, Joseph	94
		Haaland, Gunnar	115, 119
Bodel, John P.	2	Haaland, Randi	115, 119
Boyce, Mary	28, 29, 31, 32, 33, 34, 66, 67, 75, 106, 107	Haroutunian, H.	2
		Harrison, Margaret	4, 64, 65, 66, 68, 72, 78, 85, 89, 96, 97, 98, 103, 117, 118, 119
Branigan, K.	85		
Briant, Pierre	28, 29, 32		
Brody, Aaron J.	1, 3, 30, 49, 50, 51, 61, 73, 74, 77, 78, 92	Hershman, Debby	75, 76
		Herzog, Zeev	99, 100

Holladay, John S. Jr.	61, 63, 71, 110, 119	Nakhai, Beth Alpert	2
		Negbi, Ora	69
Hopkins, I. W. J.	25, 117	Notley, R. Steven	24
Insoll, Timothy	9, 11, 12, 14, 64, 82, 114	Oestigaard, Terje.	117
		Olsson, Birger	94
Japhet, Sara	21, 22, 39	Olyan, Saul M.	2
Joyce, Rosemary A.	8, 11, 12, 62, 63, 115	Ortiz, Steven M.	130
		Overholt, Thomas W	7, 8, 10
Kaliff, Anders	74	Pagán, Samuel	40
Kelm, George L.	123	Parker, Bradley J.	18
King, Philip J.	2, 91, 92, 100, 101, 136	Pfoh, Emanuel	7, 9
		Polak, Frank H.	36, 37
Kitchener, H. H.	116, 118	Poorthuis, Marcel	35
Kletter, Raz	70, 71, 72, 103, 128	Pyschny, Katharina	61
		Rainey, Anson F	24
Kloner, Amos	24, 26, 130	Rainville, Lynn	18
Koehler, Ludwig	41	Renfrew, Colin	12, 13, 14, 15, 46, 63
Kottsieper, Ingo	36, 37		
Kuhrt, Amélie	27, 30, 31	Richardson, M. E. J.	41
Kyriakidis, Evangelos	13, 14	Ritmeyer, Leen	37
Langgut, D.	50	Ritmeyer, Kathleen	37
Lapp, Eric Christian	142	Roaf, Michael	3
Lapp, Paul W.	57	Sáenz-Badillos, A.	36, 37
Lawrence, Louise J.	10	Scarre, Chris	83, 84, 85
Lemos, T. M	7, 10	Schniedewind, W.	36, 37
Levine, Lee I.	94	Schwartz, Joshua	35
Lipschits, Oded	24, 37, 38, 50, 52	Schmitt, Rudiger	2, 8, 19, 47, 58, 61, 63, 66, 69, 70, 71, 73, 74, 76, 77, 78, 82, 105, 135, 139, 141
Llinares García, Mar	8, 10, 13, 63		
Magen, Yitzhak	40		
Marcus, Joyce	15		
Mazar, Amihai	123		
McAnany, Patricia A.	110, 111	Schoville, Keith	23, 40
McCown, Chester C.	4, 64, 65, 66, 68, 72, 78, 85, 89, 96, 97, 98, 103, 117, 118, 119	Shepherd, William R	25, 28, 30
		Silverman, Jason M	19, 31, 32, 34, 35, 50
		Stager, Lawrence E.	2, 35, 92, 100, 101, 136
Meyers, Carol	2, 4, 19, 137	Stamm, Johann J.	41
Muilenburg, James	4, 64, 65, 66, 68, 72, 78, 85, 89, 96, 97, 98, 103, 117, 118, 119	Stavrakopoulou, F.	2
		Steinmann, A. E.	23, 41
		Stern, Ephraim	1, 3, 52, 57, 58, 59, 60, 61, 65, 66, 68, 69, 70, 74, 75, 76, 81,
Myers, Jacob M	21, 22, 40, 41		

	94, 104, 105, 106, 121, 122, 123, 124, 134, 135, 143
Tal, Oren	24, 26, 129, 130
Tebes, Juan Manuel	114, 116
Turner, Joseph	35
Ussishkin, David	123, 125, 128, 129
Van der Toorn, Karel	2, 74
VanderKam, James C.	41
Von Bothmer, D.	4, 64, 65, 66, 68, 72, 78, 85, 89, 96, 97, 98, 103, 117, 118, 119
Wampler, Joseph C.	4, 64, 65, 66, 68, 78, 85, 89, 96, 97, 98, 103, 117, 118, 119
Williamson, H. G. M.	22, 23, 24
Wilson, Robert R.	9
Winn Leith, Mary J.	1, 23, 29, 30, 33, 34, 36, 37, 38, 39, 40
Wolff, Samuel R.	63, 130
Wortham, Robert	8, 11
Wright, John W.	24, 25, 26
Zetterholm, Magnus	94
Zorn, Jeffrey R.	4, 49, 50, 51, 52, 53, 54, 55, 56, 76, 82, 85, 86, 87, 88, 90, 91, 92, 93, 94, 97, 98, 100, 101, 103, 105, 107, 108, 109, 110, 111, 112, 113, 114, 118, 134, 136, 137, 139, 140, 141, 146, 160, 162, 163, 164, 165, 167, 178

www.ingramcontent.com/pod-product-compliance
Lightning Source LLC
Chambersburg PA
CBHW022020220426
43663CB00007B/1154